"A compelling story of an era in which America embraced risk to win the Cold War . . . of heroic men, armed with courage, conviction and an unfailing faith in themselves, their crew and their experimental craft, who fought the battles far from the headlines in the unforgiving depths of the oceans. . . . The story of *NR-1*'s Long Ride Home was reminiscent of the decisions my teams faced on Apollo 13. . . . As a reader I feel the survival instincts of the captain and crew kick in to meet each new challenge, confident of victory. . . . Great reading!!"

—Gene Kranz, former flight director, NASA,
New York Times bestselling author of *Failure Is Not an Option*

"Highly readable . . . informative and entertaining. I recommend it to anyone with an interest in underwater exploration spiced with adventure."

—A. J. Hill, former Navy instructor and author of
Under Pressure: The Final Voyage of Submarine S-Five

"A heretofore classified adventure story that I read from stern to stern. . . . While the *NR-1* was not as visible as our spacecraft, the commitment and heroism of the men who ventured into unknown and hostile seas below was not unlike that required in the exploration of the heavens above."

—Captain Gene Cernan, USN (Ret.),
commander of Apollo 17 and the last man to walk on the moon

"Using storytelling techniques usually found in novels, Wukovits infused his book with the sights, sounds, smells, and tastes of the battlefield and the deprivations of life in a Japanese prisoner of war camp." —*San Antonio Express-News*

"Submarine enthusiasts will love the behind-the-scenes look at how Adm. Hyman G. Rickover, the father of the nuclear Navy, pulled strings to get funding for the *NR-1*, how he handpicked the crew . . . and the tyrannical way that he got it built. . . . The genesis of the little submarine is a fascinating part of the tale. . . . A gripping narrative . . . more harrowing than many a piece of fiction."

—*The Day* (New London, CT)

"Fans . . . will devour this one with enthusiasm." —*Publishers Weekly*

"This book had me up till 3 a.m. I had thought what we did on *Hammerhead* was the most clandestine Cold War submarining, but *Dark Waters* proved me dead wrong. The tales of Admiral Rickover's antics alone are worth four times the cover price! Vyborny and Davis had me hanging on while the *NR-1* made its first voyage, from Admiral Rickover's sketchpads and budget thievery to the floor of the graving dock at Electric Boat, and from there into black secrecy as it patrolled the sea bottom. The close scrapes with near-death at depth were terrifying. All submariners and Cold War history buffs will absolutely love this book!"

—Michael DiMercurio, former main propulsion officer aboard the USS
Hammerhead and *USA Today* bestselling author of *Threat Vector*

"This enjoyable read provides insight into a super-secret operation that many in the navy didn't even know existed, and the story of the boat's development and production will be an eye opener. Recommended." —*Library Journal*

NEW AMERICAN LIBRARY

DARK WATERS

AN INSIDER'S ACCOUNT OF THE *NR-1*,
THE COLD WAR'S UNDERCOVER NUCLEAR SUB

**Lee Vyborny
and Don Davis**

New American Library
Published by New American Library, a division of
Penguin Group (USA) Inc., 375 Hudson Street,
New York, New York 10014, U.S.A.
Penguin Books Ltd, 80 Strand,
London WC2R 0RL, England
Penguin Books Australia Ltd, 250 Camberwell Road,
Camberwell, Victoria 3124, Australia
Penguin Books Canada Ltd, 10 Alcorn Avenue,
Toronto, Ontario, Canada M4V 3B2
Penguin Books (N.Z.) Ltd, Cnr Rosedale and Airborne Roads,
Albany, Auckland 1310, New Zealand

Penguin Books Ltd, Registered Offices:
80 Strand, London WC2R 0RL, England

Published by New American Library, a division of Penguin Group (USA) Inc. Previously published in a New American Library hardcover edition.

First New American Library Hardcover Printing, January 2003
First New American Library Trade Paperback Printing, March 2004
10 9 8 7 6 5 4 3 2 1

 REGISTERED TRADEMARK–MARCA REGISTRADA

New American Library Trade Paperback ISBN: 0-451-21161-8

THE LIBRARY OF CONGRESS HAS CATALOGUED THE HARDCOVER EDITION AS FOLLOWS:

Vyborny, Lee.
    Dark waters : an insider's account of the NR-1, the Cold War's undercover nuclear sub /
Lee Vyborny and Don Davis.
        p. cm.
    Includes bibliographical references and index.
    1. NR-1 (Submarine) 2. Vyborny, Lee. 3. United States. Navy–Biography. 4. Cold War.
I. Davis, Don (Donald) II. Title.

VA65.N67 V95 2003
359.9'84–dc21   2002026417

Set in Caslon Book
Designed by Ginger Legato

Printed in the United States of America

To all those who have served on the *NR-1,*
and to the many who could only wait and hope for its safe return

ACKNOWLEDGMENTS

Life is a process of continuing education, and this effort has taught me a number of lessons. Among the most important is that getting a book into print is more about building relationships and following through with good team play than it is about writing alone.

My wife, Johanna, suggested the subject and supported my attempts, while others encouraged me to keep at it whenever my enthusiasm flagged. Agents Jane Dystel and Miriam Goderich recognized merit in the kernel of an idea that I presented to them. Many former shipyard, navy, and technical personnel contributed their time for interviews and their personal memorabilia, on which much of the detail contained herein is based. Mike Walker of the U.S. Naval Historical Center unearthed invaluable documents. The Submarine Force Museum in Groton, Connecticut, opened its doors and library to us. Don and Robin Davis combined their own research with my thoughts and rough text and produced a manuscript that is both readable and downright exciting. Editor Doug Grad at New American Library had faith and confidence in an untested commodity on a promising new project. Once we had draft material, Anne Kimber provided a thorough first read and gave us valuable editorial feedback. Then copy editor Michele Alpern and managing editor Adrian Wood corrected the lapses in our grammar, syntax, and style and moved the book into production.

We labored in concert, each taking the lead at the appropriate time, then acting in a supporting role while another team member had the lead. Together we bring you the story of a little-known U.S. Navy submarine.

–Lee Vyborny

CONTENTS

Summary of Features

Missions

- Search
- Large and small object recovery
- Geological survey
- Oceanographic research
- Installation and maintenance of underwater equipment

Search Capabilities

- Side Looking Sonar
  - 600 ft (180 m) search width with 1 ft (30 cm) resolution or
  - 2,400 ft (730 m) search width with 4 ft (1.2 m) resolution
- Deep Submergence/Obstacle Avoidance Sonar (DS/OAS)
  - Compatible with Deep Ocean Transponder (DOT) for both bottom survey and local navigation
- Sub-bottom profiler
  - Variable power
  - Selectable frequency

Principal Characteristics

• Length overall	145 ft 9-7/16 in. (44.4 m)
• Pressure hull length	96 ft 1 in. (29.3 m)
• Diameter	12 ft 6 in. (3.8 m)
• Maximum beam (at stern stabilizers)	15 ft 10 in. (4.8 m)
• Maximum navigational draft	15 ft 1 in. (4.6 m)
• Box keel depth (below base-line)	4 ft 0 in. (1.2 m)
• Design operating depth	2375 ft (724 m)
• Displacement submerged	366 long tons, 409.92 short tons
• Speed, surfaced/submerged	4.5/3.5 knots
• Mean draft	15 ft 3/4 in. (4.6 m)
• Endurance	210 man-days (nominal)

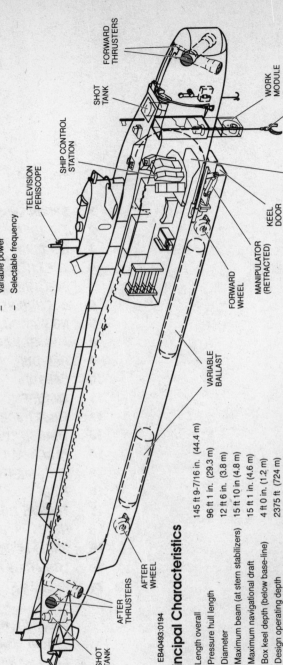

EB40493:0194

Labels: FORWARD THRUSTERS, SHOT TANK, WORK MODULE, OBJECT RECOVERY CLAW, SHIP CONTROL STATION, TELEVISION PERISCOPE, VIEWING PAD, KEEL DOOR, MANIPULATOR (RETRACTED), FORWARD WHEEL, VARIABLE BALLAST, AFTER WHEEL, AFTER THRUSTERS, SHOT TANK

PROLOGUE

*T*he Cold War was a time not only of tense relations between the United States and the Soviet Union, but also of rapid innovation and change. The twenty-five years from 1945 to 1970 was a period of technical optimism and astonishing achievement as the United States and the Soviet Union vied for strategic survival. Aviation moved from piston engines to jet propulsion for both civilian and military aircraft. Missiles evolved from Germany's simple V-1 and V-2 rockets to giant intercontinental ballistic missiles with multiple independently targeted warheads. A space race culminated in Americans landing on the moon. Nuclear energy was harnessed to generate commercial electricity and power the ships of the world's major navies. True science caught up with, and surpassed, science fiction.

The competition demanded by the Cold War was felt in outer space, in the air, on the ground, and also beneath the seas. During that intensely creative period, a number of unique submarines were conceived and produced by the U.S. Navy as it sought to stay abreast of the Red Fleet. The *Nautilus* became the first submarine to sail under nuclear power. The *Seawolf* followed with a liquid sodium–cooled reactor. The huge *Triton* carried two reactor plants, while the elusive hunter killer *Tullibee* packed an advanced sonar system. The *Halibut* had a large hangar bay on her foredeck to test experimental cruise missiles. The *Glenard P. Lipscomb*, with her direct current electric drive, was known as the fast ship, while the *Narwhal*, with a natural convection cooling system, was known as the quiet ship. Such submarines took undersea warfare

1

beyond merely shooting torpedoes, and into the shadowy world of gathering intelligence, and by doing so they earned a place among the most distinctive achievements of that tense and special time.

There is one conspicuous absence from that list—a submarine that has been intentionally kept so far off the books that it has remained hidden for decades not only from the public, but also from most admirals. It is the smallest nuclear-powered submarine in the U.S. Navy, a one-of-a-kind boat with wheels and a bewildering array of extraordinary equipment, and it dives three times deeper than any other submarine in the world.

It has neither a captain nor a navy name, no guns nor torpedoes. Its topside is painted bright orange whenever civilians might see it, but for many missions it wears black and is rendered almost invisible on the surface. When it dives, it vanishes. For thirty years, an elite handful of men have taken this submarine down thousands of feet to the bottom of the sea, and have literally driven along the ocean floor and flown through unknown canyons for up to a month at a time. This small crew of quiet, unrelenting achievers has been a spawning ground for future senior naval officers and for men who would continue to excel when they returned to civilian life. Some of their missions were of utmost military importance, while others were journeys of extraordinary scientific discovery. The possibility of disaster is their constant companion, for the chances of the crew surviving a major accident at sea are nonexistent.

Just getting the ship built was a technical accomplishment comparable to assembling the first spaceship. Keeping it afloat in the turbulent world of politics, Pentagon infighting, and budget battles was just as difficult. Almost every time it went out, the sea challenged its right to exist. Incredibly, this submarine is still in service, has become one of the oldest submarines in the fleet, and remains as much of a mystery today as ever, to friend and foe alike.

This is the story of the *NR-1*, the men who conceived and built a machine unlike any other the world had ever seen, and then sailed it into dark waters.

The *NR-1* and I began our naval careers about the same time.

I grew up in the small town of Merced in the middle of California's central valley in the 1950s, an average kid who did well in school without much effort. During high school, I worked at the county airport pumping gas, mowed the grass strips between the runways, and stared out over the flat, dry landscape, looking for some change—any change. Aviation was interesting, but did not capture my imagination. I received a state scholarship to the University of California at Santa Barbara, but had no specific academic objectives. After a year and a half of modest effort and lackluster performance, my grades were abysmal and I felt that trying to improve them was hopeless. So I dropped out.

In the early 1960s, every young man in America had a compulsory military obligation, so when I left UCSB, I had to not only make a living, but also deal with Uncle Sam. With no real job prospects and an idealistic yen to work within a small, dedicated group on some special project, I enlisted in the navy in February 1963 and signed up for the nuclear power program. After basic training in San Diego I remained there to take six months of courses to become an interior communications electrician, which would be my first step up the nuclear ladder.

Meanwhile, at the very top of that ladder was the father of the nuclear navy, a crusty admiral named Hyman Rickover, who was about to make his first tentative moves to create the *NR-1*. Eventually, Rickover would handpick twelve men to become its first crew and I would be among them.

Early in my navy career, I was only vaguely aware that about half the U.S. submarines and the men who served on them were lost during World War II. Losses among the German and Japanese sub forces were much greater. That I would live and work aboard a submarine did not bother me at all. World War II seemed like ancient history, Korea was never mentioned, and the new American submarines had excellent safety records, especially the large nuclear-powered ones. But while I was still training in California, the USS *Thresher* sank off the New England coast on April 10, 1963, and killed all 129 men aboard. That gave a stark reality to the dangers of the underwater world into which I was headed, but we joked that at least death aboard a submarine was swift and clean. There were few, if any, maimed submariners. You either came back alive and well, or you did not come back at all.

After San Diego, I was assigned to the Submarine School in Groton, Connecticut, beside the placid Thames River, where I learned to operate various systems and handle all kinds of emergencies. Those two months of classroom training were combined with practical experience in what was literally a sink-or-swim environment that seemed to emphasize eternal claustrophobia.

We practiced swimming to the surface from various ear-popping depths in a water-filled escape tower. We were locked in a special chamber, where we struggled, as water rose around us, to stop torrential geysers that were pumped in to simulate undersea emergencies. When we boarded a real submarine to get that memorable first taste of being totally enclosed in what some trainees called a steel coffin, the claustrophobia proved too much for a few of my classmates who could not bring themselves even to go down the hatch. Those who could not cope were allowed to transfer to duty aboard surface ships. Submarines were not for everyone.

There was an abrupt halt to our classes on November 22, 1963, when President Kennedy was assassinated. That black day dealt a debilitating blow to all of us and emphasized that the world itself, not just the undersea realm, had become a difficult and dangerous place.

But a young man is resilient and grows up fast in the submarine service, and for me, the practical navy training had succeeded where UCSB had failed. I had found a new home and, imbued with a spirit of determination, graduated as top man in my Sub School class. Allowed to choose my next station and the type of submarine on which I would serve for six months of intense hands-on training, I went to Pearl Harbor and the USS *Sargo*. Like generations of submariners before me, it was time to prove myself at sea and "qualify" under the watchful eyes of salty chiefs, for only after that rite of passage would I be allowed to pin on the coveted silver dolphins.

While I was busy doing that, Admiral Rickover would be bulling forward in Washington with his plan to build a new and secret submarine that could reach places no other ship could go and do things no other ship could do. The *NR-1* and I, both navy novices, were on a collision course with the Cold War.

1
SPOOK MISSION

Our nuclear attack submarine, the USS *Sargo*, was two weeks out of Pearl Harbor, gliding easily at seventeen knots some four hundred feet beneath the surface of the Pacific Ocean and headed for the east coast of Russia. The white numbers on our sail had been painted dark gray to match the rest of the ship and prevent identification, the radio room was stuffed with new electronics, and we had taken aboard three mysterious "communications technicians," ghostly figures who rarely left their equipment and spoke only to the captain. Once a day we rose to periscope depth to receive any radio messages, then immediately dove to again hide our transit in deep water. It was 1964, the world was awash in the Cold War, and after preparing the ship as if she were going into combat, we were on our way to do some serious snooping in the Tartar Straits.

The Cuban missile crisis only two years earlier was still fresh in everyone's memory, and in the short span of time since, President John Kennedy had been assassinated, Nikita Khrushchev had been overthrown as the Soviet premier, and British Prime Minister Harold MacMillan was driven from office by a scandal. America was trying to catch up with the Soviet Union in the space race, Russian reconnaissance planes were flying over Alaska, East-West tension was tight along the Berlin Wall, the Soviet Navy was growing at an alarming rate, and American armed forces were being drawn into Vietnam.

The repercussions of such geopolitical events reached even to the depths of the Pacific, where I was serving aboard the *Sargo*, a submarine that had already sunk once. Four years earlier, while tied up dockside at Pearl Harbor, a pressure hose carrying pure oxygen into the ship ruptured and an intense fire broke out. Flames shot a hundred feet into the air and the nightmare scenario of fire aboard a nuclear-powered submarine became a reality. As the inferno roared and with one sailor already dead, the captain made the drastic decision to flood his own ship, and put the stern of the crippled ship on the floor of the harbor with a deck hatch left open. The aft compartment filled with water and kept the raging fire from reaching the ship's nuclear reactor. The *Sargo* was later hauled up by a huge crane, refurbished for three months, and returned to active duty. Now she was my home, and my bunk during this four-month mission was a vinyl mattress right beside the warhead of a large torpedo.

My duty station was at the plotting table in the control room, noting the position of any ships or other contacts. It was an enviable job. Although I was one of the most junior people aboard, I was in the operational heart of the *Sargo*, just a step away from the dive station and the periscope stand. I knew where we were and what we were doing.

You lose track of the hours in a submarine, for there are no windows, and no matter where your ship may be, the clock is set at Zulu, the time on the prime meridian, the imaginary line of longitude that passes through Greenwich, England. So days and nights cease to have meaning to a submariner, for there is no sunrise or sunset, no stars or moon, just the ship's bells to signal the time for meals, working, and sleeping. After two weeks at sea, we crossed the international date line deep in the Central Pacific, hundreds of miles from anywhere, far from friend and enemy alike, and constantly challenged by the tedium of routine tasks. But we stayed on our toes, because absolutely nothing is taken for granted aboard a sub.

After several hours on duty one quiet day with no contacts to plot, I sat listening to the machine in which we lived. There is a continual din inside any ship underway—the whine of the turbines and reduction gears, the whoosh of air conditioning, the squeal of hydraulic fluid moving through pipes and valves, the bleeps of electronic devices, the straining shakes and shudders as turning screws push the ship through the water. Everyone feels the comforting rhythm that gives a sense that all is well, and instantly recognizes any change. I watched the Fathometer send out periodic pulses that returned many seconds later and showed the ocean bottom was eighteen thousand feet–more than three miles–below us. It made me wonder what it would be like to fall that far, a thought I quickly pushed aside.

The intercom in the control room came on with a request from the engine room, where a minor leak had been discovered in the hydraulic plant. Permission was requested to shut a valve to stop the leak so a hose could be replaced. It was a logical, routine decision and Lieutenant Ted Ardell, the conning officer running the sub during that watch, gave consent.

As soon as the sailor closed the valve, it felt as if a giant hand had struck the boat. The nose of the *Sargo* pitched violently down and the calm shipboard tempo instantly changed to that of a ship in serious trouble. "The stern planes have gone to full dive!" cried out the planesman, who jumped to his feet and pulled back on the control stick with all his might. "I can't get them back!" We tipped more sharply and felt the downward angle increase. I grabbed the tilting plotting table as everything that wasn't tied down tumbled forward in a sudden avalanche. Some items rattled past around our feet while other objects launched themselves through the air and crashed against the compartment bulkhead that only moments before had been the wall in front of me. With the steep angle of the boat, that wall was now well below the stations to which we clung in order to keep from falling. "Switch to emergency plane control!" yelled Ardell.

The angle only grew steeper, passing forty-five degrees. "Still on full dive!" called the planesman. Neither our captain nor the executive officer could reach the control room because the sharp angle and force of the dive had pinned them against the walls of their cabins. I glanced at the large digital depth indicator, where the numbers were changing so fast that they were a blur. In a matter of seconds, the ship drove herself down several hundred feet and the bow angle was greater than ever. The *Sargo* was out of control and heading toward her crush depth, the point at which the outside water pressure would crumple the hull. Ted Ardell, a sandy-haired young officer not long out of the Naval Academy, had to act immediately and instinctively, for if he hesitated, we would all be lost.

"All back emergency! Blow all ballast tanks!" he called, and the *Sargo* shook violently as her machinery obeyed the command. The giant propellers reversed and a thunder of compressed air blew some of the water from our ballast tanks. Everyone held on tight as we listened and prayed that the straining boat would respond. Our only chance of survival was to use every means available to stop the plunge. Ardell did everything right, and it worked. In seconds that seemed like years, we felt the rapid descent slow, and the bow began tilting back up. The ship's hull groaned under the tremendous strain, but held. Everyone in the control room looked at each other without speaking as the ship recovered. We had gone to the edge of eternity and back in less than two minutes.

The single valve turned by the sailor in the engine room had disabled both the normal and emergency steering and diving systems. There were four other Skate-class submarines just like us, and although the problem had never before been encountered, it eventually would have happened to one of them. Luckily, we survived to pass along the warning.

We quickly put things back to normal and the *Sargo* resumed the mission as if nothing had happened. Responding to emergencies is part of life underwater.

Through the East China Sea, the Straits of Korea, across the Sea of Japan and we silently entered a long body of water between the Russian mainland and Sakhalin Island, a protected sea lane that the Soviet Navy considered to be its own private pond. It was an awkward place for an American warship. While the United States recognized only a three-mile limit, the Soviet Union claimed sovereignty of the seas to a distance of twelve miles from their shore. We would work the gray area in between those distances, a disputed zone where some American subs had been discovered by Soviet warships and slammed by "practice" depth charges, as the USS *Gudgeon* had been in 1957. Those boats often returned to Pearl Harbor with large dents in their hulls and superstructures, but neither side acknowledged such incidents. The rules of engagement would change if we entered the three-mile limit, where the enemy ships would have the right to capture or destroy our boat. The chart on my plotting table clearly marked that critically important territorial line.

The Soviets were testing an early version of their cruise missiles on a range within the Tartar Straits, launching the antiship weapons from a submarine toward a group of target barges a hundred miles away. At night, we stayed well offshore, but each morning the *Sargo* crept in and waited near the supposed launch position. After a week of hearing nothing, our sonar picked up the sounds of several approaching ships, including a submarine. We moved closer after they came to a stop and were able to observe the complicated process of how they prepared the ship-to-ship missile for launch. Small, choppy waves helped hide our periscope during the short intervals when it was raised, and our captain, Lieutenant Commander Robert M. Douglass, settled down to watch.

The Soviets had no idea that a large U.S. warship had joined their observation group, her ominous bulk hidden beneath just a few feet of seawater only a hundred yards away from their ships. When the missile was ready, the eyes of all the Soviet sailors focused on the launch. Douglass then boldly raised our entire package of periscopes, cameras, and antennae. A bright sun bathed the area, and when the rocket shot away from the Soviet sub, we probably got better photographs of the test than they did. We also captured and recorded the telemetry and launch signals from the ships and the missile itself. We picked them clean, grabbing a complete top-secret Soviet launch profile while remaining undetected. Then the *Sargo* moved quietly away to await new orders.

As a reminder that this game was never easy, our luck turned bad a few weeks later when we were lurking at the far end of the missile test range, hoping to watch one of the weapons impact among a quadrangle of moored barges. When our spooks learned a shot was imminent, we worked into the area and once more settled down near the Soviet ships gathered to watch the incoming missile. But this time when the skipper raised the periscope, he saw a Soviet sailor on the bridge of one of the ships pointing right back at him and yelling something. Douglass, a tall man with a terrific command presence, simply said, "Uh, oh. I think they've spotted us. Lots of activity on deck. Down scope! Let's get out of here!"

The Soviet surface ships scattered to make room for a Kashin-class destroyer that was charging toward us. She began pinging away with active sonar, and then took up a position across the path we would most likely have to take to reach undisputed international waters beyond the twelve-mile limit. We were now the prey instead of the stalker, but Douglass, whose calm in such situations was legend, did not intend to make things easy for the Russian destroyer. Instead of heading out on the direct route, he slid the *Sargo* slowly forward, between the target barges, which made a jumble of the destroyer's sonar signals. When it became obvious that the Kashin did not have a fix on us, and was simply waiting for us to make a mistake, we angled out of the area, sticking close to the shoreline, and slipped into deeper waters.

The next item on our surveillance agenda was shadowing one of the newest Soviet missile-carrying submarines, a boat of their Echo II class, to determine if she was powered by standard diesel engines or a nuclear reactor. Intelligence sources informed us that one was leaving the shipyard at Komsomolsk-on-Amur and would be coming through the Tartar Straits to reach the ice-free port at Vladivostok, on the southern coast of Siberia.

We found a good spot and waited about a week before picking up the sounds of that sub moving cautiously on the surface behind an escorting patrol boat. A heavy mist blanketed the sea and hampered their ability to spot our periscope, and the submerged *Sargo* swung in smoothly behind both Soviet vessels, where the churning and turbulence of their own propellers masked any chance they might have of detecting us with sonar. They were making only eight knots through the fog, and we were tailgating at less than a mile, closing at ten knots and keeping the sound of their props centered dead ahead on our television-like passive sonar display. As we slipped up on them through their roiling wakes, we could hear the actual throb of their screws in the water around us.

The captain issued rapid-fire orders to maintain our speed, just two knots faster than theirs, and to start the radiation sensors, automatic cameras mounted on the periscopes, and sound-recording gear. As we overtook the Echo II, our fully extended periscopes were only ten feet beneath her hull. The *Sargo* surged ahead until she came even with the bow of the Russian sub, completing a clean sweep during which our equipment made the important discovery that the Russian boat was indeed nuclear powered.

We slowed and dove to begin our escape, and the submarine and patrol boat moved along to port not knowing that they had been electronically mugged. We had harvested exceptionally valuable intelligence and would add a complete set of photographs of the bottom of the submarine's entire hull, a power plant radiation profile, and a transcript of their engine and propeller noises to the navy's library of intelligence information. If an American sonar man ever detected that sound again, anywhere in the world, he would know exactly which ship it was. If we survived to relay it home.

Our final chore was yet another submarine chase. One of the Soviet Juliett-class diesel-powered submarines had become particularly quiet and hard to detect, a remarkable change for a type of sub that usually made quite a racket with her propellers. We had to find out why, and began our cat and mouse routine by parking off the big naval base at Vladivostok.

Since it was near the end of the tour, the crew of the *Sargo* had been honed to sharpness by the work of the past few months. One exception was the ship's navigator, a lieutenant with a sour attitude about not having risen higher in rank. He was a large man who already had gray hair at the age of forty, and was known for trying to avoid even the simplest jobs. The crew nicknamed him Satchel Ass, for the way the seat of his unkempt khaki pants sagged behind him. The nickname conjured an image of sloth that suited him well, and soon everyone, including the other officers, took to calling him Satchel to his face, though he never figured out why. Unfortunately, we had to rely on this weak link to determine where we were in the ocean.

The Juliett appeared to be conducting some sort of tests as we spent days scouting her. The sub would emerge from port, operate for a short period, then return to base. It was too risky for us to use the tactic we had employed against the Echo, for this Juliett boat moved too fast when she was on the surface, so we watched from a distance as her knife-edged bow threw water aside when she powered through her exercises. Every day we jockeyed for a better position, hoping the sub might loiter near us just long enough.

Satchel kept track of our location by taking bearings from the peaks of the snowy mountains along Cape Povorotny, and confirmed his position with readings provided by Loran Alpha radio signals, the only electronic navigation device we had that worked in the far reaches of the northern Pacific. His job became trickier as the weather changed and early summer fog obscured the view of the mountains, often for days at a time. When he could no longer see the peaks, he was forced to rely solely upon the Loran radio signals.

It came as a surprise to all of us when, on the first day of July, after taking the regular position fix, the navigator pinpointed our boat as being not a dozen miles off the Russian coast as we thought, but smack in the middle of the vast and dusty Gobi Desert. The captain immediately withdrew to deeper water to find out what was wrong. Electronic technicians swarmed over the Loran gear, calibrating and testing, and declared it to be working perfectly, only to have the Loran tell us over and over that we were a thousand miles inland, sailing beneath the Gobi sand. Meanwhile, we could only navigate by dead reckoning from the last fix the navigator made from the mountaintops, which were now hidden by the fog. Without a good position fix, we could only make rough estimates of how far the strong currents might have carried the *Sargo* along the coast, and soon had only an approximate idea of where we were.

At that moment, the Juliett gave us the opportunity for which we had been patiently waiting. She began her run back to port escorted by several ships, and all were moving slowly because of the fog. At that speed, we could catch her, extend our periscopes, photograph the hull, and figure out why she was so quiet. Captain Douglass studied the chart with Satchel and was assured that we could accomplish the mission before the enemy sub reached the protection of the three-mile limit. Using the available data, I plotted an intercept point that would allow us to come to periscope depth right behind our target.

From there, we would repeat the Echo maneuver, dive beneath the enemy sub, and raise our periscope until it was only a few feet below her hull as we moved forward. We caught up as planned and positioned the *Sargo* just beneath the Soviet sub. Our skipper got his first good look through the eyepiece and saw that the Juliett's propellers were recessed in miniature wind tunnels, which shrouded them and greatly reduced the amount of noise leaving the ship. This was another exceptionally important find, and Douglass ordered the recording and photography to begin.

But luck again turned against us. Before we could complete the pass, the Juliett accelerated, which meant we would have to increase our own speed to overtake her. We went down to four hundred feet to reduce the noise of our own propellers, leveled off, and rushed forward at full speed, planning to rise up at the last moment and finish the job.

Without warning, we hit something unseen. The whole boat shuddered and the bow rocked up like she was sliding up a boat ramp. We were all flung forward by the impact even as the captain ordered, "All stop!"

Our momentum at high speed defied his order, and although the engines went to idle and the propellers stopped turning, the *Sargo* plowed along the seabed, scraping and shuddering. "I can hear gravel scattering," called the sonar operator. We had run aground at full speed, bounced twice off the bottom, and skidded to an abrupt standstill, dead in the water. We had made so much noise that we believed it would have been impossible for the Russian ships not to hear us.

"Check the chart!" Douglass ordered. "There shouldn't be any four-hundred-foot bottom out here!" Anger tinged his voice. Our captain did not like surprises while sailing beneath Soviet warships.

The quartermaster gave him the bad news. "We're inside the three-mile limit, sir!" he said. The chart clearly showed the only four-hundred-foot depth charted in the Vladivostok area was less than two miles from shore, which made us a fair target. We were well within the forbidden zone in which the Soviets could attack us with full justification. We listened for pinging from the Juliett's escorts, or the splashes of depth charges we expected to come raining down, but only silence surrounded us. So far, we were not being hunted.

"Sonar. What are the ships above us doing?" the skipper asked in a whisper.

"The ones I can hear are still headed into port, sir. But they may have left one up there sitting quiet and waiting."

Damage reports came to the control room, the worst stating that seawater was leaking into the pump room and could not be halted while the ship was submerged. We could not just sit there idle in such dangerous waters.

"Ahead one-third, ten degrees up angle on the bow planes," ordered the captain. He had to know immediately if the ship was still maneuverable, and somehow the *Sargo* struggled back to life and responded, although awkwardly. At least our hull was still intact and we had some control, but if they were going to find us, it would be now, and we braced for an attack. Once again, nothing happened.

Douglass seized the opportunity and pulled us out of the area to the open waters some miles away, where we surfaced and stanched the leak. Then we limped away toward safe harbor in Okinawa, staying well offshore and steering by compass headings.

Inspections would later show that all of the instruments had been raked off the underside of our boat, half of the big rudder was torn away, and the eighteen-inch-thick rudderpost was bent back at a thirty-degree angle. We would have been sitting ducks, virtually defenseless and without much ability to maneuver, had we been attacked.

As we made our way slowly back to port, the skipper ordered technicians to rip the Loran to pieces, clean and test every part, and put it back together. They did, and it still worked fine. Whatever the problem was, it wasn't with the Loran set.

The lead electronics technician, baffled by the mystery, had an idea and hunted up copies of recent navigation publications. After only a few minutes of turning pages, he discovered why we had ended up in such jeopardy, sailing under a desert and slamming into the bottom a stone's throw from the Russian coast. The fault was not mechanical, but human.

Clearly spelled out in bold text in a "Notice to Mariners" was that on the first day of July, all signals transmitted by the Loran stations in the western Pacific changed to new frequencies. That was the day our Loran "failed" for the first time. The lazy and disgruntled Satchel had not bothered to read the notice nor alter the charts for the new settings.

Captain Douglass was furious. He accepted the fact that he, the ship, and his crew must work in an extremely perilous environment, but he would not tolerate incompetence compounding the risk. He ordered that the navigator be confined to his quarters for the rest of the long trip, and after that, Satchel's only contact with the outside world was a sailor who served meals to him in the small compartment. The rest of us wanted nothing to do with him. Before we reached Okinawa, those passing through the corridor outside his cabin heard the lieutenant muttering and crying, in the middle of a nervous breakdown. When we finally tied up, Satchel was escorted topside and taken away in an ambulance. We never heard from him again.

Crew members on this mission of the *Sargo* were awarded medals for operating in a war zone. The official explanation was that we had passed through the dangerous waters off Vietnam during our journey. The truth is that the potential combat we faced on our mission had not been in the warm Gulf of Tonkin, but far away in the misty and frigid waters just two miles off the Russian coast.

2

THE IDEA

At the very time that I was learning the operations of a modern nuclear submarine, science and technology were opening new vistas in underwater exploration, advances that went virtually unnoticed because they occurred alongside the publicity-laden race between the United States and the Soviet Union to send a man to the moon. With national prestige on the line, government money poured into the American space program, although many scientists felt that learning about Earth's "inner space" was more relevant than outer space.

Only governments could build huge rockets and warships in those years, but that was not true about exploring the oceans. Private companies might not be able to reach into space, but commercial interests had gone to sea for centuries. Soon after businesses decided there were profits to be made in the undersea world from new minerals and food sources and the discovery of sunken treasure, some companies started constructing and launching private submersibles.

The route to the bottom of the sea was paved by a unique partnership between the military and scientific communities. By assisting scientists and oceanographers, the navies of the world advanced their own strategic interests by learning more about the mysterious environment beneath the waves. As the years passed and technology advanced, such knowledge became critical.

The first significant underwater probe had taken place in 1934, when an American scientist, William Beebe, and an engineer, Otis Barton, rode to a depth of about a half mile in a round steel ball secured to a surface ship by heavy lines. Barton called it a "bathysphere," which can be loosely defined as a deep ball, and the two-windowed submersible was one of the remarkable inventions of the early twentieth century, for it took mankind into an unknown world.

French diver Jacques Cousteau and his partner Émil Gagnan added some mobility to sea exploration in 1943 with the invention of the Self-Contained Underwater Breathing Apparatus. Divers who had been confined to working in life-sustaining heavy suits and steel helmets now could swim about easily by wearing scuba gear.

World War II brought a quantum leap in the machines that allowed men to efficiently breathe, travel, and exist deep beneath the surface, but it was peacetime that brought about an ultimate underwater triumph. On January 23, 1960, American Don Walsh and Jacques Piccard of Switzerland boarded the U.S. Navy's only bathysphere, the *Trieste*, and submerged into the Challenger Deep of the Marianas Trench in the Pacific Ocean. They defied logic, pitch darkness, and thousands of pounds of pressure in order to plant an American flag a record 35,800 feet below the surface, in the deepest spot on earth.

The *Trieste* was the only U.S. "deep submersible" at the time, but with the explosion of commercial interest in what might be found on the ocean floor, some eighty deep submergence vehicles were built and deployed during the next decade. The navy built or sponsored only fifteen of them. The rest were the products of academic institutions and major corporations, such as Westinghouse, General Electric, Lockheed, Reynolds Aluminum, and Perry Ocean Systems. They branched away from the early diving ball concept and developed vehicles with mobility—submersibles and compact submarines that could not only go underwater, but also do independent work while submerged.

The most famous was the *Alvin*, a maneuverable submersible built around a hull sphere of pressure-resisting HY-100 steel and paid for by the navy, but operated by Woods Hole Oceanographic Institution in Massachusetts. The *Alvin*, named for a popular chipmunk cartoon character of the day and Allyn Vine, a pioneering Woods Hole scientist, set the standard for oceanographic research.

The private sector responded with a deep-sea research sub owned by Reynolds Metals, called the *Aluminaut*, which set a world's depth record for a deep submersible of 6,250 feet on its first time out.

Dive by dive, new commercial vessels, scientific boats of all shapes, and submarines of the world's seafaring nations pushed deeper into the dangerous undersea world.

The exact cause of the *Thresher* disaster was never determined. However, enough evidence was gathered to show there was a massive failure somewhere in the labyrinth of seawater piping in the engine room as the ship made a deep dive. The salty spray short-circuited the electrical system and shut down the nuclear reactor. Without propulsion and unable to restart the reactor, the ship sank deeper as her men tried to combat the flooding in the dim light from emergency battle lanterns.

The flood of high-pressure water soon overcame her buoyancy and dragged the *Thresher* deeper and deeper, until she sank past her crush depth in the unforgiving ocean.

The ship might have survived if the heat energy stored in the reactor and its coolant system had been used to drive the ship to the surface. However, strict reactor operating procedures of the time forbade such an action because it might have damaged some of the large heat exchangers in the reactor compartment. The rules stressed protecting the power plant regardless of what happened to the ship.

The death of the *Thresher* in waters a mile and a half deep caused profound changes within the U.S. Navy, particularly concerning the safety of submariners. During World War II, the sinking of ships with all hands aboard was acceptable, but much had changed since then. In peacetime, the loss of so many lives could not be ignored. The navy's investigation underscored the need for a way to rescue men trapped below the surface aboard incapacitated submarines. Even though no rescue would have been possible in the case of the *Thresher*, we submariners liked knowing that if disaster struck, our navy mates would at least be able to attempt to save us.

Like a whirling top throwing off sparks, the investigation spun into unexpected directions, including the creation of the Deep Submergence Systems Project (DSSP), the centerpiece of which was the Deep Submergence Rescue Vehicle (DSRV), a piloted minisubmarine designed to save the lives of sailors trapped in crippled subs. After the *Thresher*, neither the public nor Congress would object to spending money for that purpose.

The navy removed both the project and the proposed DSRV from the normal path of ship development and placed them in the Navy

Special Projects Office. Special Projects, already overworked with developing new generations of missiles and submarines, declared the DSSP to be an independent subsystem and dropped it on the desk of its chief scientist—a brash and brilliant young man named John Piña Craven.

There it faded from public view, and secrecy enveloped the entire deep submergence effort.

The most remarkable thing about the DSSP was that it had a budget that was large and loose. There was plenty of room beneath that funding umbrella for things other than building submarine rescue vehicles. As American submarines became tools of espionage, millions of DSSP dollars would be siphoned away and spent on things the navy would not even admit existed.

"The Deep Submergence Systems Project was the embryo of the intelligence navy," Craven would write in *The Silent War*. "DSRV was mother to quite a brood ... a classic example of the secret intelligence paradigm; the cover is real and it produces covert progeny."

The top of the chain of command in America's nuclear navy did not stop at the desk of whichever admiral happened to be the chief of naval operations at the time, for the CNO eventually would retire and turn his flag over to a successor. The decisions on anything related to nuclear power, and many times far beyond, lay with a slight, gruff, and brilliant little old man who put the fear of God into almost everyone he met—Hyman G. Rickover.

Rickover rose to the rank of full admiral despite being previously denied promotions by superior officers whom he regularly chastised and browbeat. The gulf between him and the navy's leaders was summed up in a *San Francisco Chronicle* editorial cartoon in which bemedaled admirals are gathered around a strategic map and one growls, "Gentlemen—We may be able to beat Russia any Wednesday before lunch—but what can we do about Rickover?"

His power came from a peculiar combination of jobs. On the military side, Rickover was the assistant chief for nuclear propulsion in the U.S. Navy's Bureau of Ships (BuShips). Simultaneously, he was manager of Naval Reactors (NR), in the Division of Reactor Development for the Atomic Energy Commission (AEC). Under this extraordinary and tangled organizational chart, Rickover at the AEC could order the navy's Rickover to get something done, and BuShips could not counter the directive. His Naval Reactors department became the pioneering and powerful lead agency in nuclear matters. Almost anything having to do with military or civilian nuclear energy programs passed over one of Rickover's desks.

Correctly considered the father of the nuclear navy, Rickover personally saw to the creation of the submarine USS *Nautilus*, the first ship ever to use a reactor. When Commander Dennis Wilkinson flashed the historic signal "Under way on nuclear power!" as the *Nautilus* set out on her maiden voyage in 1955, the transit of the seas changed, and overnight, oil and coal became as obsolete as wind in powering ships. Within a few years, shipyards all across the country were sliding warships of ever increasing types and sizes, from submarines to aircraft carriers, into the water, and more and more of them carried Rickover's nuclear reactors.

In testimony before Congress in 1965, when he wore three stars and already was long past normal retirement age, Rickover remarked that since he had joined the Atomic Energy Commission in 1949, Presidents Truman, Eisenhower, and Kennedy had passed through the White House that was currently occupied by President Johnson, and that he had also watched ten secretaries of state, seven CNOs, seven chiefs of BuShips, and a couple of AEC chairmen come and go. The admiral was careful to exclude his congressional allies from his acerbic comments on transient leadership because they had spent so many years in office themselves. "The other people rotate, we endure," he once told his aide and biographer, Theodore Rockwell.

Even today, long after his death, the very mention of the name Rickover sends shivers through admiralty ranks, for no other modern naval officer ever accumulated the influence of Rickover, nor had one displayed it with such arrogant ruthlessness.

The admiral was a not-so-benevolent dictator of an unassailable kingdom and was extraordinarily successful in finding the huge amounts of money needed to reach his objectives. It was inevitable that he would discover John Craven and what was going on in the Deep Submergence Systems Project.

Reports differ on when Rickover first began thinking about building a small nuclear-powered submarine that could drive along the bottom of the ocean, but he certainly was influenced by the developing technology that had created the deep-diving submersibles, as well as the new role evolving for submarines in covert operations.

As he saw it, tethered submersibles could go deep with a couple of observers, but had limited range because of the lines and electrical power cables that secured them to support ships on the surface. Unmanned underwater robots were limited because they did not carry a crew and were confined to very specific roles. As an example, the navy's Cable-Controlled Undersea Recovery Vehicle (CURV) was designed to recover test weapons and torpedoes off the California coast in depths down to two thousand feet. And the piloted miniature submarines such as the *Alvin* and the *Aluminaut* could roam freely, but not for long because of weak, battery-powered engines. Nothing surmounted all of those problems.

In November of 1964, according to one biographer, Rickover discussed the puzzle during an airplane flight with Mark Forssell, an expert on submersibles and advanced developments. Nuclear power, Rickover believed, could create a new breed of underwater vessels with unlimited possibilities. They would not depend upon batteries, would be manned by expert naval personnel, and would operate independently of surface ships. Such a boat could conquer the ocean floor, and the strategic implications were huge. By the time the flight from Schenectady, New York, landed in Washington, Forssell had orders to draw up parameters for a small sub that could go deeper than any manned submarine in existence and be powered by a compact nuclear reactor that would let it stay underwater indefinitely.

Forssell soon reported back that it was theoretically possible to construct a reactor small enough to fit into a tiny submarine. That was enough for Rickover. Almost with a snap of his fingers, he decided to create such a ship.

No one else in the navy had the power, the position, the foresight, the means, and the determination to do something so outrageous, for he went around every check and balance in the system. He saw a need and chose to fill it, doing something that most bureaucrats would never do—making a decision completely on his own.

Thus began one of the most incredible periods of rapid development in the U.S. Navy's long history of building ships. Rickover's creation, the *NR-1*, would never again move as fast as it did in the days when it lived only in his mind. With only sketchy reports in hand, the admiral launched a tour de force of political maneuvering to breathe life into the project while at the same time keeping it away from the formal channels of budgeting, review, and justification.

He won the backing of some of the navy's top technical people and then briefed the chief of naval operations, Admiral David L. McDonald, on January 28, 1965. After that, he assembled more official backers in an incredibly short time. One of his first converts was Dennis Wilkinson, the former commander of the *Nautilus*, who had become a rear admiral and was head of the navy's submarine branch. Wilkinson agreed with his old mentor on the need for a deep-diving submarine that would test a new generation of nuclear reactors and take subs to depths none had reached before, just as his *Nautilus* had once opened new worlds of navigation under the Arctic ice.

Next, Rickover won the blessing of Robert Morse, the assistant secretary of the navy for research and development, the man who held the purse strings. Then he swept Rear Admiral Levering Smith, head of the Polaris missile project, onto his team. In short order, he was able to give Secretary of Defense Robert McNamara and Secretary of the Navy Paul H. Nitze just enough information to get their approval at a time the two men were becoming overwhelmed by Vietnam.

Nitze would recall discussing costs with Rickover, who brushed the issue aside, claiming that the total project could be done for only $20 million—about one-tenth the cost of a warship. The skeptical Nitze decided to provide some leeway and pledged to recommend a budget of $25 million. Not an inch of the ship had yet been built and already the cost was escalating, something that disturbed Rickover not at all. He was confident that his political allies would support the project and the money would flow. McNamara approved Nitze's suggested figure.

Then Rickover blatantly reached into the DSSP project and stole John P. Craven, the navy's chief scientist, to be one of the managers of his new program. The cigar-smoking, poker-playing Craven was always coming up with new ideas, even at one time proposing a deep-diving submersible made of glass, and at another, considering a small submarine with nuclear power that could go very deep.

Although based in firm science, such schemes were not much more than flights of fancy—the kind of out-of-the-box thinking that constantly flowed from Craven. When Admiral Wilkinson told him that one of those ideas to create a futuristic vessel might actually be possible, the scientist was intrigued. Rickover pulled together a secret meeting with Craven, Admiral Smith, and Assistant Secretary Morse to work out the details. Again, the money issue arose, for the hasty project was being born outside of budgetary planning.

Rickover demanded to know how much money was available, and Craven replied that he could come up with $10 million from the secret budget for special projects. Morse thought he could shift over another $22 million in ship construction money already appropriated by Congress for other projects. "Good," Rickover replied. "It will cost $32 million." The price was growing almost by the day.

In fact, the total had reached a level at which Congress was going to demand some answers. Rickover was unfazed, because he had yet to play his final card. On April 18, President Lyndon Johnson interrupted a holiday at his ranch in Texas to issue a news release in which he announced the navy and the Atomic Energy Commission were developing "a nuclear-powered deep-submergence research and ocean-engineering vehicle." The president noted that Admiral Rickover would be responsible for the propulsion plant. BuShips would handle design and construction, and the Special Projects Office would have overall responsibility, a point that would keep the ship behind the veil of national security.

The protest from Congress over not being notified in advance dissipated when they were briefed. Rickover, a master of political gambits, had engineered a presidential decree. Anyone wanting to block development of his new boat now faced the unpleasant prospect of dealing not only with the daunting Rickover, but also with the White House, where President Johnson was also known for getting his way.

That the new vessel was Admiral Rickover's baby was never in doubt, for he personally gave the ship its name. It would be called the *NR-1*— NR after his Naval Reactors division, and the number 1 because he planned to eventually have an entire fleet of such revolutionary boats.

The secrecy and deception that would wrap the *NR-1* for decades began at the very start. Not only was it under the aegis of Special Projects, but it was also never designated as a warship. Even the White House announcement blandly stated the new vessel would "contribute greatly to accelerate man's exploration and exploitation of the vast resources of the ocean . . . enable scientists to examine firsthand an extensive part of the earth's surface for new sources of raw materials . . . and extend accumulation of commercially useful information on the habits of diverse species of marine life." That described a handy little ship with harmless missions. Military use was not mentioned.

In future lists of naval strength, the *NR-1* would remain an asterisk among the attack and missile-carrying submarines, aircraft carriers, cruisers, and destroyers in the U.S. Navy, and many of its missions would remain strictly classified. It was referred to only as an unarmed research vessel powered by atomic energy, presumably an extension of the navy's interest in oceanography. But it would never appear in the annual Oceanographic Ship Operating Schedules published by the Office of the Oceanographer of the Navy.

When word spread through the Pentagon about what Rickover was up to, the admirals gave it little notice or importance. Their focus was on Vietnam and meeting Cold War goals that required giant aircraft carriers, battle groups, aerial armadas, and submarines that packed strategic missiles.

Most of them felt the *NR-1* was unneeded and a waste of money, but they had no time for a dustup over one of Rickover's crazy schemes. None of the dissenters dared tell Rickover to his face, fearing that to do so might set off a reprisal from President Johnson. Rickover, confident that time would prove him right, did not try to convince them of the value of the *NR-1*.

Within a few months, the proof he needed literally fell from the sky.

The nuclear necklace that the United States had hung around the Soviet Union relied upon B-52 Stratofortresses of the Strategic Air Command, some of which were always airborne, loaded with nuclear weapons, and ready to strike at a moment's notice.

At 10:22 A.M. on January 17, 1966, one of them collided with a tanker during a refueling operation over the southeast coast of Spain, at the edge of the Mediterranean Sea. Three of the bomber's B28 thermonuclear weapons aboard fell into tomato fields near the farming and fishing village of Palomares. Although their nuclear warheads remained intact, the high explosive charges in two of the bombs detonated and spread a powder of plutonium dust over 650 acres of farmland. Some fourteen hundred tons of contaminated crops and soil eventually would be removed and sent to the U.S. for disposal.

The fourth bomb and its partially deployed parachute were caught by high winds and carried out to sea, where they disappeared in deep water.

Palomares became the center of world attention as the United States rushed to deal with what was called a Broken Arrow, the code for any accident involving a missing or damaged U.S. nuclear weapon. President Johnson demanded immediate results. Teams of scientists made calculations based on everything from weather data to the shape of the weapon and the assumed drift of the parachute, but could only estimate a possible impact point within some fourteen square miles. The area was much too large for an efficient search. Only after a local fisherman claimed a parachute had landed near his boat did the analysts designate a one-square-mile target zone they called Alpha One. It was centered over an underwater ravine with steep sides that swept down more than two thousand feet.

A search was begun for the live nuclear weapon, and a small armada of thirty-eight American ships spread over the area, shadowed by Russian intelligence-gathering trawlers. Admiral William S. Guest eventually had some thirty-four hundred military and civilian personnel under his command on land and at sea, but the job of finding and recovering the bomb ultimately fell to a handful of men aboard a couple of small deep-diving submersibles. Underwater technology that was only in its infancy was to be tested as never before.

In February, the *Alvin* and its support vans were loaded aboard Air Force cargo planes in Massachusetts and flown to Rota, Spain, then transported to Palomares. In Miami, the new *Aluminaut*, which had just set its deep-diving record, was taken aboard a big navy ship for the long trip across the Atlantic. The small, privately owned *Cubmarine* from Perry Ocean Systems was also summoned, as was the navy's remotely operated CURV, from its torpedo test range in California.

As the odd search team assembled, some 125 navy scuba divers and the *Cubmarine* examined the flat, sandy shallow fringes of the Alpha One area, but found nothing.

The *Aluminaut* went to work exploring the rolling, muddy plain that stretched along the coast from depths of three hundred to over one thousand feet, while the *Alvin* searched the deep canyon whose rocky sides disappeared down into darkness.

The differences between the two high-tech submersibles began to tell immediately as they fought the strong currents. The *Alvin* was more maneuverable, but had only one-tenth the battery life of the *Aluminaut*. Every time the *Alvin* finished a six-hour dive, precious days elapsed while it was brought back aboard the waiting mother ship and readied for another attempt. The *Aluminaut* could roam farther, longer, and faster, but also eventually had to yield to battery life. Maintenance for both submersibles was hampered by the need for long periods of idleness to recharge their batteries and to wait for spare parts to be flown out from the United States.

Art Markel, a pilot on the *Aluminaut*, recalled Admiral Guest's determination to conduct "an eyeball search" of the bottom, a directive that did not recognize the advantage of the *Aluminaut's* three different sonar devices. The *Alvin* had none.

Markel said that on one dive, the *Aluminaut* homed in on a distant sonar contact and maneuvered close enough to see it through the view ports. It was part of the tail structure of one of the crashed aircraft. Logic dictated that if the debris was that far out from shore, the bomb dangling from its parachute probably landed out even further. He photographed the debris and showed the pictures to Admiral Guest. "Kind of pissed him off," Markel said. The admiral, instead of choosing to make further sonar searches, demanded to know why the *Aluminaut* had left its assigned area.

"I told him we had searched everything there and kept going," Markel said.

"How the hell can you do this?" Guest demanded.

"We're using sonar, admiral," replied the frustrated Markel, an outspoken man who, as a civilian, could allow his tone to match that of a senior officer.

The exchange apparently made no difference. The *Alvin* kept the lead role in the search, and on March 15, on its tenth dive in thirty days, the submersible located skid marks where the bomb had slid along the bottom before dropping into an underwater canyon. The *Alvin*, at the limit of its power, returned to the surface, and another week went by before the submersible found the furrow again. Almost two months had passed since the collision.

The delay demonstrated the difficulty of navigating and maintaining an exact position while working beneath the surface. When a submersible comes out of the water, it cannot return to its starting place on the bottom as if it were on an elevator. Tides and currents play havoc with pinpointing anything underwater that does not have an attached locator beacon. Keeping contact is almost impossible when erratic, strong currents shove around both a submersible and its target.

After reestablishing contact, the *Alvin* tracked the skid marks until it found the bomb, which was covered by its parachute and perched precariously on a small ledge of a seventy-degree slope, about 2,550 feet under the surface. Again almost at the end of its search time but unwilling to give up the contact, the *Alvin* wedged into a crevasse and shut down everything but essential life support systems. By the time the *Aluminaut* arrived to take over, the *Alvin* was almost out of air and electrical power. The pilot, sitting in the cold and dark, described the approaching *Aluminaut* as "the most beautiful thing I ever saw. A great silvery-pink monster . . . with great green phosphorescent eyes coming through the water." The first underwater rendezvous of two submersibles was an unsung historic moment.

The *Alvin* went topside and the *Aluminaut* assumed the grueling vigil. "We stayed on the bomb for twenty-four hours so it wouldn't get lost, walk away, or slide into eternity," said Markel.

On the surface, the navy plotted the new position as a storm whipped the fleet, and only when the seas settled was the first recovery attempt made. It depended solely on a single nylon tether that had been attached to the bomb by the *Alvin*, and when the hoist began, the weight snapped the line and the thermonuclear bomb rolled away down the mountain. Once again, it was lost.

Another two weeks passed before the *Alvin* discovered it again, and this time, the *Aluminaut* marked the spot with an electronic transponder. Several days were wasted trying to rig a complicated recovery device, but when that proved unsuccessful, the navy brought in the unmanned, remotely controlled CURV, which had spent weeks practicing the retrieval of a similar test object. The CURV operator attached two lines to the bomb's parachute, and while trying to hook up a third one, the CURV became snagged.

"I don't think they did it on purpose," recalled Markel, who watched the recovery operation. "They got it all tangled and couldn't get free, so they just brought it all back up. At first, they thought they just had the CURV, which was all mixed up in the parachute shrouds, and there was the damned bomb, just hanging there."

On April 7, 1966, eighty days after the accident, the H-bomb was lifted, damaged but intact, aboard a navy ship. The "Palomares Incident" was the worst accident ever involving American nuclear weapons.

The manned submersibles had performed well and the entire undersea program received a boost as a result. However, in the process, a number of deficiencies were identified. A much longer duration at depth was needed for long searches, and better navigation systems were required, as was an ability to retrieve heavy objects. Dedicated support ships with experienced handlers were also required, as were more independent operations for the submersible.

To Admiral Rickover, the Palomares problems sounded like a design sheet for the *NR-1*.

3
DECISION

Preliminary design work on the *NR-1* was well under way by the time the radioactive dust settled in Spain, and the first schematic drawings emerged after hours of conferences about how to incorporate ideas that would make the little boat different from anything else afloat or submerged. The design showed a long and thin submarine with a small "sail," or conning tower, near the front tip of its cigar-shaped hull. The two-thirds of the submarine aft of the sail was allocated to the nuclear power plant and engineering spaces. A close observer would notice that the pressure hull seemed perfectly round. A flat fiberglass superstructure mounted to the top of the hull would permit crew members to walk the length of the boat. Several strange oval openings fore and aft denoted thrusters that would allow the sub to hover at an exact underwater location. Another long, boxlike section was attached to the bottom of the submarine, and on the oblique view, external view ports were visible, as were two tires lined up like bicycle wheels. The drawing showed neither guns nor torpedo tubes. Almost forty years later, despite numerous changes and alterations made for modernization, increased efficiency, and specific missions, the *NR-1* would have the same basic shape envisaged by its earliest design teams.

Rickover was bringing it all together with his usual iron hand. Some of the best minds and managers in the shipbuilding business were assigned to the project; others volunteered to become part of the unique team to build a ship that already carried an air of mystery. Still more were cajoled to join, and some were simply hijacked from other jobs.

As in the fledgling days of the space program a few years earlier, people reported to work with only vague ideas about what they were getting into. Most of the work would be done at the General Dynamics Corporation's submarine-building facility, known simply as Electric Boat, or EB, on the coast of Connecticut, at Groton.

Chuck Chorlton, whose mild appearance masked a brilliant mind, was a nuclear engineering manager at EB who thought his long experience would get him to work immediately. Instead, as soon as he and ten other civilian engineers with similar extensive backgrounds came aboard, they were shuttled to classrooms for a full year of study prior to taking both the Naval Reactors' written and oral examinations. Only after receiving passing grades were these engineers, already at the top of their profession, allowed to work on the *NR-1*.

Robert Wilkinson, whose thick glasses were a result of designing submarines and submersibles, was dispatched to Washington with a team of other naval architects for what was supposed to be a few weeks of working with the experts at the navy's Bureau of Ships. His trip lasted a year.

When a contract for the overhaul of another submarine was canceled in Portsmouth, New Hampshire, Rickover grabbed twenty-five skilled workers and sent them down the coast to EB.

Such stories became legion as Rickover assembled a growing team of specialists. His constant presence was felt at every level, and he unhesitatingly bulldozed any perceived opposition. As the project progressed, he would fly to Electric Boat from Washington for weekly meetings concerning the *NR-1* to scold, preach, and push, push, push. "I spent a year with him every Thursday afternoon," one manager recalled of those pressure-filled conferences during which the admiral frequently exploded in wrath at any sign of a business-as-usual approach to the boat.

A turning point came in the spring of 1966 when Rickover called a meeting in Washington to review the latest designs. The navy was technically in charge of the design review process through the Naval Sea Systems Command (NAVSEA), which had succeeded BuShips. About thirty people were in the conference room, watching in silence as the admiral studied the drawings.

To dive into depths never reached by any other submarine, it was vital to keep "hull penetrations"—points at which inside equipment, such as periscopes, pipes, and electrical cables, pass through the hull—to a minimum on the *NR-1*. The more penetrations, the weaker its structural strength and the less ability the boat would have to withstand the immense pressures of deep water. The original specifications called for no more than ten such penetrations, and Rickover's eyes glazed into an icy stare when he counted more than fifty. He shrilly demanded, "Why?"

He was famed for pouncing on some flaw and accusing the perpetrator of total incompetence bordering on worthless idiocy. President Jimmy Carter would remember receiving that treatment while training to serve as an officer aboard a nuclear submarine. "If I made the slightest mistake, in one of the foulest and most obnoxious voices I ever heard, [Rickover] would tell the other people in the area what a horrible disgrace I was to the navy, and that I ought to go back to the oldest and slowest and smallest submarine from which I had come."

A shrewd politician, Rickover sometimes used those frightening tirades to mask his true objective, bludgeoning the opposition into hiding, and then snapping out orders to get things exactly the way he wanted. He would use the tactic repeatedly as he shepherded the *NR-1*'s creation.

At the Washington meeting, he whipped the NAVSEA people without mercy, interrogating each in embarrassing detail about the huge number of hull penetrations and why they, personally, let such a thing happen. After they answered, he threw most of them out of the meeting. Finally, six men were left, only two from NAVSEA, in whose offices the meeting was being held. Then he demanded that they all agree to no more than fourteen hull penetrations.

It was all window dressing, for he could have ordered any number of penetrations that he wanted. After declaring that the NAVSEA representatives were obviously incompetent, he announced his true objective. "As of now, NR will be responsible for the entire ship and NAVSEA will be responsible for the funding only," he said, all but kicking the regular U.S. Navy out of the *NR-1* project, but allowing NAVSEA to continue funneling money into his private, secret, and expensive program. From that point on, his own people would be at the helm, with Rickover exercising command.

* * *

Few ships in the fleet were as unobtrusive as the USS *Mackerel*, named not for some war god or killer species, but for a common species of saltwater fish used for food. In October of 1965, the *Mackerel* entered a naval facility at Key West to undergo her fourth overhaul, and was to resume operational status in February 1966. The old, single-screw diesel boat was long past her prime and was being used as an easy, noisy training target for antisubmarine warfare (ASW) forces practicing around Key West, Florida.

A surprise change of orders saved her from returning to the tiresome assignment of being ASW bait. Instead, the *Mackerel* sailed north, entered the Thames River once again, and went home to EB, where she had been built in 1952. The ugly duckling was being handed a mission from tomorrow.

By then, many of the novel ideas for the *NR-1* were ready to come off the design boards, equipment unheard of in submarines, and a test vehicle was required. The *Mackerel* was a natural choice, primarily because of her size.

She had been the navy's first venture into small submarines in a half century. The *Mackerel* was 131 feet in length and 13½ feet across the beam and displaced a mere 250 tons—comparable to the size being considered for the *NR-1*. She carried a crew of two officers and a dozen sailors, all of whom were astonished when they saw what was being hooked up to their boat. Big lights, a grappling arm that looked like a dinosaur claw, underwater viewing ports, and *wheels*! The captain, Lieutenant Joseph Snyder Jr., was coy when asked what was done during the three months that EB workers swarmed over his submarine. Snyder, obviously proud that his boat was no longer relegated to bottom-of-the-list missions, said, "We are an experimental vessel to try out some ideas the navy has." An official news release reported that the *Mackerel* had been called back "in order that equipment associated with a special project could be installed."

The sub pulled out of Groton in June, returned to Key West, and once back at the tip of Florida, she started rolling along the sandy bottom of the Gulf to try out some of the nifty gear that would one day adorn the *NR-1*. Years later, when the *Mackerel* was finally retired, the official history remembered that she was "the first ship in the U.S. Navy to run completely submerged on the ocean bottom utilizing wheels mounted on the pressure hull."

The lowly *Mackerel* paved the way for Rickover's underwater space-ship, and the testing had cost the navy yet another million dollars.

Admiral Rickover's demand for perfection came from his firm belief that the navy's nuclear program might not survive a single accident involving a reactor. The American public would not accept a nuclear disaster aboard a navy ship, and in fact, largely because of Rickover's doctrine, which tolerated no defects, there has never been one. On the other hand, a severe radiation leak aboard a November-class Soviet nuclear submarine in 1965 hospitalized an unknown number of crewmen and reminded everyone involved in the U.S. nuke world of the correctness of Rickover's personal construction mantra that quality always came before cost.

However, that iron rule was about to be bent, for the growing price of the *NR-1* had become a source of concern, even for the admiral.

Even while the *Mackerel* was being retooled to conduct her tests, Rickover did something completely unexpected and out of character. He listened to the advice of others instead of trusting his own instincts, and by doing so made a rare mistake that would haunt the *NR-1* for many years.

It began with the admiral boarding a sport fishing yacht in Miami and roaring out to where the submersible *Aluminaut* was investigating the waters of the Gulf Stream. He went aboard the deep-diving vessel, the hatch was closed, and Rickover paid rapt attention as the pilot guided the little submersible through a full demonstration of its capabilities.

He had not yet finalized the design of the *NR-1*, and was desperately looking for ways to keep it small and also to reduce costs. Listening carefully to the men who ran the *Aluminaut* and watching the submersible at work, he reached a decision that was faulty in logic and impossible to accomplish—the rising price of the *NR-1* would be shaved by using commercially available equipment or military grade material that already existed. He would soon ban developing anything new on the boat other than the nuclear power plant. Under the new guidelines, the non-nuclear guts of the *NR-1* would be off-the-shelf gear available to almost anyone in the industry.

That abrupt verdict stunned those who knew him best. Jack Leonard, the veteran Electric Boat project manager for the *NR-1* and a longtime Rickover admirer, observed, "Somebody sold him the idea that there were a lot of deep submersibles that already went a lot deeper than the *NR-1* would go, and they all used commercial equipment. It would be readily available and relatively cheap. They took him for a ride."

The most obvious argument against the pronouncement was that the *Aluminaut* and all other commercial submersibles had entirely different missions from those planned for a navy submarine. Their dives lasted only a few hours, they had very limited mobility, and they surfaced frequently to be tuned up again by experts aboard support ships. Some sort of repair was needed after almost every dive, and time was not critical for the submersibles.

By contrast, the *NR-1* was to be a military submarine, which would dive to untouched depths under enormous sea pressure, then change depths, and surface and dive repeatedly. It would encounter wicked weather and currents as it roamed the oceans completely on its own and cut off from all support for up to thirty days at a time. The technology for building such a revolutionary craft simply did not exist, and no review panel would ever have approved sending the boat to sea with anything that did not measure up to the most stringent military specifications. But Rickover was the only review panel that counted on this one, and he had decided to alter his own quality versus cost rule in order to cut some financial corners. While finding millions of dollars for the overall project, he chose to do a number of things on the cheap.

As a result, some of the equipment installed in the *NR-1* was more Stone Age than Space Age. The oven in which we heated meals was the same as those used on commercial airliners, only not as efficient. The manipulator arm that would be used to pick up items from the ocean floor was a leftover from another naval project. The computer navigation system that would guide our underwater voyages was adapted from one that did not even work well on the transatlantic airline flights for which it was built. Instead of a steering wheel at the maneuvering console, we had four control sticks converted from fighter planes. The crew would have to make do with cramped spaces, frozen food, and few personal facilities. The captain would have neither a cabin nor a private bunk and would often sleep on the deck to remain close to the control station. "There are more amenities aboard a fishing boat," said one distraught designer who was trying to figure it all out.

The most unusual aspect of the *NR-1* would be its ability to drive along the bottom. NASA was spending big dollars to create a lunar exploration buggy with wheels that were a woven mesh of fine zinc-coated wire with treads of titanium. But it was decided that we could roll a four-hundred-ton ship across a treacherous terrain just as unknown as that of the moon, but three thousand feet underwater, on a set of Goodyear truck tires.

It did not take Jack Leonard long to prove at Electric Boat that although the new "make-do" directive might work on some ancillary components, it would never pass muster on other vital parts of the boat. Few people knew more about building submarines than Leonard, who had worked at EB and with Rickover for the past twenty-four years. He had been the nuclear project manager for the *Nautilus*, the *Skipjack*, and the *Narwhal*. And he was one of the few people who knew how to deal with the admiral, even when the admiral was wrong.

After examining some of the commercially available equipment, Leonard expressed doubt that it would work on the *NR-1*. So Rickover told him to get a propulsion motor of the sort used by submersibles and "pressure cycle" it to duplicate the enormous strains of a long-duration submerged mission. If it were to be used on the *NR-1*, repairmen would not be able to coddle the motor every few hours.

"The only thing we had was an old sixteen-inch gun barrel left over from a World War I ship, so we rigged a system to put the motor in it, then let the pressure build up," Leonard said. "After a few cycles, the whole thing blew apart. It was such a mess that we couldn't figure out which part had failed first."

As he stood looking at the debris of what had once been a precision motor, Leonard was certain that what worked elsewhere might never be adapted to the *NR-1*. "That was the end of that show. Forget all this commercial stuff," he said. The program, already past normal submarine design and development, was entering an unknown phase of shipbuilding. "After the propulsion motor incident, they had to change everything."

It was only the first of many lessons the engineers and designers would learn the hard way, and failed experiments became almost routine. What Rickover wanted and demanded seemed impossible to deliver.

The navy was forced to send Congress a gloomy "reprogramming action" for its projected budget for the upcoming 1967 fiscal year, claiming "substantial changes and additional engineering work will be required" to build the mysterious *NR-1*. It admitted that hull construction and assembly procedures for conventional submarines could not be used and that available state-of-the-art equipment "did not provide sufficient reliability" for the submarine.

The *NR-1* was originally planned to be 97 feet long, but the new length would be 135 feet. The proposed submerged displacement went from 230 tons to approximately 364 tons. "Because of these developments, the estimated cost has increased to $58.3 million," stated the budget request. The planned delivery date of the sub to the navy was slipped back a full year and a half.

Nothing had yet been built, but the *NR-1* had grown bigger and longer and was becoming an entirely different ship from Rickover's original scheme. Rickover would hew to the cost-cutting line whenever possible, but things had taken a radical and expensive new turn. Skirting the navy budget by wearing his Atomic Energy Commission hat, Rickover shifted $7.5 million of AEC money into the design of the minireactor. It still would not be enough.

Brian Wruble was an admitted space junkie, and was hooked on what unfolded in the early 1960s as the United States and the Soviet Union launched rockets that carried machines, monkeys, and men into that far frontier. It wasn't the rockets that grabbed his attention as much as the men who built them. He was only twenty-three years old, held a master's degree in electrical engineering from Cornell University, and was imbued with the desire to become involved with a great big project that would allow a small group of men to explore the unknown. The slightly built son of a research scientist in Kalamazoo, Michigan, Wruble knew that most engineers who supported the space program were locked to drafting tables, doing little more than pushing paper. Because his wit and personality demanded the company of other people, and his heart responded to adventure, he did not want to march into an office every day to work with slide rules and T squares. So instead of heading for Cape Canaveral, he decided to become a field engineer for the Sperry Gyroscope Company, where going to work could mean trips beneath the sea on the fast attack submarines and missile boats of the U.S. Navy.

Field engineers and technical representatives, or "tech reps," are specialists who bring their expert knowledge to bear on developing and maintaining specialized equipment that is beyond the operational realm of most sailors, who have enough demanding duties aboard ship without having to master scientific theory. It remains common, even today, for technologically sophisticated submarines to carry engineers and tech reps on missions. It is not a job without risk. Seventeen civilian specialists, including several from Sperry, were aboard when the *Thresher* sank with all hands.

One of Wruble's missions took him out on an early trial of the Polaris missile submarine USS *Francis Scott Key*. Never at a loss for words, he got into a procedural dispute with a grizzled old chief petty officer. "After our return to port, I was ordered back to Sperry headquarters in Great Neck, New York. Three guys in suits called me in. I thought they were going to fire me, but instead they said, 'We have an opportunity for you if you're smart enough to grab it.' They were interviewing oddballs like me for the job," Wruble said. The men described a one-of-a-kind operation the navy was putting together that sounded much like the pioneering days of the space program. "You can be one of the guys," his bosses said. Wruble took the job on the spot, and became the computer expert for the *NR-1*.

In keeping with Rickover's dictum to use available technology whenever possible, Wruble found himself wrestling with a computer that was absolutely archaic by today's standards, and was hardly state of the art even in 1966. Sperry originally built the two-part MK XII aircraft computer for Pan American, but when it did not work for the airline, it was pulled out of service. The lightweight, small computer was renamed the Mark XV and found its way out of commercial obscurity through Rickover's drive not to create new equipment, and was pressed into military secrecy for use aboard the *NR-1*.

It had reels of magnetic tape and was so fragile that some parts included hair-thin wires actually *sewn* into the machine by seamstresses. The total memory—random-access memory (RAM) and program storage—of the Mark XV was only twelve thousand twenty-one-bit words, or "bytes." By comparison, even the earliest desktop computers would have several million bytes of total memory, while current laptops commonly have more than ten thousand million bytes, making them about a million times more powerful than the computer that first ran our boat. In the *NR-1* computer, every memory location was highly valued real estate, since there was no room to add more. Trying to pack all that was required of the computer within such a limited space would be a long and frustrating exercise in abstract thinking for the engineers. The small memory was a killer.

There was no operating system for it, such as today's Windows and yesterday's DOS programs. The only instructions Wruble found showed the computer had a maximum of fourteen possible operations, all primitive machine language commands. It could add, subtract, and multiply but could not divide one number by another until the programmers taught it how. If there was going to be a book on how to operate the puzzling unit, the Sperry programmers were going to have to write it.

Wruble and the others had to convert the machine that had balked aboard airplanes into a sophisticated computer that could communicate with almost everything aboard a highly automated ship that would be run not by electrical engineers, but by sailors guiding the boat across the floor of the world. When he set up the equipment for testing in the giant Sperry plant in Great Neck, he discovered the computer wouldn't work any better for him than it had for Pan Am. The two separate pieces did not even talk to each other.

In moments of despair, Wruble realized that programming and storing all of the mathematical functions needed for complex underwater navigation was a long way off, if it could be done at all. He and his team began working sixteen-hour days to convert the Mark XV into a machine on which submariners could bet their lives.

The Sperry facility in Great Neck was a single massive structure with mile-long hallways that were so wide workers rode bicycles between distant offices. There were special dust-free laboratories in which technicians in white coats put together precise instruments for use in ship navigation and gun-missile fire control, but the general layout was a haphazard mix of offices and laboratories. Maps were useless, because almost in a matter of minutes, shoulder-high portable walls were rearranged on a bumpy floor of vinyl-covered two-by-four timbers to create a maze of spaces sectioned off into hundreds of rabbit warrens. When someone called out a name, dozens of heads popped up from inside the various cubicles. Wruble was so deep in his work during one overnight shift that he did not realize until morning that while he was trying to debug the latest problem in the Mark XV, an entire room had been created around him, four walls with no door.

At least, the engineers believed, the march of scientific progress made one important part of their job easier. The computer world was changing rapidly, and they were absolutely confident that the tiny memory system of the Mark XV would be replaced within a few years with something many times more powerful. Therefore, they decided to save some vital memory space by using only one digit to represent a year–1966 would be a "6" and the other years would be similarly designated "7" and "8" and "9" until the end of the decade. No zero was written for 1970, since the old hardware was certain to be replaced by the end of the decade, by which time it would be a technological antique.

Thirty-five years before the end of the twentieth century, when a computer-webbed world stumbled through the Y2K scare, Wruble and his team unwittingly set the stage for what would happen if a computer could not tell the proper time. Only instead of Y2K, the problem would be Y70. Sometimes the *NR-1* was too far ahead of its time.

EB Project Manager Jack Leonard called Sperry's top brass early in the project to alert them that Rickover was coming to their plant. Before hanging up, he asked, "You have grapes for the admiral?"

"Grapes? What grapes?"

"You gotta have grapes and peanuts and stuff for the admiral," warned Leonard. "He demands them. You better get some, or you're dead before you start."

A Sperry executive telephoned Leonard in a few hours to assure him the crisis had been resolved. Grapes were on hand for tomorrow's visit.

"Are they seedless?" Leonard asked. Stunned silence at the other end of the line. Sperry, then one of the biggest defense contractors in the nation, swung into action again and seedless grapes were on the table when Rickover arrived.

While at Great Neck, the admiral wanted a demonstration of the computer over which Wruble had been slaving. As Rickover watched, the young engineer put the machine through its whirring and blinking paces in an air-conditioned room, and it actually did what it was supposed to do. Brian Wruble thought things went extremely well.

"Sure, it works like this," snapped Rickover, unimpressed with the performance. "But how does it do running continuously for thirty days at 120 degrees and in 100 percent humidity?" Wruble knew the answer. Any computer, particularly one as sensitive to its surroundings as this airline makeover, was bound to fail under such conditions. Rickover blew up, shouting that it had not been properly tested at all, and that the Sperry people in general, and Wruble in particular, were imbeciles. He ordered that the computer be put through maximum, not minimum, tests.

It was a major setback for Wruble and Sperry. They now had to come up with creative ways to protect the delicate Mark XV from environmental adversity that was well beyond its design limits. It was already compact and lightweight, but now they had to make it virtually indestructible. Computers in those days were generally huge and pampered machines, and while the NASA people were packing a lot of computing power into a tiny space capsule, NASA also had a virtually unlimited budget and swarms of technicians and engineers. Big submarines had air-conditioned computer rooms, gentle surroundings, and men who gave their computers tender loving care. The *NR-1* had Wruble.

As Rickover left Great Neck that day, he barked at Jack Leonard to "Get those Sperry people on the straight and narrow." The seedless grapes had not mellowed the man a bit.

Wruble and other Sperry engineers were left to find a method of running thirty-day tests at high temperatures and 100 percent humidity. They erected a big plastic tent inside the Great Neck building, secured the flaps to the floor, filled it with steam, and hauled the Mark XV inside. That impossibly sweaty chamber became Brian Wruble's world.

4

THE CREW

*I*n addition to his dedication to developing nuclear power for both the military and civilian worlds, Admiral Rickover was a passionate educator. Throughout his life, hours of hard work and continuous study on a vast range of subjects paved his way to personal success, and he was unrelenting in passing along what he learned. He read voraciously, and peppered his public addresses with arcane quotes and facts, bombarded subordinates with clippings from publications, and wrote a number of books, several on American education. He was openly contemptuous of the educational methods of his alma mater, the U.S. Naval Academy, where he had graduated in 1922 as number 107 in a class of 540 midshipmen. His single-minded attitude toward continual work and study was well demonstrated when he was a lieutenant stationed at the navy's Office of the Inspector of Naval Material in Philadelphia during 1933. Rickover not only performed his assignment, but also used the job as an opportunity to carefully observe American manufacturing methods, and in his spare time, he translated the book *Das Unterseeboot* (*The Submarine*) by World War I German Admiral Hermann Bauer. The work became a basic text for the U.S. submarine service. As Rickover achieved power, he established some of the most stringent training programs and schools the military services had ever seen.

My next stop after the *Sargo* patrol was at one of those Rickover academies, the navy's nuclear power school at the Mare Island Naval Shipyard in Vallejo, California. For six months, all officers and men who would operate nuclear reactors on ships had to pass through the classroom regimen at either Mare Island or the other nuclear power school, in Bainbridge, Maryland. It was a sort of technical basic training, but was not easy, nor was it designed to be. The emphasis was on academics, day and night, and the heavy course load was almost identical for officers, some of whom did not hold engineering degrees, and enlisted men, many of whom had only high school diplomas when they were thrust into courses equal to anything offered by an engineering college. Not everyone made it through, but Rickover never lowered the standards.

Classes were conducted eight hours a day, five days a week, in a large, cream-colored building on an isolated, treeless, wind-swept spot at the north end of the shipyard. We had a minimum of four hours of homework each night, all designed to give the students the theoretical, scientific, and technological background we needed for the safe operation of nuclear power plants. The subject matter was pure hard science, including courses in math, physics, chemistry, thermodynamics, metallurgy, reactor dynamics and core characteristics, shielding and radiological fundamentals, and reactor plant systems and operations.

I continued to find it much easier to assimilate knowledge within the structured military environment than at college, for at training sites such as Mare Island, outside influences were kept to a minimum. All I had to do was make my bunk in the morning, show up at the appointed classrooms, and focus on the subject at hand. Others took care of the daily routine of life while we hit the books.

Although extracurricular activities were not encouraged, we played cards occasionally in the lounge, managed a few ski weekends in the nearby Sierra Mountains, and even formed a ragtag team to play in the Mare Island seven-man flag football league. We called ourselves the North Gate All Stars, and played in shorts and T-shirts, sometimes in bare feet, against well-established, well-muscled, sponsored, uniformed, and rubber-cleated teams such as the Marine Corps Barracks. Not surprisingly, we were crushed in the first game. Also not surprising for a bunch of pretty smart guys, we quickly figured out the folly of playing head-to-head against the local mastodons. So we put a new strategy in place by the second game, continually shuttling in fresh players who were quick on defense while our offense introduced a spread formation that relied on passing, speed, and using the whole field. Instead of trying to go through the big boys, we went around and over them, never lost another game, and so learned to adapt and work as a team, a lesson that would pay big dividends in my future.

I went across the country again for the next six-month phase of my training and arrived at the Nuclear Power Training Unit (NPTU) in Windsor, Connecticut, on February 16, 1965. The unit was hidden in a heavily wooded area amid a sweep of fields and drying sheds that produced fine shade-grown tobacco for cigar wrappers. The NPTU was home to the prototype of the S1C nuclear reactor that powered a class of small hunter-killer submarines called the *Tullibee*, and we received hands-on experience with that model power plant.

While we worked in Connecticut, other students were learning the S3W reactor at Arco, Idaho, and the S3G in West Milton, New York. The *G* in the name of a reactor signified that General Electric had built the plant, the *W* stood for Westinghouse, and the *C* designated a plant from Combustion Engineering. Each reactor-training site housed power plants from different types of ships.

All of the reactor prototype and training units were located in rural locations, and we wore civilian clothing when going off-site to reduce public awareness of such military installations. At Windsor, unless you knew the prototype was there, it didn't exist. The access road doglegged through the trees, and we would park in a designated lot and show our badges to the security guard at the main gate to enter. A large building with vertical metal siding housed the prototype reactor, its shielding, and its instrumentation, and the offices of the nuclear physicists who monitored its operation. From the back side of the structure protruded the large, round hull of the replicated submarine engine room. Nearby was a long single-story building that housed the classrooms and the navy site administrative offices.

The prototype consisted of a fully functional nuclear reactor and ship's engine room, identical to that used on the class of boat for which it was designed, so our training mirrored reality. It was used not only to train future power plant operators, but also to test any changes on the full-scale reactor under carefully controlled operating conditions on land, rather than risk introducing untested designs on a ship at sea.

We spent three months in the classroom to learn the theory of operation, then went to rotating shifts and worked in the "engine room" just as if we were aboard ship. At this point, the courses became very specialized, for we had to learn the skills particular to our own field of expertise. On a submarine, we would be specialists, with very different duties to perform and control panels and equipment to operate. With the large number of men being pushed through to man the rapidly growing nuclear fleet, there was very little time for cross training.

As an electrician, I learned the Electric Plant Control Panel, which brought the generators on line, synchronized the power loads, and distributed electricity to the nuclear plant and the rest of the ship.

Reactor operators mastered the Reactor Plant Control Panel. They would take the reactor "critical" by pulling out the control rods until a self-sustaining nuclear reaction was achieved.

Machinist's mates operated the Steam Plant Control Panel to control the supply of steam to the turbines that drove the ship's propellers. They would operate the steam generation and distribution equipment, systems such as hydraulics, heating, and ventilation, and the seawater distilling plants. Further, some of them were trained to perform water chemistry analyses of the reactor's primary coolant and the "boiler water" in the steam generators.

In addition, we all had to become maintenance experts in our fields.

Meanwhile, the officers learned to supervise all of the panels, as well as the operations and maintenance of the entire power plant. When serving as engineering officers of the watch (EOOWs), they would coordinate the various operations and lead the response to emergency conditions such as fire, flooding, and failure of power plant equipment. The EOOW was stationed behind the panel operators in the maneuvering room so he could see all of the displays and indicators at the same time.

We ran drills over and over until we could instantly recognize a problem and take the actions demanded by established, well-tested procedures, for we were never allowed to vary from the Reactor Plant Manual. Rickover's experts had assembled it carefully over the years, and virtually all situations you might encounter were included. If a new or unusual problem cropped up, the Book had to be changed before you could go ahead. You went by the Book, each time, every time, or God help you because Rickover and his henchmen wouldn't. It became our Bible.

Our instructors were former students who had placed at the top of their classes, both at the nuclear power school and at the prototype.

They were the cream of the crop, for only about one out of a hundred was selected to remain behind to train others. To my surprise, upon finishing the prototype course, the navy did not reassign me back to another boat in the fleet as I had expected. As Honor Man of my class, I was chosen to stay on as an operator-instructor myself. I was only twenty-one years old and without realizing it had just achieved one of the mandatory ticket punches that would be needed a year down the road to join the crew of an entirely new and secret submarine.

As the *NR-1* was coming off the drawing boards, Rickover started the process of choosing the dozen men—three officers and nine enlisted—who would be the first to take it to sea. The admiral liked to bring a "commissioning" crew together early in the process so they would grow along with the submarine, and learn their boat as it was assembled and tested.

That was true even with the big nuclear-powered vessels, where the men concentrated on specific assignments. But special care was given to whom he chose for the *NR-1*, for this handful of selected sailors and officers would have to know not only their own jobs, but those of everyone else, too. The lack of cross training at the NPTU had to be overcome, so that a machinist's mate could handle the ship's electronics, an electrician's mate could drive the boat, and an officer could fix a leak. Instead of concentrating on a narrow field, we would have to know how to do everything.

The determining factor on the number of crewmen was the size of the little boat, since the tight space meant it would go to sea with only seven or eight men. If those eight were divided in half to stand twelve hours of watches a day, then no more than four men would run the entire submarine at a time. At an absolute minimum, one man could run the entire reactor plant while just two other people stood watch at other positions.

Just finding people who could get along in such cramped quarters for long periods was a problem. Submariners are among the most equable people anywhere, finely trained not to panic, not to yell when facing a stressful situation, and to get along with others for months at a time while running underwater. John Craven described how psychological tests that jammed such imperturbable men together under conditions envisioned for the *NR-1* often ended in fistfights between the more aggressive ones after a few days.

Rickover's determination to keep his *NR-1* away from the structured, slow, and bureaucratic ways of the official navy extended to choosing this first crew. Having bypassed the oversight and review process on construction, he would do the same on personnel. The Bureau of Personnel, known as BuPers, normally handled the assignment of officers and sailors, but it was frozen out of this selection process as Rickover established a criterion that few could meet.

First, any candidate for the *NR-1* had to be qualified in submarines. That eliminated everyone in the surface fleet, and no aviators need apply. Then he had to be a qualified nuclear power plant operator, a requirement that narrowed the field sharply because of the specialized schooling needed for certification. The final screening component was that a candidate must be an instructor at one of the few nuclear power training units.

The genius in Rickover's selection process was that the only people who could possibly qualify were already under his command, and that allowed him to put them anywhere he wished. He didn't want to consult BuPers, didn't have to, and didn't.

A general memo was circulated among the NPTU instructors, and although the wording was vague, the idea of joining a one-of-a-kind team for a unique, secret mission appealed to me. During a round of interviews in Washington, some of the candidates had to face the admiral himself. I was one of the fortunate ones who did not have to undergo that particular test, although I was thoroughly grilled by some of his aides who seemed well trained in his methods of verbal terrorism.

The interviews for the enlisted men were not as bad as the ordeals faced by our officers, whom Rickover was simultaneously vetting for possible future command positions. As power plant instructors, we had been thoroughly schooled in how to conduct Rickover-style oral interviews ourselves, and had often been on the other side of the table in such sessions. We would ask a candidate technical questions until we discovered an area of weakness, then bore in to expose his lack of knowledge. So during my one-on-one interviews with Rickover's assistants, I knew the best response was to be concise, never venture beyond what was asked, and promptly say so if I did not know. Any attempt to guess or make up an answer was bound to fail, as you would be trying to explain something you did not fully understand to someone who did.

At the beginning of the selection process, only about 100 men among the 650,000 in the navy at the time possessed the needed credentials—less than a tenth of 1 percent. The twelve finally selected represented less than one-hundredth of 1 percent.

The *NR-1* commissioning crew was announced on October 13, 1966, and to my surprise, I was on the list along with Jim Turner, another NPTU Windsor instructor. Being chosen was kind of numbing, but only for a short time. Jim and I celebrated with a pitcher of beer at a local pub.

The NPTU gave us commendations, but there were no big parties, no loud cheering, for the media spotlight was pointed the other way, toward the heavens, where American astronauts were orbiting in a two-man capsule. While astronauts were usually unveiled with a maximum of publicity, my selection was written up in my hometown newspaper, the *Merced Sun-Star,* on an inside page, with a two-column headline that stated, MERCEDIAN IS CREWMAN ON NEW RESEARCH SUB. Jim and I had a week to get our stuff together and report to our new duty station.

Rickover kept his *NR-1* and its people under wraps for years to come. Even when we went aboard other navy ships, we would occasionally be whispered about as being CIA spooks. Nobody knew who we were or what we did, and we couldn't tell them.

I had finished at the top of my class in the navy's basic electronics school and in Sub School, and then after I qualified aboard the *Sargo,* did the same at Nuclear Power School and at reactor prototype training. But when I walked into a small classroom at the Knolls Atomic Power Laboratory in Schenectady, New York, to meet my fellow crew members of the *NR-1,* I found myself among a group of men who had academic résumés and service records that equaled or surpassed my own.

We were all in civilian clothes, but there was no doubt that the quiet fellow who stepped forward to shake my hand was our skipper. He was Lieutenant Commander Dwaine O. Griffith from Shoshone, Idaho, an old guy who had recently turned thirty-one. This low-key man who smoked a pleasant-smelling pipe had admiral stamped all over him. In his long naval career, Griffith would command not only our little boat, but also the ballistic missile subs USS *Casimir Pulaski* and USS *Sam Rayburn* before becoming director of the navy's Deep Submergence Systems Division and serving as a rear admiral on the staff of the chief of naval operations. He also held a ranking job in naval intelligence. Rickover hand-selected this unpretentious graduate of the University of Idaho to be the first officer-in-charge of the *NR-1,* and it was a good choice.

The other two officers were also slightly older than the rest of us, both out of the Naval Academy at Annapolis. Steve Perry was a topflight nuclear engineer with a reputation for excellence in training those who worked for him. Jack Maurer was a supervisor of nuclear power plant operations and the son of an admiral.

They were a stark contrast in almost every way. Perry had blonde hair and somewhat of a baby face, while Maurer was dark, with a perpetual five-o'clock shadow. Steve was open and outgoing, while Jack seemed brooding and formal. The one thing they had in common was that both were terrific naval officers.

There were eight other enlisted men in addition to me, all in their twenties, and in the months to come, we would become close friends and trusted partners who would ride together to the bottom of the oceans. Discipline was rarely a problem, for if we had a disagreement, we sorted it out among ourselves. You never wanted to carry a grudge three thousand feet below the surface, where lives depend upon mutual trust and cooperation. None of us would let a personal problem with another member of the crew interfere with the job.

I assumed they were all smart, since they had passed Rickover's screening, and I was right. We looked forward to learning and understanding the coming avalanche of new material, although we were embarking on an unknown boat for unknown missions in unknown places. Many of us never even took notes.

We were products of our time. There were no minority races represented, our haircuts were high and tight, we wore narrow ties, some had thick glasses, about half were married, and all of us seemed to have avoided the discontent that was seeping into American youth in the mid-1960s. We had spent so much time in navy schools and aboard ships that we did not feel part of the outside world, where changes were troublesome and many. There wasn't a hippie in our bunch, we didn't discuss politics, and nobody did drugs. For the twelve men meeting for the first time that day at Knolls, such things just were not important to us.

Griffith, Perry, and Maurer, along with Jim Turner, Bob Lunt, Dean Paine, Danny Gunter, John Claytor, Larry Kammerzell, Dave Seaton, Don Marks, and I, had only one thing on our minds—getting ready to run the navy's smallest nuclear-powered submarine.

Our biggest problem was that there was no manual on how to run a ship like the *NR-1*, since it was the only one of its kind, and still more an ephemeral idea than hard steel. Assumptions could be made about how things would work, but no one really knew. One of our most important tasks would be to determine and document the operating procedures for this ship through trial and error, in that abrupt area where theory meets reality.

5
ELECTRIC BOAT

*T*he nuclear submarines of today glide through the eastern end of Long Island Sound and ride up the Thames River like slow shadows, with green water cascading over their bows and peeling away from the round hulls. They are steel creatures of prey that have been away for a while–few know where, doing things–few know what. Returning to their nest, their compact forms move with menacing grace toward the sub base at Groton, Connecticut, home of the big black boats.

The scenic waterfront town of New London is on the western shore of the deep estuary as they pass by, and on the eastern side are the tightly packed seventeen acres of the legendary Electric Boat shipbuilding facility, where entire flights of nuclear-powered boats have been built. Three miles from the mouth of the harbor, the subs slide beneath a railway bridge and the twin spans of Interstate 95 that separate the upper reaches of the river from its lower harbor section. The bridges are a convenience for ground transportation but pose a military hazard, and for many years, the navy kept a few subs docked at the State Pier on the ocean side of the span, which would be a natural target in case of war. Otherwise, if an enemy missile brought it down, much of the American submarine fleet would be bottled up and helpless.

Jack Leonard had neither the desire nor the time to watch any incoming subs on a chilly day early in 1967 as a winter wind hummed down the harbor. He had seen a lifetime of ships, and as he walked from his office on the Hill down to the EB yard, his mind was focused solely on the baffling project that Rickover had given him. Leonard, a burly dark-haired Scotsman with the personality of a bulldog and a no-shit attitude, was considered the best manager in the company for submarine design and construction, but the *NR-1* was driving him nuts.

EB had been turning out boats since the early 1900s, when it crafted custom yachts for millionaires, elegant pleasure vessels powered by quiet electric motors that did not offend the ears of wealthy clients. When World War I began, the company converted its expertise in batteries, electric motors, and diesel engines into building more than eighty submarines. In World War II, EB produced another seventy-four subs at Groton and oversaw the construction of another twenty-six. After that, the company helped develop new generations of submarines and made history in 1955 with the *Nautilus,* on which Leonard had been the shipyard's nuclear project manager.

As he crossed Thames Street toward the guard shack, his senses were assaulted by a persistent, cloying chemical smell from the Pfizer pharmaceutical plant that bordered EB to the south. It smelled like rancid peanut butter. The time was just after lunch, and his boots crunched over thousands of bottle caps that glittered on the pavement, debris from the midday break when thousands of thirsty shipyard workers had crossed the road to reach the lines that stretched outside of bustling taverns. Bartenders had rows of shots and beers waiting, so a worker could pay for his drink, belt down the whiskey, grab a bottle of beer, and return to the rear of the line to do it all over again. Welders swore that the alcohol somehow cleared their lungs and nasal passages from the chemical stench of their trade and the Pfizer odor.

Leonard shaded his eyes and did a quick scan over the clutter of warships. Both the North and South Yards were hives of activity. Attack subs, submarines to carry Polaris and Poseidon missiles, high-speed subs, and deep-diving subs were on the ways and at the wharves and the piers, in various stages of construction, conversion, refitting, or overhaul. The *Triton,* the world's longest submarine, was due in soon to be decommissioned. Big cranes on railroad tracks hoisted steel sections, and the normal cacophony of shipbuilding noise rose to meet him—grinding, drilling, hammering, shouts. Twenty-five thousand men were at work down there, some three thousand engineers elbow-to-elbow in the brick building he had just left, and hundreds more in the nuclear engineering building. Sperry engineers were working in make-shift offices aboard an old ferryboat that had been rented and hauled up to an EB pier when the yard ran out of available office space.

Leonard paused a bit when he glanced at the covered South Yard building ways that sat right beside the river. It was there that the *Nautilus* had been built in secret, and it was there that the *NR-1* would be assembled. Just as when they had built the historic *Nautilus,* this new boat also was to be completely shielded from public view—if it ever reached the point where some construction might actually begin.

It seemed to Leonard that with all those people at work, all of the equipment, and the decades of knowledge available to EB, the little submarine should have been as easy to build as the seven previous research subs the company had produced. But submersibles like the *Aluminaut* and the *Sea Cliff* and the *Turtle* were child's play in comparison to the *NR-1*.

As if the logistical, design, testing, and construction puzzles were not enough, Admiral Rickover was pounding on everyone to move faster. What are you going to do about the thruster motors? What are you going to do about batteries? How are you going to feed the people? He not only demanded that every item on the boat meet, and in many cases surpass, military specifications, but he would not compromise on his edict of using cheap, off-the-shelf equipment whenever possible. "Keep it simple!" the admiral would shout during his weekly visits to Groton, and, almost in the same breath, bark, "We're going to be up and down for years and I want to know if this stuff will take it!" He even had the bathyscaphe *Trieste* take some of the external equipment down to twenty thousand feet for durability tests. The admiral wanted a unique military ship at the best commercial price, and Leonard knew there was no way that could work.

Entire new laboratories were being built just to test parts for what was now being derisively called Rickover's Rubber Duck. More testing meant more money, and it was devouring huge and unanticipated blocks of time. "We had to test everything," Leonard recalled, "and everything we tested had a problem." As modern technology collided with the reality of money, the size of the boat kept changing to accommodate the hand-tooled equipment. Top management at the shipyard worried as costs escalated, but there was nothing they could do except press ahead.

This day's major crisis involved perhaps the most important part of the entire boat, the pressure hull. Without it, there could be no ship. Submarine hulls are usually just long, round, empty steel tubes, affectionately called sewer pipes, a series of carefully molded rings that are joined and capped with round hemispheres at each end. Over the years, the shape had proven to be the best method to withstand the immense pressures exerted by water at depths.

Never before, however, had any hull required the exacting standards demanded for the *NR-1*. In order to survive great depths, the long cylinder had to be an almost perfect circle, the most precise ever turned out by Electric Boat. Forty flawless plates of top-grade HY-80 steel, with no impurities whatever, were given tender love and care during the manufacturing process at the Lukens Steel plant in Coatesville, Pennsylvania, and arrived at EB aboard special flatbed railcars. Each weighed four tons.

Huge machines rolled those big plates—eight feet wide, ten feet long, and two and three-quarters inches thick—again and again, squeezing them with tons of pressure. The top roller was smaller than the bottom roller, so with each pass, the steel plate was gently curved a bit more until it formed what would be one-quarter of a circle. Like pieces of a jigsaw puzzle, four of those plates would be put together to become a cylinder. The cylinders would be welded together to form the hull.

The major problem was that EB had to be so exact in this process. Normal submarine hulls could be a little out of shape, with an acceptable circular tolerance of several inches. But Henry Furuno, the head of the EB hull design department, calculated that for the *NR-1*, the twelve-and-one-half-foot diameter of each cylinder could vary by no more than one-sixteenth of one inch—virtually a perfect circle of heavy steel. Only then would it be able to withstand the immense pressures of the deep ocean. The latest plate being bent wasn't even close, proving that the machine was not rolling the HY-80 tight enough. It was once again time to improvise.

Leonard sighed as he showed his security badge to the guard who controlled access to the *NR-1* area. He saw Test Manager Dick Patenaude, an up-through-the-ranks machinist-turned-engineer who understood how things were done on the yard, waiting on the other side of the tall fence and reaching for the spiral notebook he kept stuffed under his belt at the small of his back. To Leonard, it was almost as if Patenaude were drawing a gun, for that damned notebook never contained anything but bad news.

The first day that our crew spent at the Knolls Atomic Power Laboratory, tucked away outside of Schenectady, we were introduced to the reactor plant that would power the *NR-1*. It made me a little uneasy. The nuclear principles were the same, but this seemed more like a toy or some science fiction gadget than the sort of huge reactors that I had studied, worked on, and taught.

We were all veterans of the big boats, submarines on which nuclear reactor compartments were equipment-filled caverns devoid of life, while adjoining engineering spaces were manned by dozens of specialists every hour of the day. The reactor room on a typical nuclear sub was about two stories high, and the pressure vessel that contained the reactor was some twenty feet in diameter and surrounded by lots of lead shielding, multiple pumps and valves, and panels of intricate control instruments.

The dozen of us who had gathered in the small classroom at Knolls listened incredulously as General Electric scientists, engineers, and physicists described what they had invented for the *NR-1*. The ship would have a miniature pressurized water nuclear reactor and power plant, and could be run from a single control panel by one man! The reactor, its surrounding pressure vessel, and its shielding would be about the size of an office desk, hang from a bulkhead, produce only about one-hundredth of the power of a normal ship reactor, and turn out a maximum of only 130 horsepower, of which 60 could be used for propulsion. Just turning on the heat in the forward compartment would cause a jump in the power readings, and the top speed would be only five knots, about as fast as a man could walk. These days, you can buy an outboard motor that produces 100 horsepower for about $5,000.

A sculptor once asked his mentor how to carve an elephant out of stone, and was advised to get a big rock and chip away everything that did not look like an elephant. The GE engineers were following a similar path in designing the minireactor. They started with a normal plant and chipped away everything that didn't look necessary, and had left us a bare-bones nuclear reactor unlike anything that had ever been created.

In an age in which nuclear plants had been growing ever larger and more powerful to propel bigger ships, reversing the process to build a reactor to absolute minimum specifications was a challenge for the engineers. Although the reactor was yet to be built, they were enthusiastic that the technical and theoretical problems were being overcome. The crew was not quite as sanguine as we listened to the lectures and studied the design, for this was more than a classroom exercise to us. We viewed their work to date as creating more of a teakettle than the big, reliable plants of the boats on which we all had sailed. Our different view was colored by the fact that our lives would depend on it.

Naturally, there had been limitations on what GE could do. In line with Rickover's cost-saving orders, they had to build the reactor from standard components that were used on navy nuclear power plants of the day. In addition to the minimum number of control rods, the designers had to use the fewest pumps, valves, instrumentation, and components that would allow safe operation.

One engineer said there had been some early hope of going all the way with this reactor, making it totally automatic and able to answer the propulsion commands from a computer. Admiral Rickover immediately squashed the idea of a machine talking to a machine about reactor operations. A human had to be in control, he ordered, for only a human could react to unanticipated emergencies.

The eventual result of the design was just what Rickover wanted—a low-power reactor that could be operated by one person, with the instruments associated with all three of the usual control stations on a big submarine condensed to a single panel for the *NR-1*. In the end, the GE engineers would be proven correct. That little reactor packed enough muscle to successfully push the *NR-1* around for almost forty years of incredibly strenuous sea duty. The small reactor represented an immense technological achievement.

During the intense classroom sessions, our instructors were not telling us how nuclear power worked, just explaining how to operate their invention. Only a few weeks earlier, we had been instructors ourselves, so they treated us as equals who had a full comprehension of the technical and scientific data laid before us. The crew grasped the concepts easily, for this was a single pump in a single coolant loop with the added capacity to remove sample water for testing. After working on the big plants, we could virtually see this one work. It was like stepping down from maintaining a Ferrari to working on a Model T Ford.

An esprit de corps and an unusual sense of fraternity settled upon our crew during our studies, for our three officers were right beside us, learning the same material at the same time.

We all had been used to the rigid structure of military life, in which one's place and function are well defined. It was clear that the manpower requirements for the *NR-1* would force us to transcend those historic relationships, for there would not be much room for saluting.

We developed organizational and operating concepts on the fly. The officers helped the enlisted men and vice versa, and we realized that the cross-training everyone had been denied because it was unneeded on big boats was going to be an absolute requirement aboard the *NR-1*. Electricians would have to care for mechanical equipment, and machinist's mates had to be up to speed on reactor controls. Our knowledge would expand far beyond the confines of the nuclear reactor plant, for each of us would have to know everything about the boat.

The designers envisioned that the single engineering control panel operator would be an officer who would simultaneously run the power plant reactor and all of the electrical and steam systems while directing the efforts of an enlisted helper. But that assumption was the result of traditional thinking, which the *NR-1* was proving wrong at almost every turn.

Since our crew had only three officers, and the captain would not be standing watch, that would leave only two people to man the EOOW position all day, every day on missions that could last for weeks at a time. It was obvious that some of the enlisted men would have to be qualified to handle some duties that usually were limited to officers, exactly as Admiral Rickover had intended.

It was one of the first signs that we were expected to be more than a crew. We would have to become a team unlike anything else in the navy.

As we ended our two weeks at the atomic laboratory, we thoroughly understood the miniature nuclear plant from an intellectual standpoint, but that was all. There was no prototype available on which we could practice, for the reactor itself was still being built. When we departed Knolls, our instructors could go back to overseeing the development, testing, and delivery of the reactor to the ship. Until then, it was still all theory.

We still had not seen anything more than a sketch of the ship, a drawing that didn't tell us much, and were anxious to reach our next training stop, Electric Boat in Connecticut, and get a look at our new submarine. The schedule that had been given to us showed that the ship should be about halfway built by this time. It wasn't exactly waiting at the pier. In fact, it didn't exist.

The schedule for building the *NR-1* was as flexible as rubber. Frustrated managers took their latest problems to the planners and explained that, once again, more work was needed on some aspect, and therefore a new timeline had to be made. "What do you want to hear this time?" one planner usually responded, knowing that any date he projected was nothing but a number on a calendar as far as the *NR-1* was concerned.

Things were in a jumble, and had fallen so far behind schedule that when we showed up for three weeks of training in late 1966, we were about nine months too early.

The EB engineers gave us classroom instruction on the nonpropulsion systems that would be aboard the little submarine. We learned about waste management, the thrusters, the anchors and lead shot, the manipulator arm, the lights and the tires and many other mechanical designs. Of course, we were cautioned, that's the way it is all supposed to work. Won't really know until it all comes together.

The closest we came to touching any part of the ship was checking out a crude wooden mock-up that EB put together as part of planning the interior spaces. Pieces of colored plastic were tacked up to represent various dials and gauges, and the unpainted wood brought a new dimension to the "plank owners" term applied to the commissioning crew of any new ship. As we squeezed into the plywood replica of the space in which we would work, there was no doubt that the *NR-1* was going to be a tight fit.

Then we sat in the dark for hours and watched grainy 16-mm movies of the *Mackerel* running around the sands off Key West, purposely bumping over rocks and coral. Submariners never like to see a ship hitting underwater rocks. Surely, I hoped, the *NR-1* would run more smoothly than that.

As we discussed it quietly among ourselves while having a few beers in one of the nearby taverns, some of us began to wonder whether this boat would ever get built. Everything about it was foreign and different from anything we had ever seen before. But our skipper, Dwaine Griffith, reminded us that our job would be to run it, not build it. We would just have to leave that to the experts.

The final stop on our introductory training trail was down at Great Neck, New York, where the engineers at Sperry were producing the ship's instruments. The nuclear plant was behind schedule, the shipyard was almost off the chart, but maybe these engineers would be on top of things in designing the instruments.

For the next five weeks, they took us through all of the navigational, ship control, and oceanographic equipment, and it was all new territory for a bunch of nukes like us. At one point, we approached a large plastic tent that sat in the middle of a spacious area, and a sweat-soaked engineer named Brian Wruble came out to greet us. He swallowed a handful of salt pills and drank a large container of water as he explained that they were having "some problems" with the navigation computer. He escorted us into the tent, where unbelievable heat and humidity slammed my face, as if I had just entered a tropical rain forest. We were sweating within moments.

A row of eight-foot-high cabinets on each side contained the navigation and electronic instrumentation that would be the brain of the *NR-1*, just as the nuclear reactor would be its heart. This was "front of the boat" stuff, and the engineers, not wanting to endure another Rickover tirade, were challenging every piece of the equipment. They even dunked electrical components in a swimming pool in a crude, but effective, test to ensure their containers were watertight.

Roger Sherman, a stocky engineer, was at the semicircular control panel between the rows of cabinets. Sherman is a jocular and gregarious man whose spirit is almost impossible to dampen, but the constant testing failures had even gotten to him. He looked up, wiped his forehead, and told us, "Stuff is crapping out right and left around here."

When the muscular veteran of Polaris and Poseidon boats had signed up for our project because he thought it sounded interesting, Sperry sent him to Great Neck for a tour of a few weeks that eventually turned into eighteen months. Shortly after he arrived in the big building, he heard a loud, high-pitched scream that increased in piercing volume as he got closer to a room in which engineers were testing the four-hundred-cycle converter that would go aboard the *NR-1*.

The higher cycle rate allowed the use of smaller components, but that didn't impress Sherman. "All it was doing was converting electricity into noise," he said. Over the WHHEEEEE of the converter, Sherman had shouted to another engineer, "WHAT ARE YOU GOING TO DO ABOUT THAT NOISE?"

"WHAT NOISE?" the engineer yelled back.

"THAT HAS TO GO ON A SMALL BOAT!" Sherman replied. The shrill whine was splitting his skull. "YOU EXPECT PEOPLE TO LIVE WITH THAT?"

The engineer shrugged, and the screech of the converter followed Sherman as he hurried away with his hands over his ears. Sperry would improve and test the unit for some three hundred hours, and although they managed to reduce the volume somewhat, it never lost its loud, grating voice. It screamed at us throughout every voyage, and sometimes we slept right in front of it.

We also were introduced to Fred DeGrooth, an engaging first-generation Dutch American and former F-86 Saber jet pilot who had briefly worked on the Apollo space program before being laid off along with three thousand other engineers. When DeGrooth started looking for work, he stopped when he saw the "Sperry Gyroscope" sign while on the Long Island Expressway because his father, a merchant marine captain, swore by the accuracy of Sperry compasses. DeGrooth pulled into the parking lot, was interviewed, and was hired on the spot. By the time he joined the *NR-1* team, he was twenty-eight years old and a veteran field engineer aboard submarines. We often wondered how the tall, angular Dutchman ever could have folded himself into the tight cockpit of a fighter jet.

Wruble, Sherman, and DeGrooth would follow their packages of electronics right aboard our boat and become inseparable members of our tight team. They rode into the ocean depths with us, fixed whatever went wrong with the delicate instrumentation, shared our discomfort, risked their lives, and became our close friends. We would never have made it without them.

When the crew finished our classroom work at Great Neck, we still had plenty of time on our hands. The reactor wasn't ready, the boat wasn't ready, and the instruments weren't ready. Since the navy abhors a vacuum, it decided to keep us busy by expanding our skills to deal with the stem-to-stern operations of the *NR-1*, and ready us for those inevitable moments when we ran into trouble and there was no one around to help.

Because there was no room aboard for a corpsman, some of us underwent weeks of intensive emergency medical training. After watching gory movies that showed various types of wounds, we practiced suturing open injuries by stitching up chicken skin. Two of our enlisted men went to an advanced electronics course and another was dispatched to welding school.

Three of us—Larry Kammerzell, Don Marks, and I—were assigned to the Navy Dive School. After several months of having done little more than attending classes, talking with brainy engineers, eating three meals a day, and sitting on my butt for hours, then drinking beer after work with my new buddies, I had put on about twenty pounds. A mirror showed that I had indeed become rather pudgy. That had not mattered in the academic training environment, but now I was totally out of shape and heading for one of the most physically rigorous courses in the navy.

6
GETTING READY

On a blustery February morning that was ear-biting, New England cold and darkly overcast, Larry Kammerzell, Don Marks, and I drove over to a low, nondescript building that housed some of the support services on the submarine base just north of Groton. When we stepped into the Dive Locker, it was as if we were entering foreign territory without passports. The stuffy air reeked of seaweed and rubber, and the ugly weather outside was balmy compared to the atmosphere inside. Several navy divers sat around drinking coffee and pointedly ignoring us—three wimps from some secret project.

We weren't welcome, didn't particularly want to be there, but had to prequalify in order to attend the dive school in Florida. A chief petty officer emerged from a small office, read our orders, threw us a look of disdain, and growled, "So you think you want to be navy divers? Well, it ain't gonna be like that Jacques Cousteau stuff you see on TV."

Kammerzell, the biggest member of the *NR-1* crew and habitually good-natured, sometimes bit off more than he could chew. Like now. He tried to explain that we would be conducting underwater maintenance on a new submarine, but the edgy chief snapped that was what his boys did all the time. Kammerzell stammered that, sorry, he couldn't say anything more, because this was a secret project, we couldn't talk about it, and anyway, we would sometimes be working in remote parts of the world. "Don'cha think we like to travel?" the chief groused, sweeping his hand toward the other divers, who nodded in agreement. In the navy, it is not wise to piss off a chief.

"I don't like doin' this, but you got orders," the chief said, looking through our papers again, as if hoping to find a loophole so that he would not have to deal with us. "Let's go down to the boat." We trooped across the road and he immediately chose Kammerzell to go into the water first.

Other divers stuffed Larry into a heavy and dirty canvas dive suit without warning him that he was about to get wet. Except for his jacket, Kammerzell kept on everything he was wearing, even his shoes and wallet. Before they screwed the faceplate down tight on the bronze hard hat, the chief told him air would be pumped in through a hose, and then he placed Larry's hand on a valve to control its flow. "You let in too much air and the suit *will* blow up like a balloon. You *will* pop to the surface." His leathery face changed into an evil grin. "And you *will* be disqualified."

They hooked a big cable to a harness, and the bulky package that was Larry Kammerzell was hoisted off the deck. He swayed for a few moments like a man being lynched, then was plopped into the dirty, frigid river, where he promptly sank, leaving only a trail of bubbles behind. Something else the divers had not mentioned was that they use the oldest canvas suits around for the prequalification tests, wasting no sympathy on neophytes. The older suits had holes worn into the knees from years of hard use. Leaking is not an apt description for the way the water poured into the suit.

Kammerzell, thinking the suit was watertight, became alarmed when he felt his feet get cold and wet. An experienced "hard hat" diver would have immediately increased the air pressure within the suit to keep any water below knee level, but Larry didn't know that. We could tell by his voice that he was shaken by the unexpected flush of chill water, and was trying to control a bit of panic. "I'm okay, but the water is filling my suit," he said through the intercom. It climbed to his knees, then past his thighs and all the way to his chest before stopping. Larry, as terrified of coming to the surface as of drowning, tried to control the rising water by feeding in only tiny increments of air as it rose toward his chin.

For an eternity of ten very long minutes, he hung suspended in a twilight world, soaked and shivering as the water sought to reach his face while the bubble of air in his helmet forced it down. Eventually the smirking divers hauled him up and extricated him from the suit. He was exhausted, pale, freezing, and soaked. The chief handed him a towel and said begrudgingly, "Congratulations. You're going to dive school."

He looked at me. "Next." Don Marks and I had paid very, very close attention to Kammerzell's trial by water and convinced ourselves they would not let us drown. Probably. By conquering that fear, we had a much easier time weathering the water-drenched, claustrophobic experience, and got our tickets to Florida.

The three of us arrived at the U.S. Navy Underwater Swimmer School in March, basking in the warmth of Key West. All submariners go through "wet training" early in their tour, and after the pre-qual tests, we all felt comfortable in the water. So did our classmates–big, strong guys who seemed to be part fish and were absolutely at home in the sea. Some had already chosen to be hard hat divers and deepwater salvage specialists, while others were to become SEALs, the navy's elite commandos, and had "Vietnam" stamped on them. Just as at the Dive Locker, we were viewed as academic interlopers and nobody was betting money that we would survive the course.

Each morning for the next month began with rigorous calisthenics followed by a five-mile run through the city's deserted streets, sometimes carrying scuba tanks on our backs for extra weight. The flab we had gained vanished quickly as our bodies hardened and tanned, but it was a struggle to keep up with the better-muscled swimmers, and the instructors kept threatening, "You fail to complete a swim, you're out of here."

Daylight ocean work, although extremely tiring, was really quite pleasant as we swam through sun-drenched blue waters, surrounded by fish of every shape and color. We dove down to 110 feet through clear, purple-blue water, then ascended and hung motionless at specific intervals to decompress, feeling as if we were in a giant, warm-water aquarium.

The night swims could be horrifying. We were dropped from landing craft known as Mike boats a mile off the beach and had to swim toward a solitary light barely visible on shore. Salt water flushed into our mouths and lungs, causing some of us to throw up while we swam, while long tendrils of oily eelgrass grazed our skin and seemed intent on trapping our legs. Toothy barracuda watched among the weeds, and we knew that sharks and large numbers of the dreaded jellyfish called the Portuguese man-of-war were lurking nearby. Concentration, determination, and training kept us focused. The only goals were to keep a rhythmic kick going and make sure you and your swim buddy reached that light. Forget the darkness. A jellyfish only hurts like hell, it can't kill you. Keep swimming.

I have seldom felt as vulnerable in my life, and thoroughly understood why some of the swimmers simply gave up. There are easier ways to make a living. The distances and the duration of our swims steadily expanded over the weeks, but Kammerzell, the ever determined Marks, and I simply would not quit. We kept paddling and eventually got to where we had to go. Not quitting was part of our plan.

Early in the Key West training, back when we were feeling buffaloed by the tough guys, I asked an instructor how our final grade would be determined. It was all I could do to suppress a smile when he answered that 75 percent of the ranking would come from classroom work, where we studied topics including safety, the effect of compressed gases on the body, and procedures for effective diving. Only 25 percent would be graded by the swim and dive instructors.

Thinking happily back to the football days when we outsmarted the bigger teams, I hunted up my *NR-1* mates. "Look guys," I told Larry and Don. "We always do well in school and have scored high on navy tests for years, so let's focus hard on the classroom work. Then all we have to do is just be sure to finish each swim and dive. We don't have to be first, or fast, or physically impress anyone out there. All we have to do is *finish*!" We all slapped hands in agreement.

When our class graduated on March 27, 1967, the top slots went to the three *NR-1* sailors, much to the chagrin of the macho types who *knew* they could swim better than us. They were right, of course, but it didn't matter. We wished them well in their future endeavors amid the slime, eelgrass, and barracuda, and headed back to Connecticut.

Back to the boat that still wasn't there.

The desire to build small submarines was not new. The first American sub to go to war, the *Turtle*, was a human-propelled egg designed to let the one man inside the boat drill a hole into the hull of a British ship and plant a time bomb. Although she failed, the Revolution succeeded.

The Confederate Navy's *Hunley*, which carried eight men, destroyed a Union warship but sank herself with the same torpedo. The U.S. Navy began its own submarine fleet with the purchase of the *Holland* in 1900. She was only 53 feet long.

In World War II, "midget" submarines saw extensive use. The Japanese deployed pencil-thin subs in their attack on Pearl Harbor. Four-man British X-Craft put the German battleship *Tirpitz* out of action. Small American subs scouted the D-Day beaches.

The Germans took the idea of underwater craft a step beyond their dreaded U-boats, and tested a minisub called the *Seeteufel* (*Sea Devil*), which had tanklike caterpillar treads that allowed it to crawl along the bottom or move onto firm beaches. The Russians later expanded the *Seeteufel* concept and developed tiny subs that could lay mines, deliver commando teams, and perform as quiet sentries. During the Cold War, a Soviet civilian research ship was seen carrying a nonmilitary miniature sub equipped with tracks for underwater mobility. A British author reported the Soviets had some two hundred little subs assigned to a variety of missions, including underwater photography and tapping communications cables.

Suspicious tire imprints were detected on the sandy bottoms around ports from San Francisco to Sweden, and South Korea to Japan. When the Swedes accused Moscow of violating international limits, an arrogant Soviet official challenged them to "Present proof, if you can," and the Swedish diplomat responded that the Kremlin must want everyone to believe the tracks had been left by some prehistoric centipede.

It would not be long before we would be leaving some suspicious tire tracks of our own, and doing much more than some battery-powered, creep-and-peep midget.

Electric Boat finally erected the first *NR-1* hull section in a keel laying ceremony on June 10, 1967. Two years had passed since Rickover persuaded President Johnson to champion the *NR-1*. Another year and a half of daunting work lay ahead before it would be launched.

The steel cylinder was empty except for a few frames that provided added strength, and it lay on a cradle in building ways made to handle ships five times our size. As seemingly small as it was, that single cylinder triggered a sense of momentum in the South Yard, as if a huge boulder were teetering on a downhill slope. Things were leaning forward, in a big part because so much time had passed. The specialists, engineers, crew members, and technical representatives who had been dispatched to other places for training and design and the testing of equipment were returning now to help in the assembly process. We had done everything asked of us, had waited and waited, and were eager to move this boat beyond the design stage and get to work.

The experimentation by the venerable *Mackerel* had been successful and the old rolling mills had finally curved the steel plates to the necessary tight diameter. Knolls was finishing the baby nuclear reactor. Westinghouse Electric in Baltimore was providing the remotely controlled manipulator arm that would pluck items from the ocean floor, and our friends at Sperry in Great Neck were debugging the navigation and ship control system with its pesky computer. Progress was slowly being made, but nonetheless, it was progress. Although many of the pieces that would comprise the boat had not even yet arrived, the materials managers at EB hustled to find warehouse space around town where they could store the parts. There was an air of certainty that indeed this thing called the *NR-1* was more than an idea.

The latest technical drawings had refined the earlier schematics to include all of the changes that had been made. They showed that our boat would have the sleek look of a combat submarine, with the cylindrical pressure hull and diving planes on the sail. The sub was only 135 feet long, most of that set aside for the reactor and engineering spaces, and the diameter was a mere 12 feet 6 inches.

It would be powered by twin screws, and have a conventional rudder and four X-angled thrusters, set in pairs forward and aft for maneuverability. Beneath the bow were three thick viewing ports, powerful external lights to provide illumination for the television camera and the remotely controlled manipulator arm.

Still, it remained mostly a paper ship, and despite the enthusiasm and beginning of construction, there was little for us to do. As spring approached, the crew totally appropriated the EB wooden mock-up so at least we could practice drills. The seats, the cabinets, and the control stations with their paper dials and switches provided a realistic training space, once we got past the feeling that the plywood panels were a stage set.

Dick Patenaude, the EB test manager, added a realistic touch when we ran a drill to determine if we could shut the hydraulically operated valves in less than one second to cut off all seawater coming into the ship. Patenaude realized that none of us could react and operate the levers fast enough, and he also knew that there was no way to close the valves any faster. His advice was, "Oh well, if you have a double break in the seawater piping, just bend over and kiss your ass goodbye."

The mock-up constantly demonstrated how different our craft would be. It would not have traditional helmsmen, but a "pilot" and a "copilot" who would sit side by side before a wraparound console. The primary and backup TV screen displays that would show images from the cameras located in the bow and stern, and the periscope TV camera on the mast above the bridge, were in the center, where both men could see them. Secondary displays would have the communications and navigation instrumentation. Each man would have two control sticks: one for lateral motion—surge (forward and back), sway (motion sideways), and heave (up and down)—and the other for rotational motion—the pitch, roll, and yaw of the vessel.

Scott Carpenter, one of the original seven Mercury astronauts who became a deep submersible diver himself, visited our mock-up and was briefed on the *NR-1*. He was awed by its diminutive size, the power plant, and the daring conception of such a boat, and how much its controls resembled those aboard a spacecraft. He recognized the hurdles that had been surmounted to make it all real, and he understood the value of deep submergence and extended missions with an unlimited source of power. He told Nuclear Test Manager Herb Berry, "Oh, my God! There's a hell of a lot more going into this program than the one that's sending us into space!" When the ship was completed, Rickover barred Carpenter from coming aboard.

Of course, one of the huge differences between the craft taking astronauts into space and the *NR-1* was that they had to rely on fuel cells for power, which limited their mission time, while we had a nuclear reactor that allowed us to stay at sea as long as necessary. The thought of using nuclear energy to propel the rockets seemed unthinkable for weight and safety reasons but only three years later it was a fuel cell that exploded and caused the *Apollo 13* near tragedy in space.

One of our biggest challenges was the weekly letter that our captain, Dwaine Griffith, was required to send to Admiral Rickover, a daunting one-page typewritten update that could not contain the strikeover of a single letter, not a white-out nor an error of any kind. Margins were exactly prescribed, tabs and spacing had to be accurate. It was murderous, and Rickover would tolerate nothing less than perfection. To me, the extreme neatness seemed like a waste of valuable time. There were intelligent men on this crew, who had a demonstrated ability to face down the Russians and a nonpareil knowledge of nuclear energy. In the words of one skipper's wife, we were "steely-eyed killers from the deep." But none of us could type! Everyone took a crack at the letters, and we all failed miserably. We spent hours hunting and pecking on a typewriter keyboard, slowly getting a paragraph at a time until we could celebrate when the entire page was done. Finally, we coerced the captain of another ship to lend us his yeoman (clerk), who spent about fifteen minutes typing it up each week.

Besides the letters, Griffith had to call the admiral three times a week. He spent hours in preparation, whether or not he had anything to say. Once when the skipper was away, Executive Officer Steve Perry had to make the call and Griffith briefed him on the protocol. If he had nothing to report, his line was to be, "No." The call went this way.

Rickover: "Go."

Perry: "No."

Click.

Then there was the problem of supplies and spare parts. We had no supply officer, as every other ship had, and could not master the bureaucratic labyrinth to get what we needed. Again, we tried, and failed. At one point, when Kammerzell had to build some shelves for a shack we had been given as a storage area, he filled in what he believed to be the correct requisition forms, and in about a week, two tractor-trailer rigs rolled up, stacked with giant twelve-by-twelve posts and two-by-twenty-four planks. Kammerzell built some of the heaviest and sturdiest shelves in naval history. They may still be there. A supply chief would become the first person added to the *NR-1* support team.

Even with the extra training, time lay heavy on our shoulders. We wanted to work, to get the *NR-1* out to sea. But because of all of the delays, we were still on the scene months too early. We would spend most of 1967 and 1968 just waiting for the ship to be built.

* * *

Upon my return from diving school, I had moved into an apartment building in Stonington, Connecticut, with a bunch of other sailors. But the demands on an *NR-1* crew member did not mesh easily with the hard-partying guys from the regular navy, and during the late spring of 1967, I rented an apartment of my own.

Shortly after moving in, I was having trouble using the oven one evening and when I stepped out of my door to go find the manager, I almost bumped into a young woman passing in the hallway. She was petite and trim, with huge Audrey Hepburn eyes and dark hair cut in a stylish pageboy.

From that moment, I knew I had to engage her in conversation, to find out who she was. Nuclear training was of absolutely no help, and all I could think of was a lame "Do you know anything about stoves?" She paused, took a look through the open door into my bachelor apartment, replied, "No, I don't," and walked away without looking back.

Fortunately, Stonington is not very large, and I soon met her again at a cookout. She was not as curt this time, but I was still rather tongue-tied in her presence, and once again we did not hit it off well. Nevertheless, I learned that her name was Johanna Jane Roden, and that she was intelligent, independent, confident, and a cut above the other young women I had met.

The relationship remained somewhat rocky for a while, and early on she considered me juvenile and an obnoxious know-it-all. Since she had left a job as reference librarian at the University of Pittsburgh to become head of the Stonington Library, I shot back that she was a snob. In reality, I was smitten and so was she.

Somehow, the relationship grew, although I loved *Star Trek* and she didn't watch TV at all, only movies with subtitles, and I hated to read a movie. When I took her for a ride on my Triumph motorcycle, I showed off by doing a wheelie and dropped her off the back end. She laughed, forgave me, got back on, and off we went. On another occasion, after ignoring her advice, I dumped the bike while moving slowly through soft beach sand, and the tip of her shoe touched the spokes of the spinning back wheel. Two of her toes were dislocated. I loaded her back on the bike and zoomed to the emergency room.

Despite everything, she stuck with me until we developed a strong bond and mutual respect, and found our independent lifestyles were complementary. Our time together became a welcome respite from our working worlds. Like several other single sailors in our crew during that time, I began to think about life beyond the boat.

Admiral Rickover prided himself on never believing the "sales brochures with their excellent futuristic artistry and claims that are presented by the sales managers of our large companies." His rule was that nothing would get aboard his submarines that could not pass the sternest tests. He even dropped some equipment out of tall buildings to see how it survived hitting the sidewalk below.

He needed that reputation now more than ever, rather than having to admit he may have been wrong in lowballing many items after his trip aboard the *Aluminaut.* "I had read advertisements claiming that equipment such as *NR-1* would need for submerged operation was available," he told a reporter, dodging the question. "Upon investigation, I found that very few items of reliable equipment were actually available . . . That is one reason why *NR-1* costs so much."

The muttering of critics only made him more determined to get our little ship completed, despite all obstacles. His mood, sour even on good days, worsened.

By the mid-1960s, the nuclear fleet had grown to include more than a hundred vessels, from attack submarines to guided missile cruisers and even aircraft carriers. More were under construction or authorized, and Rickover monitored them all, along with the emerging civilian use of nuclear energy. It was an incredible test of endurance, dedication, and mental agility, one that few men would have been able to accomplish, certainly very few who had already passed normal retirement age. Still, he kept the *NR-1* in his crosshairs, often walking through the ship when he came to EB. His impatience was nearing the level of a reign of terror. No one wanted to pick up a telephone that might have him on the other end.

Rickover might take a train up from Washington late on Wednesday night and have a midnight meeting to berate the EB managers. Or he would take a plane and spend the flight to Connecticut ripping apart newspapers and various magazines. His pockets would bulge with articles on education and anything involving the U.S. Navy by the time he deplaned, and he left the debris stuffed into the seat back, the seats around him, and even the barf bags. It seemed that he was always lurking somewhere—a mean little poltergeist who would give no one a moment of peace.

One *NR-1* subcontractor in California just gave up after being flayed so many times by Rickover and his minions. Finally, whenever the admiral would telephone, a receptionist would respond politely that her boss was out surfing. A navy captain in the Deep Submergence Systems Project (still the financial cover for the *NR-1*) was a favorite target, and Jack Leonard remembered how the admiral was "always telling the guy that he was such a dumb this and that, so much until the poor guy didn't know whether to shit or go blind."

Rickover actually had a personable side but kept it under close wraps. On a Wednesday late in November of 1967, Rickover was sharing box dinners of grapes, turkey sandwiches, and apples with the EB managers when he remembered that the next day was Thanksgiving. "We're not going to meet tomorrow!" he suddenly announced, and the managers believed they might get a nice holiday weekend. Rickover squelched those thoughts. "We'll meet again Friday."

Electric Boat chartered a plane to return him to Washington to be with his wife on Thanksgiving, and when he flew back, his attitude had lightened remarkably. Nuclear Engineering Manager Chuck Chorlton recalled of that rare meeting, "He didn't want to talk any shop at all. Instead, he spoke about philosophy and leadership. When I came out of that room, I could have walked on water. It totally motivated me."

President Johnson stripped the federal budget to pay for his Great Society programs, and the voracious demands of the Vietnam War were leading the U.S. Navy into stormy seas. Then the admirals were rocked in January 1968 when a Soviet November-class submarine got onto the tail of the aircraft carrier USS *Enterprise* and stayed there for days, at times reaching speeds as fast as thirty-one knots. The unwelcome realization that the Soviet Union had subs that were faster than anything our intelligence and naval communities had ever suspected ignited a battle in Washington that would rage for years. The fight to create a fleet of fast, quiet nuclear submarines of our own drew the Pentagon, Congress, presidents, and secretaries of defense—and Admiral Hyman Rickover—into near brawls over design and monumental costs.

Cash-strapped admirals were resentful that the crisis did not deter

Rickover from pumping increasingly scarce funds into his pet project, the *NR-1*. Even more pressure was on him to get the boat done, and the only way he could solve problems at this point was to keep throwing money at it. That led inevitably into a trap, for, as he told some congressmen, "A design is not enough. You learn the real lessons when you start building. It is then that the real difficulties come to light." Congress was approached for more money, because more "significant design changes" had forced the latest *NR-1* cost estimate to climb to $67.5 million.

One day, when Rickover did not show up as expected, Jack Leonard's telephone rang in the shipyard. "There are some people, financial types from Washington, over in the Supervisor of Shipbuilding office, and they can't understand why the price of the *NR-1* has increased so much," he was told. "Can you go over and talk to them?" Leonard believes Rickover knew the team was on the way and chose not to be around for the confrontation. "Somehow I survived it," Leonard said. "But jeeezz . . ."

Johanna and I were married on July 6, 1968. By becoming my bride, she joined a select sorority of women who, as the wives of submariners, chose a life filled with uncertainty and waiting. When the *NR-1* was on a mission, there would be little communication between us, and none at all when we were on the bottom for weeks at a time. Even when we were together, there was little I could discuss with her about what I did and why my job required so much time away from home. Only women with extraordinary confidence in themselves do well in filling such roles.

To make things even more unusual, the *NR-1* crew and their families lived within a bubble of isolation during some of the most turbulent times in our nation's recent history. Fire destroyed the *Apollo 1* spacecraft on the launch pad, killed three astronauts, and brought the space program to an abrupt halt. Our work went on. There were some 475,000 U.S. troops fighting in Vietnam, and the bloody Tet offensive took the war into the living rooms of Americans. Senator Bobby Kennedy was assassinated while campaigning in Los Angeles for president, and civil rights leader Dr. Martin Luther King was murdered in Memphis. Throughout all this turmoil, our routine continued without a halt as the *NR-1* inched toward reality.

7
NO WAY OUT

We had front-row seats to an incredible industrial ballet. With the precision of Swiss watchmakers, the rough-and-tumble EB welders, electricians, grinders, riggers, crane operators, metalsmiths, and managers brought together the individual cylinders to fabricate the strongest hull structure ever built for a U.S. Navy submarine.

Grinders spent long days using noisy air-powered rotating disks laced with diamond dust to bevel the edge of a curved plate of high-strength steel into an exact, sharp-edged V. Streams of sparks flew from their tools and the acrid scent of burning metal smelled like the aroma of progress.

When two cylinders were done, the riggers and overhead crane operators would position them so the points of each V would touch, forming a notch. Then the electricians moved in to preheat the edges, followed by teams of welders in heavy leather aprons who sweated for hours behind tinted face masks, laying down strand after strand of weld bead. Bright rainbows danced in the arcs of their torches as they labored in the noisiest and dirtiest place in the shipyard.

After each layer of weld, the grinders returned to smooth them out and to remove any slag, then the welders put down more bead. Weeks were needed to fill a single notch, and if the X-ray inspectors found a flaw, that portion of the work would have to be done again.

The *NR-1* was an entirely handcrafted ship. The designers had no computers and worked with T squares and slide rules, while secretaries used manual typewriters. There wasn't a robot on the EB lot, and all of the welding and grinding was done by men who took a sense of pride in the fact that their skills allowed them to work on the special project. The *NR-1* mystique was firmly in place—something out of the ordinary was being done here.

The overhead cranes moved the completed hull sections to the South Yard Building Ways Number 11, where another crane placed them on the wooden cradle next to the sections to which they would be joined. Sheets of canvas and plastic sealed the area to prevent curious passersby or snooping satellites from seeing anything at all.

Once on the cradle, the sections were spaced about twenty feet apart to allow insertion of equipment, pipes, cables, decks, tanks, and foundations for other gear to be slipped into place and welded tight. Then the sections were brought together and seamlessly connected.

The same routine went into preparing the middle, or engine compartment, and the tail end, which stayed off until the nuclear reactor and engine compartment equipment could be installed. As the various sections were joined, we finally saw something that looked like a submarine.

Once it became a single unit, the only things that could come aboard would have to fit through the single hatch opening in the pressure hull, a hole that measured only twenty-five inches wide. Removing anything larger than that would require cutting the hull apart, so the EB managers had to be right the first time, every time.

That lone hatch inside the fiberglass sail would also be the only entrance and exit for the crew, and if anything happened to it, the game would be over. There were no other hatches, and no way for the *NR-1* to mate with a submarine rescue vehicle.

Although we tried not to pay attention to that fact, it was impossible to ignore in the face of what was happening in the submarine world at that time. The Soviet submarine *Leninsky Komsomol* lost thirty-nine sailors during a fire near the North Pole, and several months later, another Soviet sub sank off Severomorsk, and another ninety men lost their lives. We could not be cavalier about those accidents and just blame Russian technology or anything else, for on May 21, 1968, it happened to the U.S. Navy as well. The USS *Scorpion*, returning from a mission in the Mediterranean, sank in about ten thousand feet of water southwest of the Azores, killing ninety-nine Americans. That loss of our fellow submariners made an impression on us.

Our Sperry field engineers—Roger Sherman, Brian Wruble, and Fred DeGrooth—were constantly aboard the *NR-1* to get the electronics and instrumentation on line, and were convinced that gremlins lived in the wiring and the TV displays. If something went to Great Neck for repair, engineers there would try several methods until something worked. "Which one fixed it?" Sherman asked about one problem, because he needed to log the procedure for future reference. "We don't know," was the reply. Sometimes the Great Neck workers would add something new and unexpected rather than confining the fix to the problem. In another instance, while trying to repair a problem at sea, Sherman discovered that an intricate $50,000 compass had broken because someone at the plant had installed a cheap $28 relay rather than the one called for in the specifications.

The engineers devised a three-part strategy to combat their problems. The units were built to be replaceable as a whole, rather than by individual spare parts. So one unit would always be on the boat, one would be in a support van either at the pier or aboard an escort ship, and the third would be in Great Neck for repair. In a breakdown, the unit on the boat would be swapped with the one in the van. The unit from the van would be replaced by the one sent up from the factory, and the broken piece of equipment would be sent back to Great Neck with plenty of time for repair. That redundancy, although expensive, would work well in coming years.

The small nuclear power plant was never considered a real problem because everyone was so familiar with its functions, but it cost almost $12 million by the time General Electric delivered it to the boat. Great care was taken while installing, then testing it, because while it was conceptually simple, it was unique in construction.

The hydrostatic tests for structural integrity, the radiation tests that gave some unexpected results and required adjustments in the shielding, the filling of the elegantly simple main coolant system for "cold" and then "hot" operations, were all done while the boat still lay in pieces, with the aft pressure hull and tail section off. The loading of the radioactive core was especially dicey because the procedures were so different from how things were done on other nuke boats. Only when the core was tested and certified could the boat be buttoned up and have its final weld. Then we seasoned the reactor and its coolant system with another cold operation, then a second hot operation, and finally we had ourselves a submarine nuclear power plant ready for inspection.

That was a major step, for Electric Boat had to deliver the reactor compartment as a single, complete product, and as months fell from the calendar, word had come down that the project was running out of money.

The managers felt good about a design and build-out they thought was "breathtaking," then George Barfoot arrived to do a final inspection. Barfoot spent days combing through the reactor compartment, then went back and wrote up his report. He had found some thirteen hundred deficiencies, causing almost that many heart attacks among the EB brass and managers. "We all got thoroughly thumped for that," recalled Nuclear Engineering Manager Chuck Chorlton.

"Management was saying, 'What are you doing, George?' But he did such a thorough job that when all of those deficiencies were corrected, that was it—no expensive rework. What George was doing was saving them oodles and oodles of money."

The General Accounting Office of Congress ran a special audit on the *NR-1* and lambasted it as being one of the worst managed programs it had ever encountered. The admiral replied in a curt single-page letter on August 6, 1968.

On 23 July 1968 you requested my comments on the draft *NR-1* audit report.

The subject report puts me in mind of the review of D.H. Lawrence's *Lady Chatterley's Lover* which appeared in the November, 1959, issue of *Field & Stream.*

'This fictional account of the day by day life of an English gameskeeper is still of considerable interest to outdoor minded readers, as it contains many passages on pheasant raising, the apprehending of poachers, ways to control vermin, and other chores and duties of the professional gameskeeper. Unfortunately one is obliged to wade through many pages of extraneous material in order to discover and savor these sidelights on the management of a Midlands shooting estate, and in this reviewer's opinion this book cannot take the place of J.R. Miller's *Practical Gameskeeping*.'

It is evident to me that the reviewer lacked comprehension of the primary occupation of the gamekeeper as described in *Lady Chatterley's Lover*.

A cursory review of the subject report leads me to conclude that its authors, likewise, lack comprehension in the manner of accomplishing Research and Development. Therefore, I believe no useful purpose would be served by detailed comments on my part.

* * *

Non-nuclear testing also had its problems. The batteries became a major issue, and sent Rickover into screaming fits that literally left some engineers in tears. Moving parts that would be exposed to seawater during near bottom operation were tested in a saltwater slurry that contained bits of clamshells and sand that seeped past vital rubber seals and caused the pumps and motors to fail. To keep out the debris, oil-filled pressure compensating systems were added to each motor. By keeping the pressure of the oil inside the slightly stretched bladders a pound or two higher than the pressure of the surrounding sea, the oil would leak slowly out rather than allowing seawater and its abrasive material to leak in. Electrical connectors corroded and leaked under pressure, and there were even difficulties with painting. To reach the inside of one small tank, two husky men dangled a midget upside down by his ankles for a while, then he painted a few moments, was pulled back up to get a breath, and was lowered into the tank again.

"Everything had a problem, and the quality control inspectors were looking at it with a fine-tooth comb," Jack Leonard said. Every day seemed to bring another emergency, but one by one, the dragons were slain, and EB moved closer to completion.

Around the circular pressure hull, the workers mounted the box keel; ballast tanks; thrusters; foundations for our lights, cameras, and sonar; and a fiberglass exterior along the top. Then the fiberglass sail was bolted on, the final major construction step.

One of the things that determined how long the *NR-1* could stay down was the amount of food needed for the crew. Large submarines have galleys that can serve hot meals, brew fresh coffee, and even make desserts. There was no kitchen on our boat. Our meal preparation area consisted of a sink, a hot water dispenser, and an oven to warm TV dinners.

Electric Boat, keeping to Rickover's orders of buying off the shelf when possible, first tried out a small commercial oven. When the harsh testing began, it lasted about five minutes and was gone. Then the admiral contacted NASA about what kind of food was used to feed astronauts, and six experts arrived at Groton to show us their wares. It was like tubes of toothpaste that you would squeeze right into your mouth. That did not last long either, particularly when it was tested on shipyard workers.

Then came the former airline oven, which was somewhat better, although not much. We had a freezer that could turn a can of Coke into a delectable slush in exactly twenty minutes, and we stuffed it with enough TV dinners to last thirty days. The test was to have anyone who was around help themselves to a package of food, warm it up in the oven, which took some twenty to thirty minutes because our industrial-strength freezer had turned it into a block of ice, and chow down.

Instead of having specially prepared meals, we would go to the market prior to a voyage and fill a shopping cart with frozen meals similar to the kind available to any homemaker in America. Salisbury steak and spicy Oriental and Mexican meals were very popular, but no one would eat the Virginia ham. Since leaving the *NR-1* some thirty years ago, I have never eaten another TV dinner.

We would go to sea repeatedly with a bare-bones cupboard, and thought that pouring almost hot water into a bag of dehydrated Lobster Newburg from Vietnam-style long-range-patrol rations was a feast. Several years later, when Bruce Heezen, the famed oceanographer, began to ride the boat, he simply would not accept such meager fare. Heezen was known to the world for mapping the ocean floor, but we will fondly remember him for turning the *NR-1* into a nuclear-powered delicatessen. Weighing better than 250 pounds, he arrived for his voyages with strings of preserved sausages, sweetbreads, canned delicacies, and jars of treats that he stuffed into any crevasse he could find and hung from overhead pipes and cables. It was a tragedy some years later when Heezen suffered a heart attack aboard the *NR-1* and died on the boat. But for months thereafter, the crew would find little memorials from him—a jar of anchovies or a tin of peaches that he had stashed away for safekeeping.

Another major need was water, and for that, we had a distilling unit that was fed seawater, was heated off the turbine steam line, and could make up to a hundred gallons of fresh water per day. That was the theory. But the still was originally designed to operate off the hot exhaust of a large motor yacht, not low-pressure steam. We ran it constantly and kept our drinking water tank topped off, but it was difficult to get water pure enough for reactor use. There was no shower aboard, so the warm, nearly pure water that we did get was saved in buckets and used for washing socks and for the occasional sponge bath that was usually taken in concert with donning one of the four changes of clothes in our lockers.

We were into recycling water years before it became popular. The so-called gray water from the sinks in the kitchen and the head was actually dark brown, shading toward black, and smelled putrid. It was used for our single Pullman-type commode, which folded down from the sink cabinet in the head. To drop the toilet for use, it had to be unfastened, lowered, and a valve turned to allow some gray water into the shallow bowl before tending to business. Afterward, you again faced the toilet and lifted it slowly to allow the waste to slide directly into a 110-gallon holding tank.

Naturally, the whole arrangement had been thoroughly tested. Twenty-one engineers were assigned to use that toilet for thirty days during their working shifts, under orders not to use their bathrooms at home before coming to work. They were not pleased. In another test, cans of dog food were dumped into the toilet to see how waste could be flushed.

To move around the accumulated "brown mountain" of human waste, we used a decidedly low-tech method that could be aptly described as stirring shit with a stick. The capacity of the waste tank was, in truth, the single most important factor in determining how long the boat could remain submerged.

Finally, it was all done, and the NR-1 sat in the building ways ready for launch. Four years had elapsed since Rickover first raised the idea, and building it took a year longer than the most pessimistic timetable. The price tag was almost $100 million—some $67.5 million to build the boat, $19.9 million for the oceanographic and sensor equipment, and $11.8 million for research and development, mostly related to downsizing the nuclear power plant.

It was an extraordinary amount of money to spend for a little orange sub with no periscope when the navy was struggling to maintain its fleet of warships, was saddled with a massive commitment in Southeast Asia, and was trying to keep pace with the Soviet Navy. The Russian bear, it was said, was learning how to swim, and was even conducting naval exercises in the Gulf of Mexico. The admirals thought they could have found a much better use for that $100 million Rickover spent on the *NR-1*. Very soon, the U.S. fleet would consist of 932 active units, including 156 nuclear and diesel submarines . . . and us.

At this point, Rickover was not to be denied. The *NR-1* could not be stopped, no matter what the cost, and he was absolutely fierce in protecting the project. Jack Leonard advised him that a navy "habitability team" was coming to the shipyard. "What the hell is a habitability team?" Rickover demanded.

"They come aboard before launch to see if people can live on the ship," Leonard answered.

Rickover thought deeply about the absence of comforts aboard the *NR-1* and snapped, "Don't they think we know what we're doing?" In response to the challenge, he changed the rules of the test and decided to inspect the inspectors from Washington.

"Leonard, go get me a dead mouse," Rickover ordered. "I want it still warm, and you give it to the captain to hide and we'll see if these guys can find it." As Leonard headed for the door, the admiral shouted, "Hey, get two!"

A couple of EB men drove to a local pet shop, bought two mice, and put them into a shoe box with a pinch of rat poison. The rodents died on the way back to the ship, and their still-warm bodies were promptly hidden in hard-to-locate places.

When the habitability team finished its inspection, they had found one of the little corpses and showed it to Rickover, intending it as a rebuke. Instead of an apology, they got a table-thumping, volcanic lecture about being incompetent and how they had done a terrible inspection and the navy didn't need officers who couldn't do their jobs right: "I know there were *two* dead mice on that boat," Rickover roared. "I bought them! You only found *one*! Get out of here!"

The officers slunk back to Washington, suddenly worried more about their own fitness reports than the living conditions aboard the *NR-1*. Leonard shook his head in wonder at the latest Rickover triumph. Sometimes you had to admire the guy.

A launch date was set, then postponed, then reset, and more last-minute problems arose, problems that EB solved by throwing overtime pay at the workers when navy managers panicked that the project would be delayed yet again. No one cared about the money anymore; they just wanted to move the ship into the water.

Rickover, wanting to maintain his secret to the last possible moment, considered launching the *NR-1* on a weekend night to keep it from public view. As the launch time grew closer, press interest rose, and one reporter wrote that media attempts to get details about the *NR-1* "were almost entirely fruitless." The press loves a mystery, and rumors spread, including one that the sub would be able to dive to twenty thousand feet. Evelyn Archer of the *New London Day* reported that shipyard spokesmen were not allowed to divulge the name of the keynote speaker, nor the name of the funding agency, nor the date and time of the launch. Rickover critics leaked the information to the media.

"Pentagon civilian executives, frequently on the receiving end of Rickover's slings and arrows, were wearing wide grins over the affair Friday. The most popular theory for Rick's would-be black-out order on the launching was that the father of the nuclear submarine was embarrassed over the ballooning costs of the *NR-1*," wrote columnist Robert Waters in the *New York Times*. The sources said costs had tripled since the original estimate was made in 1965, although Rickover had never set an exact figure, but had grabbed every nickel he could find.

"How he intends to launch that thing with nobody seeing it is beyond us," one official commented.

The *Los Angeles Times–Washington Post* news service reported, "Pentagon executives chortled when asked about Rickover's rising costs. Only recently he had said, 'Defense procurement policies must be tightened if the public interest is to be protected.'"

On January 25, 1969, a dreary Saturday that was bitterly cold on the waterfront, a small, select crowd arrived early at the south gate of the shipyard. Few nonessential people were around for the formal launch of the *NR-1*, and those who were there were still holding their breaths, hoping that it would get into the water okay. Only the night before, it was found that a bubble of air would form in front of one of the view ports, requiring a team of workers to stay on the job all night to fix the problem.

I was the warmest person there that day, inside the *NR-1*, comfortably keeping track of the idle nuclear reactor. The power plant was off-line, but someone had to be there, just in case. The only other "white hat" (enlisted man) aboard was Larry Kammerzell, who was freezing his butt off standing at attention in the sail beside our skipper, Dwaine Griffith.

Misinformation surrounded us. We were not the USS Anything, for to give us such a title would deprive the fleet of a slot for a warship. The navy said two scientists were on the crew, although none were. We did not really have a captain, for the program stated that Lieutenant Commander Griffith was merely the ship's "prospective commanding officer." He had been with the boat from the concept stage and still did not have the title.

The launch area was draped in bunting that fluttered in a stiff wind that also whipped up a chop on the Thames River and froze the smiles on the faces of the dignitaries who were launching the boat. A band played the national anthem, a priest gave an invocation, and hurried speeches were made as the spectators shifted in their cold seats.

Robert A. Frosch, the assistant secretary of the navy for research and development, predicted the *NR-1* was a "unique vessel" that could lead to the development of "the deep fleet of the twenty-first century."

"Most of the details of this ship are classified," he said in wonderful understatement, since hardly anyone on the platform knew much about the boat. He praised the development of the miniaturized nuclear plant and said our wheels made the *NR-1* "the first submerged amphibian." His speechwriters obviously had been given little with which to work. Joseph D. Pierce, general manager of Electric Boat, noted that the *Nautilus* had been launched from the same building ways almost exactly fifteen years ago, and he acknowledged that the *NR-1* "has been a difficult technical undertaking."

Pierce also paid respects to the Man Who Wasn't There, Admiral Hyman Rickover, who did not attend the launch of the little boat that had been such a big dream for him. Rickover never attended launchings, but would catch up with us soon for the coming sea trials. Instead, Captain William M. Nicholson, manager of the Deep Submergence Systems Project, and Rear Admiral Edward J. Fahy, head of the Naval Ship Systems Command, represented the official navy on the platform. Their presence that day was about as close as either of the agencies that paid for the vessel ever got to it.

Alice Cooper Morse, the wife of Robert W. Morse, who as an assistant secretary of the navy had given Rickover a green light on the project in 1965, was the ship's sponsor. She handed her bouquet of red roses to a friend, grabbed a bottle of champagne, and pushed up the sleeves of her warm mink coat.

The crowd counted off the final seconds, but instead of the familiar space-age backward countdown, they went forward, from one to ten. Two workmen, who had been hopping from one foot to the other to stay warm, popped their acetylene welding torches to life and sliced through the final small strips of steel holding the ship in place. When Mrs. Morse smacked the bottle of bubbly onto the starry red, white, and blue bunting that covered the bow, the welders made their final cuts. The *NR-1* quivered and started to slide away from the dignitaries on the stand.

Griffith and Kammerzell saluted in the sail, the crowd erupted in cheers, the band tooted, shipyard horns blared, the boat slid backward, and Chuck Chorlton whispered, "God, is it going to float?" It went quietly into the choppy river, and floated free. Inside the hull, I experienced that singular, unforgettable moment of a ship leaving land for the first time and becoming one with the sea.

Jack Leonard watched with almost fatherly pride as the *NR-1* bobbed alone in the water until a yard tugboat nestled close to move it over to Wet Dock B. He recalled the fantastic problems, the extreme cost overruns, the screaming by Rickover, the sweat-stained testing, and the years of plans that never seemed to work on a construction project that never seemed to end.

"It was a lot of fun," he said. "But painful."

8

A WORLD APART

If the Soviets were worried about our progress, they would not have been quite as concerned had they known how lousy the *NR-1* would be as a truly secret weapon. One major goal in submarine construction is sound-isolating almost everything, for noise can help an enemy find and kill you. Aboard the *NR-1*, noise was incessant. The small turbine generator, which spun at thirteen thousand revolutions per minute, twice as fast as a jet engine, was attached right to the hull and produced a continuous background roar. The infamous four-hundred-cycle converters screeched, the hydraulic pipes squealed intermittently, and almost everything on board vibrated. Suppression of noise was not a design factor for our boat, and sound ricocheted inside the hull. We made quite a racket. When on a dive outside the ship, I could hear the noise in the water, and by touching the hull, I could actually feel the vibration. After several days aboard, I would get off the boat with my hearing so desensitized that I could drive my Corvette all the way home without hearing the thunder of the automobile's big engine.

Then there was the problem of speed, for the *NR-1* could only make a maximum of five knots, hardly enough to escape danger. If discovered by an enemy in a wartime situation, we would be helpless.

But first an enemy would have to find us, and once we submerged, that would not be easy, for the ocean is a very big place, even for a noisy boat, and we could go very deep and stay down for lengths of time that were unprecedented for deep submersibles. On future voyages, even our own support ships would have difficulty staying in contact once we burrowed into a maze of canyons or other hiding places. Time on the bottom, not firepower, would be our weapon.

Again, that was the theory. For while the *NR-1* had been launched, another nine months would pass before it became operational, and even more time would elapse before it was delivered to the U.S. Navy.

Our planning and work to this point had been focused on just getting this very expensive and long-overdue boat into the water. Now that it was afloat, the next plateau was the pending sea trials in August. Beyond that, none of us had any idea about what we would be doing. For now, we had a boat, and not much else.

The remaining dock work was as intense in the months following launch as it had been during construction, and testing continued around the clock. Many of the systems still failed. At one point, our third officer, Jack Maurer, thought a test of the navigational instruments did not accurately reflect what we would experience underway, so he intentionally dumped a bucket of seawater onto a supposedly watertight container known as the "suitcase," in which Sperry's vital instruments were taken to the bridge when we surfaced. Since Maurer, as navigator, had to rely on those gadgets, he wanted to be sure the suitcase worked as advertised when rough seas broke over the sail. When everything in the suitcase shorted out, an angry Sperry engineer demanded to know just how much water had been emptied onto the delicate equipment, and Maurer answered, "About a tenth of a wave." The real world played havoc with well-engineered plans.

Due in large part to Executive Officer Steve Perry's creative training and drills for us in the wooden mock-up, we passed the Naval Reactors Operational Readiness and Safety Evaluation with flying colors and took the nuclear reactor to initial criticality on April 1. Then we spent another 137 days in and out of dry dock getting ready for sea trials, for problems still plagued the boat. Weird screeches and squeals came from various pumps, motors, and electrical equipment. Cells of the troublesome silver-zinc battery ran hot and had to be replaced. Insulation came loose and was repaired. Radiation levels spiked unexpectedly high and shielding had to be adjusted. We had a brush with fire when a welder's hose, spitting burning sparks, got loose and twirled like a striking cobra in the tight interior of the submarine.

Hanger points were welded to the exterior hull to hold more equipment. Our movie and still cameras and the television system for use in viewing and recording what we found, the remote grappling arm, and hundreds of other items, large and small, were rushed to completion by trial-and-error installation.

External items fell off with alarming regularity. A heavy steel ball, hook, and chain snapped from an overhead crane and slammed down only five feet from Roger Sherman, hitting so hard that its pattern was imprinted in the thick timbers. And when a technician on board removed a drawer filled with electronics, he accidentally triggered the release of *everything* on the outside of the submarine. Anchors, tons of the lead shot that we used for weight, the manipulator arm, and the big wheels fell to the dry dock floor in a rain of metal. It is a wonder no one was killed.

If the boat was at the wet dock at such times, it was up to the divers to fetch and replace the fallen items, and the amount of underwater work that was needed helped a couple of shipyard divers earn more overtime money in two months than their annual salary. We three divers from the *NR-1* crew did similar work just for our navy paychecks. It was miserable to dive in the frigid cold of the Connecticut winter, and our lights were of little use in the gray-green, mucky Thames. As we approached the bottom, powdery silt swirled up at the slightest passing motion and wrapped us in inky clouds of floating mud. Whatever we were hunting would disappear right before our eyes. As the waters warmed in springtime, long river eels chose the inside of the *NR-1* ballast tanks as their spawning ground and we had to push a path through the wriggling creatures to get at our work. It was like swimming through a bowl of spaghetti.

When astronaut Neil Armstrong set foot on the lunar surface in July of 1969, a breathless, watching world marveled at the accomplishment. No single event in history gathered as much media coverage as the moon landing, but on that same day, another incredible event took place in the deep oceans, virtually unnoticed.

At almost the same moment Armstrong touched his boots to the lunar surface, our distant cousin the *Trieste II*, the navy's last bathyscaphe, settled on the sea floor some ten thousand feet beneath the surface, just beside the lost *Scorpion*, to examine the wreckage. Many scientists claim that that feat was just as important an achievement as the lunar voyage of *Apollo 11*, for mankind has often been back to work on the ocean floor, but despite all of the glory and headlines, the moon was visited only six times, then abandoned.

I felt sorry for all of the other astronauts who had worked so hard for so long but did not get to go to the moon. It must have been miserable in that highly competitive occupation to realize that after all of the training you would be left behind. Our situation was just the opposite—we had our ride from the very start.

During the long months of waiting, watching, and practicing every drill imaginable, the familiarity between the officers and the enlisted men of the *NR-1* further blurred the navy's usual rigid line of authority. How we functioned mattered more than standard protocol. For instance, on large ships, a steward takes care of the officers' shoes. There was some early discussion about who would have that duty on our boat, but none of us nuclear-trained specialists volunteered. "Shine your own shoes" was our answer, and our officers did, without complaint, thereby gaining even more respect in our eyes.

We were a small family, with Griffith as the head of the household, the ultimate supervisor. He, and every following captain of the *NR-1*, would go on every cruise, usually sleeping only when the boat was also at rest on the bottom. We trained together constantly and bonded so closely that duty aboard ship became as much a part of our existence as breathing.

As incredible as it seems today, we never even took vacations, and felt guilty if we took any time off at all, for once the nuclear reactor was installed, four of us had to be on watch twenty-four hours a day, seven days a week, with no exceptions. The crew was so small, only a dozen men, that if anyone fell out of the rotation, everyone else had to take up the slack. Only once did a crew member take leave, early in the process, and his absence created such a void that no one else ever attempted to put together a collection of days off. Getting sick and missing work felt like we were committing a crime.

Most of the crew married during the three years we spent at the shipyard, and Johanna and I set up housekeeping in the White Sails Apartments in Stonington, a mile from her library. The new *NR-1* wives naturally had difficulty adapting to the hard fact that the boat came first. Eventually, these tolerant young women accepted our weird hours and careers as just being part of married life, as if we worked at some peculiar factory, and they came together as almost a separate unit. It helped if they had jobs of their own; not many women pursued their own careers in those days. One way they soaked up the time was to gather for weekly dinner parties to socialize and demonstrate their cooking skills. One side benefit of that was sometimes they would drive out to the boat and bring a decent meal to a husband pulling watch.

August 19, 1969, was sink or swim time for us and we could not wait to get going. We had the best submersible in the world, a state-of-the-art submarine, and we wanted to go out and do things with it, to prove in the sea trials that the boat actually worked. The *NR-1* was festooned with strain gauges that would measure how the hull would perform, and laden with extra instrumentation and recording devices of all sorts. But those would just give us statistics and numbers, which would be meaningless if we did not please Admiral Rickover, who was in charge of this final, critical test.

Before dawn on Saturday, the admiral and a team of other navy, shipyard, and Atomic Energy Commission heavyweights came aboard, their khaki uniforms soaked by a torrential shower, and the little submarine headed out under the cover of darkness to keep away from curious eyes. A few canvas chairs and temporary sleeping mats had been provided, but with thirteen people aboard, it was standing room only. "We were asshole to elbow," said Carl Olson, the *NR-1* project officer for the navy's Supervisor of Shipbuilding.

It took twelve long hours for the support ship *Sunbird* to tow the *NR-1* into a deep-dive area some two hundred miles south of New London, at the edge of the continental shelf. Rickover stayed quiet and unobtrusive during the transit, sitting at the small galley table and reading *The History of the English Working Class.*

When Jim Turner, who had the roving watch, was sent to get some crystals to replace those in a balky radio, he found Rickover was in his way. The smallest member of our crew summoned his courage. "Excuse me, Admiral," he said, fearing instant retribution. "I need to get into the bench locker you're sitting on to get some spare parts." The admiral, with little to say when things were going well, stood aside as Turner rummaged through the locker and found the crystals. Surprisingly, he did so a second time, also without protest, when Turner returned the crystals to the locker.

Rickover's mood changed abruptly when we finally were on station, and he was anxious to get the dive under way. He abruptly halted a time-consuming exchange of routine information about the trials by personally radioing the support ship. "This is Admiral Rickover. We're going to do what we're going to do. Now shut up and get off this thing and stay off! We know what we're doing over here, so you just do your job!"

A few minutes later, the *NR-1* ducked beneath the surface of the Atlantic Ocean, and everyone aboard got the ride of a lifetime.

The *NR-1* maneuvered so smoothly that it imparted the unique feeling of airborne flight, a sensation not felt aboard large submarines, and our "pilots" talked of "flying" the boat.

An "Alpha Trial" such as this usually stays within tight limits, with the primary purpose to test the propulsion, the hull compression, the various doors and lockers, and a multitude of technical things. A submarine on its first sea trial never approaches its full submergence depth. Except this time. Rickover didn't want to just bob around. He wanted the full show, and ordered the *NR-1* to go to its maximum depth of three thousand feet, then to the bottom. Years later, we agreed that the ship went much deeper than planned, actually passing below test depth. The actual numbers were never recorded.

Anxiety is a passenger on the first submergence of any submarine, for no one really knows if the naval architects' calculations were truly correct, or whether something had been overlooked in the weight and balance formula, or if any one of a thousand other things might go wrong and cause the boat to fall to its death. So at every five-hundred-foot increment, the *NR-1* halted to allow the stresses on the hull to stabilize. Then all readings were recorded from throughout the ship and inspections were made for any leaks or problems. Each stop took hours.

When it came to its scheduled stop at the first five-hundred-foot level, Herb Berry, the EB chief test engineer, discovered a potential ship killer. While checking the hull welds in the engine room, Berry found drops of water on one of the joints. "Holy Moses," he thought. "Is this a leak? Jesus, I don't want to be the one to tell Rickover." He got a rag and wiped the moisture away just as the sub resumed its descent.

"I'll give it another five hundred," Berry thought, as beads of water started to form again on the weld and beads of sweat formed beneath his curly hair. Usually quick to comment on almost anything, Berry became ominously silent.

Rickover, meanwhile, was standing in the forward control area, leaning against the battery cell–monitoring panel, watching everything like a hawk. Jim Turner, carrying a clipboard, once again nervously appeared at his elbow. "Sorry, Admiral, but now I have to get to that panel behind you and take my log readings." Rickover shifted over without saying a word.

As the NR-1 descended, Herb Berry was about ready to report that the water droplets were still seeping from the very metal of the hull weld, knowing he had moments to either solve the problem or reveal it. "How deep is the Old Man going to take us?" he wondered. To tell Rickover would be bad enough, because it would be a major embarrassment for the shipyard, but if the boat went deeper, the hull might fail and the NR-1 would be crushed. In a moment of desperation, Berry reached out, touched the water, and brought his fingertips to his lips. It tasted fresh, not like seawater. There was no leak. Berry exhaled in quiet relief, realizing that it was just condensation forming from all of the body heat being generated.

Down the boat went. Jim Turner had been so busy that he had not taken an opportunity to visit the toilet. "I had to pee something fierce," he remembered. Turner hurried to the head, and without knocking, threw open the door. Vice Admiral Hyman G. Rickover was on the small Pullman commode with his khaki pants down around his ankles and instantly recognized the intruder. "I hope you don't think you are going to move me from here, too," he said. Turner closed the door, held his aching bladder, and waited his turn.

Exhausted men sometimes make mistakes, and at such moments, the admiral always liked to ratchet up the pressure as high as possible. One of his favorite tactics was to create a make-believe catastrophe. "You're dead . . . You're dead . . . You're dead," he would declare, poking his finger into the chests of some officers and ordering them to go sit down and no longer participate during the exercise. It was totally arbitrary, just as combat casualties would be arbitrary, and whoever was left standing had to keep the ship running. After the thousand-foot inspections on the *NR-1*, he sprang that trap on our officers, who had been hard at work all day and were obviously tired.

Dwaine Griffith and Steve Perry, the skipper and XO, were in the pilot and copilot seats driving the boat, when the admiral leaned down. "You know, Captain, I don't think I have seen an enlisted man at the controls all day."

"Admiral, they have all been busy at other watch stations," Griffith replied with a growing sense of unease.

"Well, the enlisted men have been trained to operate the ship, haven't they?" Rickover's voice was iron. Part of his whole philosophy of the *NR-1* was that sailors could run it.

"Of course, sir," Griffith said, trying to evade the inevitable. With so much at stake on the sea trial, he did not want to let the boat out of his own hands. "They have had the same training we have. But they are all on watch or resting. I don't want to disrupt the watch schedule to get one up here."

The admiral glared at him. "Captain, signal the escort ship that we are surfacing and returning to port. We will redo this sea trial when an enlisted man is available."

Griffith was tempted to defy the directive rather than give an order he felt might endanger his ship, although by doing so, he probably would end his naval career on the spot. But he knew what his troops could do, and if that was what Rickover wanted, then by God the *NR-1* would give it to him. "Let's not be too hasty, Admiral. We can get one of the guys up here."

Rickover was concerned that his demand had been anticipated and the crew's most qualified man was standing by. He decided to choose the enlisted man himself and pointed to the only one with whom he was familiar—Jim Turner. "Good! How about him?"

Turner's knees went weak. Everyone aboard, especially Admiral Rickover, watched him replace Dwaine Griffith in the pilot's chair. Griffith hovered close behind as Turner checked the planes and rudders.

"Get back! Leave him alone!" Rickover yelled right into the skipper's ear. The abashed Griffith quickly stepped away, but the admiral didn't want the captain anywhere around. "Get out of here! Go to bed and get some sleep!" Griffith reluctantly retired to the bunk area, but sleep was out of the question, as the most junior man aboard prepared to run the ship.

When XO Steve Perry then tried to quietly coach Turner, Rickover climbed all over him too. "You! Outta here!" Perry also moved aft, and Rickover slid into the copilot's chair. The three-star admiral and the electrician's mate were alone at the control station, and no one dared approach.

Rickover leaned close to Turner and whispered so as not to be overheard, "You do know how to operate this thing, don't you?"

"Oh, yes, sir, Admiral! I sure do." Without hesitation, Jim read the screens before him, pushed the right control stick full forward, and the *NR-1* tilted into an incline. "Leaving one thousand feet, coming to fifteen hundred feet in accordance with the sea test plan!" Turner crisply reported. He piloted the ship all the way to three thousand feet, as far as it was designed to go.

Admiral Rickover rode along in the soft chair beside him and actually smiled, although only Jim Turner saw him do it.

The results of another vital test, the recovery from a reactor shutdown, also demonstrated to Rickover how well the enlisted crewmen were trained on the *NR-1*. Larry Kammerzell was standing duty as the engineering officer of the watch, controlling the nuclear reactor, when Steve Perry was ordered to intentionally trip the scram breaker, which took the reactor off-line. The test was to determine how effectively the crew could get it back in operation. As Kammerzell immediately began the recovery operation, Bob Lunt, who was rummaging through a nearby tool locker, jumped to help by checking that every valve in the engine room was in the proper position for a start-up. Kammerzell quickly completed his prestart checklists, and the reactor was returned to normal operations in an incredibly short time. Less than 1 percent of the battery power was used—a very small amount compared to the 35 to 40 percent of capacity regularly lost in similar tests aboard large subs.

The ever suspicious Rickover was convinced the recovery was so fast that the test had been rigged and that Lunt was planted in the engine room on purpose to provide emergency help. He thoroughly chewed Perry out and demanded that the test be run again, adding that if Perry interfered, he would drum the lieutenant commander right out of the navy.

Two hours later, one of Rickover's staff members tripped the scram breaker. This time Jim Turner scrambled from the forward compartment to assist Kammerzell in the recovery procedure, which went even faster and smoother than before. The admiral, who never counted on operations exceeding his own strict standards, had no choice other than to accept the result.

The *NR-1* prowled the bottom for two days, riding ridges, driving into canyons, and nosing into unknown territory. Rickover was like a kid with a new toy, and spent hours lying on his stomach at the center view port, watching the unknown world go by, bathed in the boat's bright floodlights. He had the boat come to a halt and back up so he could see the tire tracks in the soft bottom sediment, found an underwater trench that wasn't shown on any map, and saw a big, fat, bewhiskered cod that would not move out of the way. In a canyon on the continental shelf, a sea snake some fifty feet in length swam by and Rickover had the *NR-1* give chase. He brought the boat to a dead halt while he watched two giant crabs fighting or having intercourse—no one could tell which.

The rest of the inspection team grew tired of the tight quarters, the lack of sleep, and the tepid food that soon began to taste the same, no matter what it was supposed to be. Two days of this was long enough, but Rickover had just the opposite reaction and seemed invigorated by the time on the bottom. The ocean had become his personal aquarium.

It was with reluctance that he finally ended the trip, for he knew he probably would never ride the boat again. Before he stepped into a whaleboat to be ferried to the *Sunbird*, he gave Dwaine Griffith the equivalent of a rousing cheer. "Good trial," Rickover growled. Then he was gone, a small white-haired figure wrapped in a bulky orange life preserver.

The *Sunbird* towed the little sub back to port, this time on the surface and in the sunshine, through coveys of civilian pleasure boats from which people waved and gave thumbs-up signs to the men aboard a strange orange thing with a rope on it and the white letters *NR-1* tattooed on the low conning tower. Two months later, in October, the ship was delivered to the navy, but was never truly commissioned. Congress had authorized a specific number of nuclear-powered warships and we were not to be one of them.

After the sea trials, the feared but fatherly presence of Admiral

Rickover seemed to pull back from the *NR-1*, as if he was finally content after his ride on the bottom. His idea had come to life. Although he would stay closely involved in the boat's operations during the coming years, other things were demanding his attention, such as fighting for the new fast attack submarine. Even Hyman Rickover had to sleep sometime, and he at last allowed the U.S. Navy to have a say about the *NR-1*.

We became part of Sub Squadron Two, but not really. We were a nuclear submarine and a deep submersible, but not really. We were an undersea research vessel, but not really. We had $100 million worth of unique boat ready to go. But where? And do what?

9
DAY TRIP

*W*e went out on our own for the first time in early November 1969, a simple trip from Connecticut to Rhode Island and back. The entire mission would be run on the surface and during daylight hours, always within sight of land and along a well-marked course in some of New England's safest waters.

It was a technical assignment. Any ship built with a steel hull creates a magnetic field that an enemy might use to find, identify, and destroy the boat. Therefore, every new ship in the U.S. Navy traverses a range where that field is measured, so a shipyard can then reduce the magnetic signature. On the East Coast, the "degaussing" range is located along a picturesque section of Narragansett Bay.

Although this was to be a routine voyage, it would test the ability of the *NR-1* to operate alone, which had been one of Admiral Rickover's major selling points. The USS *Papago*, a sturdy sea-going tugboat, had been assigned to give us close escort until Rickover found out about it and canceled the order. He wanted us to do this all on our own. But Dwaine Griffith worked out a quiet and sensible compromise with the *Papago* skipper to keep us in sight, from a distance. Just in case.

That was only one of the measures our officers took to make sure the trip would be a success even before we left the pier. The *NR-1* was receiving enough official scrutiny without screwing up an easy trip, and we wanted perfection. They spent days poring over charts and tables of coastal tides and currents while the crew double-checked every piece of machinery.

A primary consideration was our lack of speed. Large submarines have enough brute power to propel them forward at better than twenty knots, either submerged or on the surface, but the small power plant of the *NR-1* trundled us along at less than five. Therefore, our trip was meticulously timed to take advantage of the strong currents that sweep through Long Island Sound and the coastal waters beyond.

We started the nuclear reactor the night before we cast off, and as we pulled into the Thames the next morning, I took the readings at the control panel. The smallest nuclear power plant in the entire navy was humming.

A bright sky provided good visibility beneath banks of high clouds as we left the sub base at New London, went beneath the bridge, and passed the bustling Electric Boat shipyard. The water temperature was in the low sixties. A slight wind from the west-southwest was expected to strengthen before dark, but by then we should be well along the leg home. There was every reason to expect a pleasant day trip, and a group of people who had helped build the boat had gathered on the sandy beach at Avery Point, where the Thames flows into Long Island Sound, to wave as we departed.

We went by Point Alpha, a lighthouse that looks like a small Victorian brick hotel built on a concrete pier, and headed into the calm waters of the sound, which is protected by land. Just beyond that was the most formidable obstacle in our path, a churning section of water known as the Race, which runs between Fishers Island and Great Gull Island, on a rock shelf that is an extension of Long Island. In that stretch, wicked currents could affect our progress, but we made it through without a problem. We took that as a good omen, then set course for Newport.

Once beyond the Race, I received permission to go to the bridge and eagerly climbed into the bright sunshine. Even on the surface, the *NR-1* was mostly submerged, with only two feet of the submarine's hull above water. The conning tower, or the sail, in which I stood was so stumpy that my head was only seven feet above the moving sea, which gave me the feeling of surfing along the water rather than sailing through it. The air was clean and crisp and I could see the waterfront houses on the Connecticut shore and the deep thickets of trees that surrounded them. What could go wrong on a beautiful day like this?

* * *

A few hours later, we arrived on schedule in Narragansett Bay. When we turned into the busy channel that was used regularly by big ships heading to the piers in Providence, our sense of tranquility came to an abrupt end.

"Captain, you should see the size of this ship!" The excited voice of XO Steve Perry sounded tinny over the intercom from the bridge of the *NR-1*. His startled comment was followed by his quick order to stop the engines.

As we coasted to a halt, Griffith hurried topside and Perry pointed to a large container ship that was approaching at about twenty knots, riding straight up the channel we were trying to cross, quite oblivious to our presence. From the pilothouse of that ship, our tiny submarine probably appeared to be just another blob of flotsam, and she did not alter her course an inch as every passing moment brought her closer. To Griffith and Perry, rocking on their small perch in the middle of the bay, the ship looked like a charging elephant.

"I don't think he sees us at all, and he couldn't stop in time even if he did," the skipper said, judging the shrinking distance. He knew that the slightest bump from such a behemoth could break us in half, and that it was too late to take effective evasive action. It was going to be close.

Griffith called down on the intercom to tell those of us below what was happening, checked to be sure the hatch was secure, then the two officers watched the wall of steel storm past, far too close to the *NR-1*, the stacks of multicolored containers on her deck towering above the submarine. "We're like a turtle crossing a freeway," Perry said. "We don't belong in the same channel with these guys."

The *NR-1* rode well enough in long, gentle swells, but steep and choppy waves would wash right over it and totally flood the inside of the conning tower. At the bottom of the sail, openings allowed quick drainage but also let water enter, with the result that when a big wave hit, the conning tower filled up from both ends.

The large wake of the container ship arrived, and while the crew inside the sub felt sharp surges and rolls, all hell broke loose on the bridge as the first wave hit. It rose over the hull and exploded in geysers that shot high into the air when it hit the sail, then fell back on Griffith and Perry. Simultaneously, more water rushed into the conning tower at their feet, and in seconds, the two officers were up to their chests in water.

Before that first wave drained away, a second surged over the top of the boat and gurgled up from the deck area, again completely filling the conning tower. Then as suddenly as it arrived, the wake passed and the sub steadied again. Griffith and his XO looked at each other in amazement as they gasped for breath. Tan uniforms that had been crisp a moment before now hung on them like wet khaki laundry. The navy's newest nuclear submarine had almost been run over by a tramp container ship that didn't even know we were there.

We considered the bizarre incident nothing more than a freak accident, and since the ship was not damaged, we got on with our business of the day.

The *NR-1* ran the degaussing range as planned, then turned for home and smoothly cleared the sheltered waters of Newport, within sight of the bluff-top mansions built by industrial barons at the end of the nineteenth century. A freshening wind blew directly against us and we were running behind schedule. The seas were building as Jack Maurer, the navigator, prepared to take over the bridge watch starting at four o'clock in the afternoon.

Just getting into the sail was a problem. From inside the sub, the hatch did not open directly onto the deck, but into what we called the Doghouse, a compartment at the bottom of the conning tower. Only three feet high and about four feet wide, the Doghouse was such a tight fit that anyone entering it had to squat. The boxlike structure acted much like an air lock on a spaceship. The hull hatch at the bottom of the Doghouse led into the ship, while another on top of it gave access to the sail area. To keep seawater out of the boat, both hatches would never be opened at the same time when underway.

The top of the Doghouse formed the floor of the bridge, and once standing atop that platform, the man on watch was no more than seven feet above the surface. A wave only ten feet high would be three feet above the top edge of the sail. That usually was not a problem in the open ocean, where there normally is a long interval between waves, allowing the ship to float up and over the crests. But when seas were steep and packed tightly together, as with the wake of the container ship, the *NR-1* did not have the time and space in which to react properly, so the waves passed over us as we bobbed along like a nearly submerged log.

Although the hatches could be sealed, the sail could not be, for if it were totally enclosed, the thin fiberglass structure would be crushed by underwater pressure when we dove deep. Sensors beside the hatch alerted whoever was coming up to the amount of water in the compartment above them. In anything but a calm sea, some water was guaranteed.

To be sure that it was safe to open the inner hatch, Maurer checked two sensor lights on the bulkhead. Red meant seawater was covering the hatch, while green meant it was mostly clear. Timing was everything.

As I stood beside him to help, he saw green, popped the hatch, and the several inches of water that had collected below the sensor cascaded onto us. That deluge was expected, and we had surrounded the ladder with a large plastic shower curtain to catch the flood and guide it into the bilge. Maurer scrunched into the Doghouse, we tightened the pressure hull hatch below him, and then he opened the bridge hatch and climbed out to relieve Perry.

The *NR-1* was plowing into choppy seas. Frothy water foamed over the deck and flung a fine spray into their faces. Perry pointed out that the rising wind was working against the current and creating quite a chop, trimming our forward speed to almost nothing and laying waste to our carefully planned timetable.

Inside, we had already figured that out, for the boat was lurching sharply. With our round hull, the ship rolled back and forth when on a choppy surface, sometimes tilting twenty degrees to each side. I couldn't walk without holding onto something.

"It's going to be a long trip home," Perry observed before ducking into the Doghouse and going below. Maurer scanned the horizon through his binoculars. The *Papago* was still on station about a mile behind us, staggering with the rhythm of the sea. The trip home would be not only long, but rough, too. As daylight faded from an autumn sky which had turned from blue to ominous gray, Jack Maurer was glad the big tug was nearby.

Dwaine Griffith got the radio call from the *Papago* captain shortly before dark. Inexplicably, that hardy vessel, capable of riding out the worst of storms, had sprung a leak in the rough seas and perhaps had cracked a couple of ribs. The tug had to run for safe harbor at Point Judith and make emergency repairs. On the bridge, Maurer watched uneasily as the *Papago* faded into the gloom. It was as if our only life preserver was floating away. The *NR-1* was alone, and heading into darkness.

We could not duck into the nearest harbor, for nuclear-powered ships are restricted to certain facilities, and the nearest was our home port in New London, about thirty miles away. The latest weather forecast called for increasing winds and heavier seas in the western reaches of Block Island Sound, growing worse overnight. Not good for a little boat caught in the open in exactly that spot.

We weren't built to handle the rough stuff up top, but even a hurricane usually causes little concern aboard a submarine. You simply flood the ballast tanks, dive, and ride out the storm in the calmness of the deep. But when we considered diving to get out of the weather, we found that we could not perform that most basic operation for a submarine because the ballast tank vent valves had been secured by big padlocks.

Those valves are kept locked in port to prevent inadvertent sinking at the dock, and since this short voyage was to be run completely on the surface, there had been no need to prepare for a dive. So the keys to the padlocks were still back in our New London office, and that meant we could not let the air out of the ballast tanks, so water could not get in and add the weight needed to take us down.

For the duration of whatever Mother Nature was going to throw at us that night, we would be stuck on the surface. And the rolling of our ship started to make many members of this particularly sturdy bunch of veteran submariners very queasy.

Steve Perry suited up in survival gear shortly before eight P.M. to relieve Maurer. While at the foot of the ladder, waiting for a chance to go topside, the suffocating warmth of the heavy suit and the sharp rocking made him seasick. While he and I watched the red and green lights blink erratically to indicate the water level in the Doghouse, he began to puke into a clear plastic bag of the sort that we used for many things aboard ship. He handed the full bag to me; I tied it off and put it into the freezer beside the full barf bags from other crew members. There was no way to get rid of the stuff.

Red light. Short green. Red, longer, then a flash of green. Red again. Perry needed to reach some fresh air quickly and the instant the next green flashed, he threw open the hatch, and a torrent of water cascaded down, sloshed over us, and almost filled the shower curtain. By the time that water drained into the bilge, Perry was scrunched over in the Doghouse, his head knocking the underside of the deck above as we sealed the main hatch below him. Then he popped the top hatch and turned to climb the three steps to the bridge when a wave slammed aboard and filled the conning tower. Steve felt as if he were climbing from the bottom of a swimming pool.

He rose to stand beside Jack Maurer, who was cold, wet, and exhausted and told Perry the ship was only a few miles from the forbidding rocky shoals at the eastern end of Fishers Island. The sea was pitching the boat madly, and Maurer was barely able to point out pinpricks of navigation lights along the shore whenever the sub crested a wave. Perry needed to watch those lights to keep us away from the hazards. The temperature had dropped after sundown, and a harsh cold wind punished their exposed skin. Maurer went down into the sub, barely able to stand up.

Then we found that we could not alert anyone on shore to our problem. The hundred-watt radio was useless because its signal was unable to reach more than a few miles in such poor conditions. And the only alternative was a set of walkie-talkies that we had used to talk to the *Papago*, which was now out of range.

About midnight, our slow, jerking progress had taken us west, past the tip of Block Island, where the wave action increased substantially. The broad island had taken some of the fury from the seas that were rolling up from the southwest. Now, without that landmass to deflect them, the hard waves from the deep Atlantic struck with full vengeance. The *NR-1* took on more pronounced rolls, often tilting some thirty degrees to each side. Papers, books, coffee cups, and anything else that wasn't nailed down tumbled about.

During the next four hours, the storm grew into a wicked, genuine New England autumn gale. Steve Perry, who had been battered during his entire watch, was to be relieved at midnight. But when the time came, it was impossible to bring him down.

Maurer and I watched helplessly at the ladder below as the warning light glowed a steady scarlet. It no longer even blinked green. Thinking the sensor may have broken, we pushed on the hatch with all of our combined strength and found it impossible to lift because the Doghouse was filled with surging, heavy water. Steve Perry got the bad news on the ship's telephone from the skipper, who told him that he would have to stay where he was until things calmed down.

The exec faced a nightmare, for in the darkness the approaching waves could not be seen. Shouldered along by a thirty-knot wind, they arrived without warning, steep and packed closely together, dealing hammer blows to the bridge and to the man stuck out there. The only warning Perry had was a rattlesnake hiss a split second before a wall of water exploded against the conning tower.

With each wave, the cold green sea buried him from above and flooded up through the conning tower below, sandwiching him in a churning maelstrom. Each time he heard the small hiss, he barely had time to duck his head and take a deep breath before the wave smothered him until it passed by. Then he would take another deep breath to prepare for the next one. He had held on for four hours and now, exhausted, learned that he would not be relieved.

A small folding seat was attached to the inside of the conning tower, and since he could not use the seat anyway, Perry disconnected the thick nylon straps that secured it and tied himself to the steel supports. This nuclear-age sailor was not unlike a mariner of old who lashed himself to the mast of a sailing ship in a storm.

Perry was hit by another big wave, a huge green-water monster that covered the entire boat and submerged him for so long that he thought the submarine might be sinking beneath his feet. His lungs ached for air as he hung on for dear life until the water passed. The mast with its periscope TV camera emerged first, then his head, and he sucked in air as the ship slid down the far side of the wave. Then it happened again. And again.

He tugged hard on the makeshift straps, tightening them as much as possible. "At least they'll find my body," Steve Perry thought.

Inside the boat, I had climbed into my bunk, feeling the boat being attacked by the roiling sea. Sleep is precious on a submarine and you grab it any time you can, even in times of peril. With a full crew on watch in the limited space of the control room, there was no room for me there anyway, so I tried to rest, to divorce my mind from what was happening, as the *NR-1* shook madly around me. Even lying down, I had to hold on. Sleep was impossible.

As his ordeal by dunking continued, Steve Perry discovered still another problem. Even with the true condition of the ship obscured by the pounding action of the waves, he sensed that the *NR-1* was riding lower in the water than it should. He called the skipper on the ship phone and, over the howl of the wind, screamed that because of the precipitous rolls, air in the ballast tanks may have bubbled out of the flood ports on the bottom of the ship! Water had replaced it, made the boat heavier, and was pulling it deeper. Standing only a few feet above the surface, Perry had no room to spare. Griffith ordered a thirty-second blow of compressed air into the tanks, forced out the extra water, and the ship steadied slightly.

We were only about two miles from the calmer waters of Long Island Sound, but still needed to get through the Race, which was difficult even in good weather. There was no possibility of waiting outside of that treacherous stretch of water, because Perry could not hold out much longer, and the hatch light still glowed bright red. The tortured exec and the worried skipper conferred again on the phone. Safety was an hour away, but it would be a hard hour.

Griffith asked if Perry could see any navigation lights, and the executive officer reported that he glimpsed a few whenever the boat danced to the top of a wave. Just as he hoped the worst was over, all the lights on Fishers Island went out, including the lighthouse marking the Race. The lights had fallen victim to the storm, and in that moment he thought we would as well. It was pitch black until the emergency generator kicked on at the Race light and it flickered back on.

The skipper looked at the chart again. Although the Race was several miles wide, only about a mile at the eastern end was suitable for passage of even a small vessel like the *NR-1*. A long granite ledge lay just beneath the surface along the rest of the opening, a clear threat to any ship. Except for best guessing, we didn't really know where we were.

It was one of those terrible moments when command weighs like iron on the shoulders of a captain. The smart thing to do was stay outside the Race until dawn, and go in on the rising tide. But that choice risked losing Steve Perry, which was unthinkable. Although the crew was being tossed about inside, we knew that Steve was in much worse trouble. There was really no choice, because we would not abandon our shipmate.

Griffith gave the order, relying on Perry's determination, seamanship, and last reserves of strength. "Position the ship the best you can," the skipper ordered, "and take us through the Race."

I was back on duty below as we went in, bucking over the great waves as Perry held on for his life. Cold and weak from fatigue, he picked up the landmarks to keep us from the shoal water and called down the steering directions. I knew that he had to be reaching his absolute physical limits, and time seemed to stand still, for our lives depended on his.

He fought the elements for another hour as the NR-1 inched forward until we finally felt the sea start to lose its savage edge. Perry had somehow guided the submarine perfectly through the treacherous Race during the dark, cold time before dawn.

By the time the sun rose, the sea gods were finally smiling on us. The bouncing eased as we moved into quieter water, which let us rescue Steve Perry, who had been trapped on the bridge for more than twelve hours. His skin was blue with cold, his eyes red and brows frosted with thick salt, his face raw from the lashing wind, and he barely was able to croak out a few words. The storm had taken everything he had.

A short time later, we passed Point Alpha and entered the Thames, and it felt incongruous that everything seemed normal again. The sun was up and the weather had moderated. There were the Electric Boat docks, there was the bridge, and the sub base was straight ahead. By the time we tied up, the images of our stormy passage were already fading. We were a few hours late, but we had all survived.

There were no hurrahs, no outpouring of emotions, and no awards for bravery. The skipper simply congratulated Steve for his good work, and the rest of us added our approval. The harrowing experience was accepted as part of the job.

We were glad to be back, glad that Steve was okay, and glad to have learned some valuable lessons, such as never leave behind the keys to the vent valve locks, get some better radio gear, and never go to sea without a support ship, no matter what Admiral Rickover wanted. Not much was said after the fact, for we kept it all as quiet as possible, not wanting to put ourselves on report for having gotten into such a situation in the first place.

I took some deep breaths of frosty New England air, went straight home, and fell instantly asleep in a large, warm bed that seemed to move with the roll of an angry ocean.

10
CANYON

Despite the rough trip through Narragansett Bay, our confidence in the boat grew in direct proportion to the time we spent putting the *NR-1* through its paces. Although we had been with the sub since it only existed on paper, we were absolutely awed by what it could do beneath the waves, when it descended to a deep bottom and drove along the floor of the world, with our bright lights illuminating dark, underwater corners of the sea never before viewed by other humans. Mysterious things swam and slithered past our view ports. We could go into a standstill hover like an underwater helicopter and pick a penny out of the mud. It worked! Unhampered by fuel constraints, we felt that we could go almost anywhere and do almost anything. The *NR-1* really could accomplish what it was designed for and no other boat in the world could match us.

We learned something new every time we went out, and when we returned to port, the guys at Electric Boat would tune her up to an even higher performance level, and we would head out again to try something else. We became intimately familiar with the little craft's idiosyncrasies. One of our earliest conclusions was that duty at the view ports, which were only four inches around inside the boat and coned outward to a diameter of sixteen inches, could be boring. You could enter the view port area only by slithering on your belly under the deck plates just below the forward control station, and then you lay there prone on cushioned mats. You never knew what you were going to see, mud or mystery.

Just beneath the surface, a lot of fish swam by to curiously examine this new creature in their midst, but surface light normally vanished by the time we reached a depth of about three hundred feet. At the middle depths, it was like looking into a thin biological soup, although there were not many fish in it. Then, in the deepest and darkest water, strange creatures and odd little fish would show up. Overall, however, it was kind of disappointing to find that the bottom of the sea was mostly a giant mudflat. We had worked all these years to be able to drive around down there, only to discover it was like taking the family car across the Nevada desert, and the view was very similar to the pictures being brought back by the astronauts of the desolation of the moon.

The most surprising thing was that there were not a lot of interesting things down there, and the things that were interesting usually turned out to be scary. Like when we ran into the giant squid.

On an early cruise, the boat was flying about fifteen feet over the bottom when Steve Perry, at the center view port, called out to Jack Maurer in the pilot's seat, "Stop the boat!"

"What? What?" replied Maurer, reining the boat to a standstill.

"Holy shit, Jack. You won't believe this!" They switched positions and Perry took the controls while Maurer slid onto a view port pad, plugged in the intercom, and took a look outside. "Holy shit, Steve. I don't believe this!"

An elongated, undulating, purplish creature so long that all of it could not be seen at the same time was directly beneath the boat. A portion slowly wiggling in our lights stood out starkly against the surrounding darkness. Perry and Maurer switched back to their original positions and decided to give the thing a nudge with the nose of the *NR-1*. Maurer pushed, but the creature just lay there, waving slowly.

Maurer pushed again, harder, and the translucent creature came off the bottom and moved toward us, startling Perry as it passed above the view port. The thing was only a foot in diameter and he had the terrible thought that it might not be the whole creature at all . . . but just part of an even *greater* creature, perhaps a single tentacle of a giant squid such as those of sea legends. "Back away, Jack! It may be trying to grab us!" he called out. The boat immediately went into reverse and the thing moved away from us again, settling on the bottom to resume its macabre dance.

By now, someone was at each of the three view ports, and the rest of us were scrambling for turns. What was this? A sea serpent like the Loch Ness monster? A prehistoric octopus? What? We were chattering like a bunch of first graders visiting the zoo, excited and already basking in the glory of discovering a new deep-sea life form. Giant squid were known to exist, but no one had ever seen one alive. We took some pictures of the mystifying monster and then decided to find the end of it, although we were concerned that it might again react violently if we disturbed it too much. Maurer slowly moved the boat to the left, and those at the view ports saw that the monster tapered to a point at that end, so the head obviously was the other way.

Moving at a creep, we scooted to the right, and spoke in whispers, as if we might be overheard. After moving about 150 feet, one of the lookouts quietly said, "There it is!" A gaping maw filled with hundreds of small, irregularly shaped tentacles wafted in the bottom current as if gathering food. There were no eyes and no gills—just this huge mouth on something that we had measured as being as long as a football field. None of us had ever seen anything like it before, not even in oceanographic photographs, but before we could give it a scientific name, like *NR-Oneasaurus* or something, a crew member suffered a flash of recognition.

Ships often practice antiaircraft fire by shooting at long target sleeves towed by planes, and at some time in the past, one of those funnel-like targets had been shot away, had fallen into the ocean, and had sunk tail-first to the bottom, where it morphed over the years into our deep-sea creature. The mouth was just the open front end, which had been frayed into tatters by the water over the years. The *NR-Oneasaurus* was nothing but a piece of cloth. None of us were unhappy when the photographs we took disappeared.

As the months passed, we neared completion of the sea testing, and everyone aboard and in the shipyard was working hard to deliver the boat to the navy in final form and get out on some real assignments. In the middle of November 1969, those careful plans went right off a cliff.

The *NR-1* was about a hundred miles off the southern shore of Connecticut when it made a routine dive into a deep area known as the Baltimore Canyon. We steadied into a hover a half mile down, just above the seafloor, extended the wheels, let the thrusters push us down to a gentle landing, and then pumped about a thousand pounds of extra water into the ballast tanks. The added weight pressed us onto the soft bottom, gave firm grip to the tires, and kept us from bouncing as we rolled along. Then we drove off to see what we could see in places that normal submarines and submersibles could never go. A few hours into the mission, Maurer was again in the pilot's chair, and this time, Brian Wruble, the Sperry engineer, was at the center view port, wearing a communications headset and watching the mud roll by. Wruble had been aboard for several previous trips, including the rough surface transit to Narragansett Bay, but this was his first chance to log some serious bottom watching. Since it was generally believed that the bottom was as flat as a tortilla in this area, the civilian was encouraged to suffer the boredom of a duty watch at the windows, which freed crewmen for other duties. Although there had not been much for Wruble to see, he was utterly fascinated by the view beyond the small window.

Things were so normal that Steve Perry was catching a nap right next to him, snoring lightly, and the rest of us were scattered about the ship doing other jobs. I was at the reactor control panel, monitoring the dials as the ship moved forward at about one knot—a bit more than one mile per hour—which to us seemed almost a gallop.

The lights cast a hazy brightness in the path right before the boat, but beyond that short curtain of illumination lay total darkness. Wruble was there primarily to see if anything interesting came along, not to guide the ship, for that was the task of the forward-looking sonar and the television cameras in the bow that displayed what was ahead on a screen at the ship control panel.

The system worked well, and earlier in the dive, the NR-1 had discovered, then deftly dodged around, an undersea field of rotting ammunition crates still loaded with live shells, deadly relics of World War II. We charted them, and continued the mission. As we rolled easily down a gentle slope, Jack Maurer, in the pilot's chair, was working the controls to force the boat to do something it did not want to do.

The ship was so stable that it automatically tried to keep itself level, which meant that as we came down the slope, the bow tended to rise and stay even with the stern. Only the rear wheel was touching the mud as the forward part of the boat angled slightly higher. That pointed the forward television cameras up too far to see anything on the bottom. The separation of the bow from the bottom also limited the effectiveness of the sonar.

Maurer added still more water to the forward ballast tanks, which brought the bow down and put both wheels back in contact. Unfortunately, the extra ballast made the boat so heavy that the maximum upward force from the combined fore-and-aft thrusters would not be able to lift it. We rolled ahead.

Wruble suddenly noticed a slight change in the character of the ocean floor, and then saw what looked like the edge of the world crawl beneath the little window. The front wheel ran off a precipice and Wruble heard a loud *whummpp* as the boat lurched and his head smacked some overhead pipes that sliced a cut in his scalp. The sound he heard was the bottom of the *NR-1* scraping along a canyon rim. Blood ran down his face as he yelled into his microphone, "Go back! Go back! We're going over the edge!"

But our forward, downward momentum made that impossible and over we went, slowly sinking into an unknown cavern. Wruble felt his stomach turn over, as if he was falling from a great height, for he saw nothing but blackness below. The weight that had glued us to the bottom now pulled us inexorably into the void, nose first. The submarine was a half mile deep, nearly a ton too heavy, and falling.

"What can you see?" Dwaine Griffith called to Wruble, and the engineer answered, "Nothing. Nothing at all!" Steve Perry had snapped awake and fought his way out of the view port area, but could only watch helplessly as the sonar painted an electronic picture that showed the nearly vertical sides of a V-shaped canyon as far ahead as it could see. It detected no bottom. Damage reports came in negative, and the reactor panel told me the plant was still on line and operating normally, although I had to grab a handhold to stay in position as the sub tilted. Below, Wruble reported water had begun to fill in around the center view port, possibly indicating a leak, which would be deadly at this depth. Just as Herb Berry had done on the first sea trial, a quick taste let Wruble know that it was not seawater, just an enormous amount of condensation that had flowed forward to the lowest point in the boat.

Maurer applied maximum power to the thrusters, but the boat was too heavy to respond. Perry had his hands on a wheel directly over the control station, the emergency blow valve that would release high-pressure air to quickly push seawater out of our main ballast tanks. "Should I give it a shot of air?" he asked the skipper, but it was too late for that.

"Wait," said Griffith. He no longer had the option of blowing the tanks because we did not know what was overhead. If we popped up, we could hit an overhead ledge or scrape the side of the canyon, either of which might trigger an avalanche that could bury us. Down we went, and the depth indicator counted off hundreds of feet as we sank ever deeper.

We all knew there was only one way out of this boat, but there was no panic, as our training clicked in. All we could do was trust the *NR-1* and ride it out. Everyone seemed coldly calm, but our eyes and ears were on full sensory alert as we pitched down in a slow-motion nightmare. We knew we couldn't fall forever.

The bottom appeared suddenly and we hit it with a thud. The bow crashed into a pile of rocks, crushed the door to the manipulator arm housing, wrecked the arm itself, and filled the compartment with mud. The rest of the boat settled onto the mucky canyon floor, sinking in deep enough that mud covered the view ports.

We were on our own down there, and no rescue was possible. Ironically, the first Deep Submergence Rescue Vessel, in whose administrative program we had been hidden, finally had been launched, but we did not have the sort of hatch that would be compatible with a DSRV. Nobody was coming to get us.

Griffith, Maurer, and Perry discussed the few options, and they ruled out taking any action that might set off a deadly landslide, which could cover the boat or perhaps flush it farther down the canyon. The mud had us firmly in its grasp and it would be difficult to overcome that suction.

We carried eight tons of emergency lead shot to help in such emergencies, but dropping that was also deemed too risky. The door to the forward bin that contained four tons of shot seemed damaged, and if we could only drop the four tons that were aft, the submarine would pivot on its nose to an almost vertical angle. That would leave us still trapped on the bottom but standing almost straight up in the water without power, or possibly make us arrow up to the surface, backward, still with the risk of hitting the canyon wall. That option was also discarded.

Griffith decided to see if we could lighten the ballast enough to get off the bottom—and try to slowly and carefully fly out of the canyon! For two hours, we sat trapped in the mud as the single high-pressure drain pump pushed water from the tanks back into the sea. I crawled down to the view port area and asked Wruble if he thought I should sharpen my stainless steel U.S. Navy pocketknife in case we needed to commit suicide. He was not amused and openly wondered what would possess a man to work so hard to get into the *NR-1* program.

To attempt breaking free, Griffith ordered the six off-duty crew members to go as far back in the ship as possible while the trim pump also shifted some water into the aft tank. We huddled into the warren of small openings in the engineering spaces, and hoped for the best. Our weight, combined with that of the extra water, pressed the stern down and applied upward force to the bow. "Full astern on both propellers," the skipper ordered. Nothing. In the rear, we all looked at each other, but not a word was said.

"Full up on all thrusters," Griffith almost whispered. Still nothing.

We were throwing everything it had into the effort, but the suction of the mud held the *NR-1* tight.

On the skipper's order, we all scrambled from the rear of the boat and rushed headlong to the front of the sub, and clustered together there while the trim water was shifted to the forward tank. Then we all rushed back to the rear again, trying to rock the boat, and repeated the twenty-yard dash up and down the center aisle a couple of times. Except for the orders from Griffith, and the noise of our pounding feet, we made those boat-rocking runs in silence. Outside the hull, the propellers and thrusters thundered at full speed. Wruble, who had remained at the view port, saw the mud coating the window wiggle.

"We're moving!" he shouted, and the sub slid free without a sound and rose a few feet off the bottom. Griffith ordered the emergency maneuvering power turned off, and the crew scattered back to our stations to wait and see what happened next. The mud grudgingly released its grip and the ship trimmed to an up angle. Griffith ordered the engines ahead at one-third speed and eased the boat forward. Lugging along huge amounts of mud, the boat was sluggish and moved like a wounded animal.

We were free, but no one could yet breathe a sigh of relief, for we were still about three thousand feet deep, right at the boat's test depth, in a treacherous and uncharted canyon.

The sonar guided us inch by inch through the ominous chasm as we slowly navigated to the surface, staying away from the threatening, towering walls that enclosed us. Hours later, when we were finally back up on top, the skipper opened the hatch, and fresh air poured inside. We did not cheer, but were damned relieved to be alive.

The manipulator arm was wrecked and the door covering it was caved in, but everything else was operational, although we were coated with a lot of heavy mud. Griffith had the divers remove the grime from the view ports, the lights, and the sonar transducers. Despite the significant external damage, we gave no thought to ending the mission. There was a job to do, and it was not long before the *NR-1* was underwater again, driving right back down into the Baltimore Canyon.

We had added another page to the operating manual that we seemed to be creating the hard way. Henceforth the maximum speed while driving on the bottom would not exceed a half knot, and the pilot would never add more water ballast than the thrusters could lift.

In one of the few articles ever written about the *NR-1*, the *New London Day* reported on December 12, 1969, that the submarine had returned to dry dock at Electric Boat for what a navy spokesman described as "minor voyage repairs." The damage actually cost more than $1 million to fix and pushed back the final delivery still further.

Brian Wruble was summoned to Sperry headquarters and grilled by a high level of management that he did not even know existed. They were worried that somehow he might have caused the incident and exposed the company to liability for the damages. They peppered him with accusatory questions, but after having been trapped on the bottom of the ocean, sitting in a comfortable conference room with some guys in dark suits did not frighten him. Brian eventually was cleared, and arrived back in Groton feeling like a veteran and eager for his next mission on the *NR-1*.

However, his course was already set in another direction, and he told our captain, Dwaine Griffith, that he would be resigning from Sperry in January 1970, to accept a position on Wall Street.

Griffith's first thought was naturally of how his ship would operate without the resident computer genius, and he scheduled Brian to do every *NR-1* mission until the resignation became effective and tune the perplexing Mark XV to perfection. Then he took the extra precaution of asking Wruble to take his program manuals with him to New York. Since I had become Brian's unofficial assistant in handling the system,

Griffith said he would sleep better knowing Brian was available "if Lee needs to call."

Then the skipper thought about all of the hard work that had been done by the civilian engineer standing before him, the man who had literally created the brain of the *NR-1*. "Brian, for a while I was never sure whether you were crew or cargo," Griffith told him. "You definitely turned out to be part of my crew." He reached into a desk drawer and handed Wruble a pair of gold dolphins, the distinctive insignia of a U.S. Navy submarine officer.

Years later, after Wruble had made several fortunes on Wall Street, he would recall how stunned he was by that unexpected honor, which he considered the most emotional moment of his career. It was a typical Dwaine Griffith gesture.

We were not the only ones in the navy skirting danger in those days, for the balance of superpower naval forces had shifted to favor Admiral Sergei Gorshkov's Soviet fleet. At sea, the Cold War no longer seemed very cold at all.

When Admiral Elmo Zumwalt assumed command of the U.S. Navy in 1970, he found the morale of his sailors deteriorating even faster than his aging fleet. Vietnam was sapping the lifeblood from the navy, and the men of the fleet mirrored the societal changes that were dividing the country. Drug use was rampant, long held loyalties were changing, and insubordination by sailors who were against the war and by angry minorities was almost commonplace. Meanwhile, the average American warship was seventeen and one-half years old, while less than 1 percent of the growing Soviet fleet had been in service for more than twenty years.

Red Fleet vessels were literally popping up everywhere. The American submarine USS *Gato* collided with a Soviet nuclear sub at the entrance to the White Sea near Norway, and a few months later, another Soviet boat hit the USS *Tautog* beneath the waters of the Pacific. Several more Soviet submarines fell victim to internal fires, but Gorshkov never slowed down.

There were no Soviet warships involved in Vietnam, although their merchant vessels regularly brought supplies to the ports of Haiphong and Hanoi. But one place the alteration in balance of the opposing forces was quite noticeable was the Mediterranean Sea, where for the first time the U.S. Sixth Fleet found itself outnumbered by a sleek armada belonging to its enemy. The Soviet Union had seventy-two ships on station in the Med, while the U.S. had a maximum of sixty. Russian and American warships shadowed each other so closely that the mixed fleets took on the look of an international boat show. The airpower of U.S. carriers was offset by Soviet planes operating from land bases in Mediterranean countries that were friendly to Moscow. Admiral Isaac C. (Ike) Kidd, the Sixth Fleet commander, observed that his fleet "has been forced to accommodate to a new environment different from the one which it dominated for a quarter century." Sailing in the Med had become dangerous.

To drive home the point that his Red Fleet had come of age, Admiral Gorshkov launched Okean I, the largest naval exercise the world had ever seen. Some two hundred Soviet ships surged from their ports, made sweeping and fast voyages along strategic routes, and set alarm bells ringing in the Pentagon, for the exercise mirrored how a Soviet attack against the United States might begin. Our analysts knew that only a fraction of the available Soviet forces were used in the saber-rattling exercise.

So Admiral Gorshkov probably had no reason to be concerned when the NR-1 finally reported for duty with the American navy on June 18, 1970. Five hundred and ten days had passed since we had been launched. Painted orange and carrying only the firepower of a single pistol, neither side considered us to be much more than a mosquito as far as the Cold War was concerned. That was exactly where we wanted to operate.

11

ENDURE

After long years of hard work, repeated setbacks, and brushes with disaster, our little $100 million boat was almost to the starting line. We had one final examination before being allowed to play with the big boys, a thirty-day underwater endurance trial, which would put on the line Admiral Rickover's claim that the basic strength of the *NR-1* was its ability to remain hidden underwater almost indefinitely.

Seven of us were chosen to take the *NR-1* down deep and stay there, working every system we had. For a month, we would exist in the most Spartan of conditions, flying and crawling a thousand feet or more beneath the surface of the ocean, living in a steel cylinder that was twelve feet in diameter. A month submerged in a large attack submarine is not remarkable, but our test would be like spending a month in a sunken school bus with a half-dozen other guys. To make things even tighter, the area amidships was further jammed with test instruments and equipment. The only other crews ever to accomplish long-duration voyages in such tight quarters on self-contained vehicles like the *NR-1* were not submariners at all, but NASA astronauts.

Three months before we left port on Groundhog Day, February 2, 1970, the ten-day moon mission of *Apollo 12* went so smoothly that many Americans began to take space travel for granted. Two months after our endurance trial, *Apollo 13* was almost lost in space, and returned safely to Earth only through the crew's bravery and the technical expertise of mission control in Houston.

We would have no mission control team waiting at the other end of a radio if anything went wrong on our trip, and since this had to be an all-navy show, no Sperry wizards would be along to help repair the equipment. It would be up to us to fix any problem, and on any *NR-1* mission, there was never a question of *if* there would be a problem, only *when*, and *how bad*?

Problems were not really bad things in our view, for we learned something from each incident, and were able to push back the unknowns involved in operating this new ship. The rough ride to Rhode Island taught us the need for an escort vessel. Toppling from the canyon rim led to the proper ballasting of the boat and adjusting the maximum speed for bottom operations. Such lessons were part of the creative engineering for any sophisticated piece of machinery, particularly a first-of-its-kind small nuclear-powered submarine. It was our duty to make the sub ready for the crews that followed us.

We were not really concerned about the boat. The biggest test this time would not involve the machinery, but our own limits. We were about to learn the true meaning of the word "endure."

To prepare for departure, we checked the endless list of supplies that covered everything from topping off the potable drinking water to stuffing the small cupboard with dry goods, such as cans of tuna fish, boxes of drink mix, and cookies made by Jim Turner's wife, Mary Lou. The freezer bulged with tiny pizzas, pot pies, and 630 TV dinners, enough to feed seven people three meals a day for thirty days. In theory, the little hot air oven could cook three dinners at once, but in truth, it could barely manage one every half hour, and after a few days at sea, everything started to smell and taste the same. By comparison, a big missile sub usually went to sea carrying about 45 tons of food, a couple of cooks, and a fully equipped galley.

Once the inventory of supplies was finished, the *NR-1* divers had to check the equipment outside the hull. In the warmth of a portable van, Larry Kammerzell and I pulled on full-body wet suits of heavy black neoprene, including gloves, booties with hard soles, and hoods. While we dressed, a tugboat crunched through the two inches of ice that covered the Thames River to give us some working space around the *NR-1*. The morning was sunlit and bright, but the air was only eighteen degrees and I didn't want to guess the water temperature. When I opened the van door, I found Don Marks, who would be our dive master, waiting on the foredeck. His husky frame appeared even bigger, being bundled in long johns, wool socks, dungarees, a foul-weather jacket and a dark wool cap. Don's normally ruddy complexion had been whipped into a bright red by the wind. "Come on, let's get going," he snapped, shivering. "It's cold out here!"

Kammerzell jumped in with a big splash, and ice-cold water rushed into the space between the wet suit and his skin. That shock lasted only a moment, and by the time he surfaced, the heat from his body was warming the protective layer of water trapped inside the suit. Then I dropped in. The icy water flooded my suit as expected, but did not stop coming in. Something was wrong! My chest contracted, my heart clenched with shock, and I could not even catch a breath as the extreme cold knifed into my chest like an instant heart attack. I kicked to the surface, gasping and flailing, and realized my wet suit was half open. I had kept it partially unzipped while in the heated van and forgot to close it before hitting the water. Kam grabbed my arm for support as I struggled, then zipped up my suit. We clung to the boat while my body warmed and I slowly returned to the world of the living. "It's going to be a long day," he said.

The only parts of us still exposed were our faces between the eyebrows and mouths, and when we pulled on the dive masks, only our lips had no protection. The maximum time allowed for a wet suit dive in such conditions was half an hour, so we bit into the mouthpieces of our regulators, sucked air from the tanks on our backs, and ducked beneath the ice.

I kept a hand on the hull so as not to lose contact or become disoriented in the filthy, turbid water. The ship's underwater lights were on, but visibility was less than ten feet near the forward view port area, and much darker aft. Swarms of white flecks drifted through the light, and although they looked pretty, we knew these dirty snowflakes were shards of used toilet paper from the sub base sewage overflow pipe near the *NR-1* pier.

With the dive master coordinating between us and the men aboard the boat who were operating the necessary equipment, we removed the view port covers, checked the lights and cameras, and wiped off the outside of the windows and sonar transducers. We made sure the manipulator arm, the keel door, and the sample basket were operating properly and gave a thorough examination to the wheels, propulsion motors, and seawater pumps.

When the checks were completed, we climbed from the freezing water and rushed back to the warm van as rivulets of water on our suits froze into strings of dirty pearls. The dive had taken almost an hour, twice as long as expected, and we were numb with cold. "You should see your lips," Marks hooted as we peeled off the ice-encrusted gear. "They look like they have been turned inside out." My mouth was swollen and dark purple.

Marks and Kammerzell headed home for long, hot showers and good meals, but I barely had time to rinse the salt from my short hair before I took over the reactor plant watch on board the *NR-1*. For the next six hours I sat there reading dials while wrapped in a foul-weather jacket, with a wool watch cap pulled over my ears, and the heater turned up as high as possible. During the dives, I had surfaced about two dozen times, and the changing pressures had forced seawater into the dive mask and then into my sinus cavities, and it was still sloshing around in my head. When my watch was over, I ate a TV dinner, fell into the nearest bunk, and slept for six hours in my foul-weather coat, beneath two blankets.

During the past year, I had used some of the immense amount of idle time we had to qualify as an officer of the deck for in-port purposes, which was rare for an enlisted man. That made me part of the three-man watch section that prepared the ship to get underway. Somebody shook me awake just before midnight and I pulled myself from the bunk, made a cup of hot chocolate, and went forward to relieve Jack Maurer. As he briefed me, the hot chocolate triggered my sinuses and out spurted the dirty river water that had clogged my head for hours. I leaned forward and a deluge of clear liquid splashed onto the rubber mat between us.

"God, that's awful," said Maurer, taking a quick step back. "Does this happen every time you dive?"

I found a towel and wiped my face, then cleaned up the mess on the deck. "Usually. Never know when it's going to break loose. At least the salt water clears my sinuses. I haven't had a cold since going to dive school." Suddenly, I felt great and was ready to go to work.

The final step before going to sea was to bring the nuclear reactor from Cold Iron to Hot Operations, or from a complete shutdown to "going critical" and producing enough steam to power the ship.

On most nuclear submarines, the reactors are shielded by a foot of

Recovering the H-bomb

The Perry Ocean Systems Cubmarine searched down to 300 feet for the H-bomb lost off the southeast coast of Spain when a B-52 collided with a tanker in January 1966. (Courtesy of Woods Hole Oceanographic Institute)

The Reynolds Metals *Aluminaut*, which impressed Admiral Rickover, used sonar to search to the edge of the canyon for the missing H-bomb. (Courtesy of George Tyler, Science Museum of Virginia)

The *Alvin*, from Woods Hole Oceanographic Institute, located the H-bomb 2,550 feet under water. (Courtesy of Woods Hole Oceanographic Institute)

The recovered bomb and its parachute on the aft deck of the USS *Petrel* (Courtesy of Sandia Labs)

Ideas vs. Reality

An early artist's sketch of how the *NR-1* might look hovering over a sandy bottom (Courtesy of Brian Wruble)

An Electric Boat engineering sketch of a possible *NR-1* shape (Courtesy of Fred DeGrooth, Sr.)

A view of the actual *NR-1* clearly showing the starboard thruster openings, the sonar transducer, and the glass window with the lights behind them, forming the eye, nose, and mouth of the *NR-1*'s "face" (Courtesy of Fred DeGrooth, Sr.)

Under Construction

While Neil Armstrong walked on the surface of the moon in July 1969, the *NR-1* sat on the Electric Boat Marine Railway. Construction manager Ed Holt (left) and Captain Dwaine Griffith ready the boat for her upcoming sea trials. (Courtesy of Electric Boat)

The *NR-1* on its construction cradle in EB South Yard with some of the tarps used to hide its top-secret features still in place, just prior to launching (Courtesy of Electric Boat)

Launched at Last

The *NR-1* sliding down the ways into Connecticut's Thames River (Courtesy of Electric Boat)

Admiral Rickover Inspects the *NR-1*

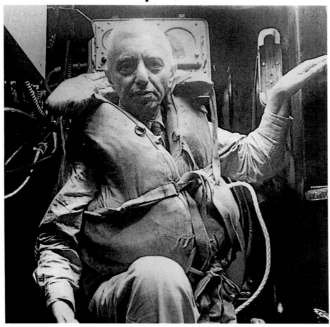

Admiral Rickover climbing out of the doghouse into the sail during sea trials (Courtesy of Electric Boat)

Admiral Rickover (right rear) and his party leaving the *NR-1* by whaleboat after the initial sea trial dive (Courtesy of Brian Wruble)

America's Secret Submarine

The official photograph of the *NR-1* provided to the press, doctored to remove state of the art equipment (Courtesy of Electric Boat)

A similar view showing the actual antennas, periscope TV camera, and sonar transducers. From left to right, Steve Perry, Jack Maurer, and Dwaine Griffith are on the bridge. (Courtesy of Fred DeGrooth, Sr.)

Out to Sea

The *NR-1* at work, riding on the surface (Courtesy of Capt. Allison J. Holifield, USN-Ret.)

The *NR-1* shadowed by fleet tug USS *Papago* (Courtesy of Fred DeGrooth, Sr.)

Hitching a Ride

The *NR-1* under tow at the end of a nylon hawser. The boat looks small measured against the tug.
(Courtesy of Richard Patenaude)

A Miniature Submarine

The *NR-1* being serviced in a graving dock built to handle much larger submarines (Courtesy of Electric Boat)

The Plank Owners

The initial crew of the *NR-1* standing in front of the ship control station mockup at Sperry Gyroscope. The arch shows the ship's hull diameter. Back row, left to right: Dwaine Griffith, Don Marks, Larry Kammerzell, Danny Gunter, and Dave Seaton. Front row, left to right: Steve Perry, Jack Maurer, John Claytor, Dean Paine, Bob Lunt, Lee Vyborny, and Jim Turner.

Family

Lee Vyborny piloting the *NR-1* (Courtesy of Fred DeGrooth, Sr.)

Johanna and Jennifer Vyborny at home in the early 1970s
(Courtesy of Lee Vyborny)

Life Aboard the *NR-1*

XO Steve Perry filling out forms and counseling a crew member at the ship's lone table and bench seat (Courtesy of Fred DeGrooth, Sr.)

Bob Lunt directing reactor plant operations (Courtesy of Fred DeGrooth, Sr.)

Dean Paine (left) and Jim Turner discussing test results at the table (Courtesy of Fred DeGrooth, Sr.)

Larry Kammerzell at the pilot station (Courtesy of Fred DeGrooth, Sr.)

The Men from Sperry

Sperry engineer Fred DeGrooth running tests in the equipment van (Courtesy of Fred DeGrooth, Sr.)

Brian Wruble (left) at the *NR-1* controls (Courtesy of Brian Wruble)

Roger Sherman (right) looking aft from the ship control station (Courtesy of Roger Sherman)

Hard at Work

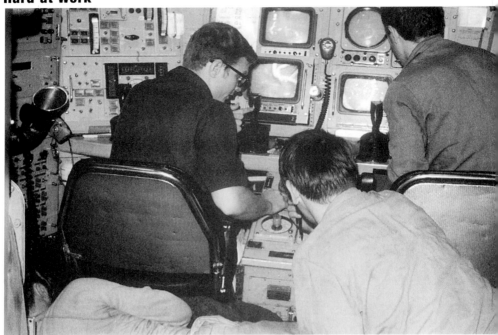

Three crew members work at the control station while the captain sleeps among them.
(Courtesy of Capt. Allison J. Holifield, USN-Ret.)

NR-1 divers (from left to right) Vyborny, Kammerzell, and Marks repairing the ship in the Azores
(Courtesy of Richard Patenaude)

The F-14 and the Phoenix

The cockpit of the F-14 ensnared in what may be Soviet fishing nets
(Courtesy of Fred DeGrooth, Sr.)

The F-14 upside down in 1,850 feet of water with the lifting pendant
attached to its landing gear by the *NR-1* (Courtesy of Capt. Allison J.
Holifield, USN-Ret.)

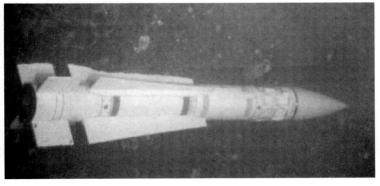

The elusive
Phoenix missile
resting on the
ocean bottom
(Courtesy of Capt.
Allison J. Holifield,
USN-Ret.)

Officers in Charge

Al Holifield (left), the third *NR-1* OIC, and his predecessor, Toby Warson (right), flank *Sunbird* CO Ed Craig beside the recovered Phoenix missile. Note the stencil on the side reading: DO NOT ROLL, TUMBLE OR DROP. (Courtesy of Capt. Allison J. Holifield, USN-Ret.)

Mike McQuown, the fourth *NR-1* OIC (Courtesy of Capt. Allison J. Holifield, USN-Ret.)

Dwaine Griffith, first *NR-1* OIC (Courtesy of Fred DeGrooth, Sr.)

lead on all sides to prevent radiation leakage. Not the *NR-1*. That sort of protective weight would have made it much too heavy to even float, and the nuclear physicists figured that the ocean's water would absorb any escaping radiation when the boat was underway and submerged. Therefore, much of the lead shielding that might be expected around and to the rear of the reactor was absent. We carried the standard foot of lead shielding only on the bulkhead forward of the reactor, which minimized the amount of radiation entering the crew's working areas.

From that bulkhead all the way back to the stern was a different story. The radiation was so hot in the area above, below, and around the reactor that it was a forbidden zone while we were under power, and was cordoned off while we were tied to the pier. Before we started the reactor, I went topside and made sure that a wire rope barrier was in place across the back end of the boat. We did not want anyone standing there when we pulled the rods.

The area was clear, and everything was crisp and exact during the start-up. Each of the 120 valves in the engine room was properly positioned, the water chemistry was precise, and the thirty dials on or around the control panel gave the required readings. The dials were read and recorded every fifteen minutes. The reactor came on line perfectly.

The rest of the crew arrived, final checks and arrangements were made, and we cast off from the pier, rendezvousing with our support ship, the USS *Sunbird*, at the mouth of the Thames. They sent over a small boat carrying the strong, seven-inch-wide nylon towline. The sailors handed Kammerzell, the biggest man aboard, a heavy titanium ball that was attached to the end of the line, and he wrestled it into the open jaws of the tow ball receptacle on the bow. The *Sunbird* turned to the sea and towed us along like a duckling on a string.

A day and a half later, we reached the deep-dive area off the New England shelf, about a hundred miles south of the eastern point of Long Island, pulled the plug, and became invisible to the rest of the world. In seconds, we were wrapped in our own universe. There would be no communication of any sort with the surface other than periodic reports to the support ship.

It was not all that bad to be out of touch, for the world was in turbulence. President Nixon was pulling American troops out of Vietnam while also preparing to invade Cambodia. Some 250,000 people had marched in Washington to protest the war, and it recently came to light that U.S. soldiers massacred civilians at a village called My Lai. The Army War College criticized officers for tolerating incompetent commanders and distorting facts to please their headquarters. General Norman Schwarzkopf would later write that he felt the entire officer corps was tarnished.

The country was totally polarized over the war, but we still felt quite separate from it. Ironically, one of our targets on this mission was a relic from another conflict, World War II, the sunken German submarine *U-550*.

Our first task was to practice navigating on the seafloor. Brian Wruble of Sperry once explained that you are just as lost and alone several thousand feet under the waves as you would be on the far side of the moon. In many ways, the deep ocean is an even more hostile environment because its movements are chaotic and prevent precise navigation.

On land, there are fixed landmarks, and navigation in outer space is done by the stars, which are so far away that they seem to stand still in the heavens. In contrast, strong tides and currents constantly rearrange the seafloor, sometimes right before your eyes. That was further complicated by the fact that we had incomplete tables and charts of the terrain over which we prowled. Pinpoint navigation was virtually impossible.

To create our own landmark, the *Sunbird* was to lower a transponder, which we would affix to the bottom, and then we would use its electronic pulses as a steady beacon to locate our position. Simple in theory, difficult in execution because a surface storm was bouncing the *Sunbird* around so badly she could not lower the transponder. That left us on our own, a situation that would be familiar to every *NR-1* crew for decades to come.

We were already into our routine, working twelve-hour days—six hours on watch followed by six hours off—but the first week of this vital test was wasted as we waited for the transponder to come down. We gorged on the best food in the freezer (pot pies, pizza, and Popsicles) and spent hours sleeping and working our way through the twenty paperback books that comprised the "Ship's Library." My initial choice was *One Day in the Life of Ivan Denisovich*, by Aleksandr Solzhenitsyn, a Russian novel about life in a Siberian gulag. It kept me engrossed for days and made me feel much better about our own living conditions. We also tried to relax by listening to the "Ship's Entertainment System," a single eight-track tape player with two small speakers and a half-dozen tapes. After a few days, no one bothered turning it on anymore because you can only listen to upbeat Irish folk songs provided by the navy wives club for so long. Although the legendary Woodstock rock festival had been held only a few months before, none of us had thought to bring along any rock and roll.

Mostly, we worked or slept, took sponge baths every few days, and checked what was happening outside the view ports. Shrimp became interesting, and watching a squid squirt its ink was a cause for marvel. A strange growth that attached itself to one of the cameras appeared to be a monster because it was so close. Crabs waved open claws to scare us away. Sonar contacts were mainly empty tin cans that had been tossed overboard by the *Sunbird*, and there was not much excitement in finding an empty tin of ham and beans.

We were bored, so instead of waiting for the transponder, we found a battered fifty-five-gallon oil drum on the bottom and used the manipulator arm to set it upright. Driving away, we discovered that our forward-looking sonar could find it from three hundred yards out, and we spent a few days playing with it as the reference point for search patterns, rather than the expensive, pinging transponder that was still upstairs. Eventually, we were able to fly up to thirty miles away from the barrel and find our way back, a remarkable achievement in bottom navigation.

Before we could do much more, however, the number three thruster began to fail, causing the boat to lurch around. By the seventh day, that thruster died completely and within a few hours we heard high-pitched squealing coming from the number two thruster, which was also getting sick. The long test was hardly under way and we were already in trouble. When we tried to move up or down, the stern moved sideways. If we tried to turn, the stern would rise or fall. We reluctantly signaled the *Sunbird* to ask headquarters if we should return to the shipyard, but they let us stay down. We terminated this part of the mission, skipped the assigned exploration of a couple of canyons that would be too dangerous to explore with faulty propulsion, and went off to hunt the U-boat.

Equipment maintenance and troubleshooting were eating up most of our time, with a corresponding erosion of morale in this season of tedium. The freshwater still salted up repeatedly and had an impact on the quality of the instant coffee that fueled our workdays. As an alternative, I carried a glass tumbler filled with my special Hummingbird Diet, a slurry of instant tea and Tang orange drink, sixteen ounces of caffeine and sugar guaranteed to keep me awake.

Fatigue, lethargy, and sleep deprivation were problems, because our patterns of rest were severely disrupted. You might sleep for a full six-hour off period or only be able to nap, and days and nights meant nothing without sunlight or stars. No mission control operator told us when to eat or sleep, and by the end of two weeks, we were careful how we spoke to anyone because we did not know if they had been working for twenty hours straight, which was pretty common, or had not slept well for several days. There was no room for flaring tempers, but we did get testy on occasion. Although we were all friends, coworkers, and volunteers and had easygoing personalities, we found it difficult to live and work under such conditions over such a prolonged period. The personal reactions were also part of the test program that would assist future crews in knowing what to expect.

To reach our search area, we flew the boat about ten feet off the bottom for several days to enter the waters off Nantucket Island where the continental shelf sloped down to several thousand feet. There we were put on hold again as our escort ships changed, with the *Kittiwake* replacing the *Sunbird*. Part of Steve Perry's job as XO was to keep up morale, so he organized the world's deepest cribbage tournament, but blunted the card game's enjoyment by mentioning that if the *U-550* had been sunk during the war, there might also be some loose depth charges in the area. Finding a lobster so big that it showed up on sonar was about the most significant thing in the voyage thus far. Endure.

When off duty, I looked forward to standing pilot-training watches, wanting to add ship-driving qualifications to my responsibilities, the final step to my becoming a fully qualified officer of the deck (OOD). I was being taught to fly this unique boat by our skipper, Dwaine Griffith. By the third week, I had completed the practical requirements in navigation, ship handling, approaching bottom objects, and landing and maneuvering near them. In midst of a watch, Griffith rose from his seat and said, "Congratulations, Lee, you are now qualified as an OOD underway on the *NR-1*. You have the conn. I'm going to get some sleep. My night orders are to maintain a search altitude of ten feet and keep looking for the remains of *U-550*. Wake me if you find it."

In that moment I achieved more than I would have thought possible a few short years before. I was the first enlisted man ever to qualify as an underway OOD aboard a nuclear-powered vessel, and I was flying it over unexplored terrain. It was a place of craters some two hundred feet across and fifty feet deep, many filled with waving forests of colorful sea anemones, crabs, cod, and scorpion fish. Hills of small shells passed beneath our keel, but no battered, long-dead German submarine.

We would need a big helping of luck to find the sunken U-boat. Its last reported position had been plotted twenty-six years earlier during wartime by a fast-moving aircraft, a combination that left a lot of room for inaccuracy. Within a few days we searched more than a dozen square miles and found nothing but junk.

Meanwhile, our days were plagued by various alarms, problems with the battery, tripping circuit breakers, and other difficulties that proved how things degrade rapidly under the pressures of the deep. The lousy food and lack of sleep had most of us nauseated and groggy. With no way to wash clothes, we became pretty rancid, and the quick wipe-downs and sponge baths had little effect. Endure.

We never did find the submarine, and by the end of the thirty days, we did not really care. We missed our families. The boat maneuvered awkwardly because of the ton of mud that had collected in open spaces during the long rests on the bottom, and we were just as sluggish from being submerged for a month. The "brown mountain," as we called the solid waste buildup in the sanitary tank, was so thick that it refused to be moved, even with the stick.

As disappointed as we were at not finding the U-boat, encountering so many equipment and mechanical problems, being unable to snoop through some ancient canyons, and suffering from sleep deprivation and the limited ways of dealing with personal hygiene, our mission was deemed a success. We had endured and by doing so had given the U.S. Navy a boat that could crawl among the lobsters, fly among the pelagic fishes, and take on missions impossible for any other ship.

The *NR-1* was everything Rickover had promised, and more.

One consequence of my OOD qualification was that I became eligible to stand the bridge watch, so I dressed with care for the midnight duty, knowing my world was about to get very cold and wet. Over a blue nylon one-piece jumper known as a "poopie suit" worn next to my skin for warmth, I donned a foul-weather jacket, heavy boots, and a kapok-filled survival suit, a combination that made me as bulky as a second grader walking to school in winter. Then I wiggled through the Doghouse and carefully closed the hatches behind me. The crisp, cold March air felt clean compared to the staleness we were living in below, and the stiff breeze had a good salt smell. Our escort was about a mile off our port bow—right where it should be—and the sea was rough, but there were no white caps to give it definition in the moon-less night. I scanned the horizon in a full circle to make sure there were no other ships or fishing boats around. The bridge remained high and dry, and I was warm inside my survival gear.

As I bent to hook up the sound-powered telephone that would let me talk with the crew below, I heard a low whooshing sound and water gurgled into the bridge around my boots. The *NR-1* does not rise very fast, but some waves do, and the water came up steadily to my knees, my thighs, and my chest. I stood up and held on.

Finally, only my head was out of the water and I wondered, "Is this ship ever going to come back up or am I going to float out of here?" Darkness was all about, and I wasn't sure what to do and there was no way to tell anyone what was happening. Slowly, the sea receded from the bridge as the sub bobbed to the surface again, and I hooked up the phone as quickly as I could. For the rest of the watch, I shivered inside my drenched heavy-weather suit and braced for the beating I knew was coming.

At dawn, there was a fitting reward. As I was relieved on the bridge, the *Kittiwake* sent over the towline, a hot breakfast of steak and scrambled eggs—real food, possibly the best meal ever—and mail, the first communication we had with anyone not associated with the mission for a month. It was strange to read weeks-old letters from home when home was just over the horizon, a hundred miles away.

12
FIRST HURRAH

*T*he sea has a proprietary interest in the seaport village of Stonington, Connecticut. The quaint town once was the home port for massive sailing ships that combed the globe in search of whales and slaughtered them by the thousands for their oil. It takes little imagination today to envision the masts of those big ships dropping below the horizon as they left on another hunt that could take months or years before they returned home. Many never made it back. For a sailor, Stonington is a reminder that, in the end, the sea often wins, no matter what technology is thrown at it.

I walked the shady streets of the village one evening in the spring of 1970 with my wife, Johanna, who had become familiar with the melancholy history of the town while working there as the librarian. She showed me Victorian homes with their mournful "widow's walk" rooftop verandas, where the wives of whaling captains would pace behind thin white railings, hoping to spy the sail of an arriving ship. Johanna also pointed out the small family graves in the yards of some of those homes. The markings indicate that mostly women and children are buried there, for many of the men never returned.

That evening stroll had a powerful effect on both of us, for Johanna was six months pregnant at the time, and I was about to board a tiny submarine for a long mission to the other side of a very large and stormy ocean. The doctors had predicted a date for the baby's arrival, and I expected to be back before she gave birth, but experience on the

NR-1 had repeatedly shown the folly of trying to plan that far in the future. It was something to think about.

Although the crew had wondered what our job would be once we entered fleet service, the boat would never lack for something to do. The navy created the Submarine *NR-1* Advisory Group to decide our assignments and already there was a long list. Admiral Rickover was no longer our ever present protector, and although he would continue to be deeply involved, the crew seldom heard from him. The regular navy types filled the vacuum.

Every mission would be handpicked by the Advisory Group, which was chaired by COMSUBLANT (Commander of Submarines, Atlantic). Final mission approval came from the desk of the chief of naval operations himself. Although the Pentagon went along with the current fiction of having scientists along, the Advisory Group ruled that "navy/military operational uses of *NR-1* will take priority over research." Years had passed since the ship was first sketched on a piece of paper, and we had not yet seen a scientist.

For our first assignment, we were sent across the Atlantic Ocean to Ponta Delgada, on São Miguel in the Azores, west of Portugal. The Azores are nine beautiful islands located atop some of the most forbidding chunks of ocean floor on the planet. The deep water has a tremendously rough bottom dominated by a chain of submerged volcanic peaks with rugged summits and sides of hardened lava that slope precipitously away for thousands of feet into uncharted depths. The islands are merely the tips of extinct volcanoes that were part of the Mid-Atlantic Ridge. They rose above the surface eons ago and are honeycombed with sulfur grottoes and steaming caverns. With so many volcanic peaks lurking below the surface, the area is a dangerous place for shipping in general and subs in particular.

Any sound going into those twisting mountain canyons bounced crazily around, the kiss of death for submarine communications and sonar, so an entire task force of ships from the various countries of the North Atlantic Treaty Organization was sent to attack that problem. The NATO group off Ponta Delgada would plant three monster communications towers on some of those underwater volcanoes in an operation known as Project AFAR (Azores Fixed Acoustic Range). Years had been spent building the towers in Europe and the sophisticated electronics packages that would crown them, but it almost seemed as if the operation had waited until the *NR-1* was ready before launching the mission. They needed our special expertise.

We were not told much about the towers other than the official line that once the stations were installed, submarines would have a better way of communicating in that area, and if sonar could be made to work there, it would work anywhere in the world. That presented a good, practical reason in that time of disinformation, and too many ships from too many nations were involved in Project AFAR to even attempt trying to keep it hidden. Few people ever learned the exact purpose of any of our missions, but some reasoned that on this one, the new towers might serve a purpose much more suited to the icy days of the Cold War. The craggy shores of the Azores were a strategic treasure, and what once was an important anchorage in the middle of the Atlantic for the sailing trade between America, Europe, and India had a military importance in the modern era.

From our area of operations off Ponta Delgada, it was a straight shot to the east, right to the doorstep of the Straits of Gibraltar. The three stations of Project AFAR could, perhaps, provide a triangulation fix on the position of any sub transiting the straits, through which it had to pass in order to leave the Mediterranean Sea. The antennae atop the AFAR towers would also have an unobstructed view of the central Atlantic, where Soviet missile boats recently had been found turning in deep, lazy circles, on station and waiting for orders to launch their deadly birds. The Western allies needed to keep track of them.

We didn't really speculate about it very much. The thing that held our thoughts was understanding that our maiden mission was going to be very difficult and dangerous, involve a lot of underwater work near the limits of our operational range, and be watched in great detail by foreign navies that had never seen anything like us.

Prior to departure, we spent several days meeting with mission planners and other specialists from the Navy Underwater Sound Lab at New London, just across the Thames from Electric Boat. Tied up next to the *NR-1* at the Sound Lab pier was the 266-foot-long USNS *Mizar*, which would be the mission command vessel as well as our support ship and carry the equipment vans containing our backup electronics, a small radiological control lab, and assorted spare parts.

On the bright summer morning of June 27, 1970, our families were allowed onto the Sound Lab pier to say good-bye. Johanna, in a green-flowered maternity dress with a short skirt, did not remind me of my promise to be home by the time our first child was born. We both knew there would be no choice in the matter and we were not the first, and would not be the last, navy couple to face this exact dilemma of a man being away at sea when he was needed at home. The ship came first.

Only ten days after the *NR-1* was officially incorporated into the navy, we shoved off for the long voyage across the bumpy Atlantic. Dusk found us sailing past Nantucket, where an unusual glowing globe appeared in the twilight sky and bathed us in light. I watched from the sail as the circular object steadily grew brighter and larger, until it reached many times the size of the rising moon, then dissipated and vanished. I had no clue as to what the odd atmospheric phenomenon might have been, other than perhaps an omen of the many mysteries that lay ahead.

It was slow going, even being towed behind the rugged *Mizar*, which earlier in her career had hauled supplies through the Arctic ice before her conversion to an oceanographic research vessel. With the *NR-1* acting as a huge sea anchor behind her the *Mizar* could make an average speed of only 9.3 knots, so it took almost two weeks for us to reach the Azores, a dozen days that seemed like forever inside the toss-ing little sub. We slept as best we could, on our backs with fingers inter-laced on our chests—elbows splayed like outriggers to prevent us from falling out of our bunks. About halfway over, the seas began to ram-page when a storm barreled up from the south and crossed behind us, and since we were on the surface, the OODs who conned the ship from the bridge once again faced the perils of being up there during heavy weather.

Gale force winds and waves more than thirty feet high rolled in on the starboard beam, and both the *Mizar* and the *NR-1* would ride up and over each wave approaching from the side like two corks attached by a string. Except for occasional spray, the bridge stayed relatively dry, and the OOD sat in a small swing seat suspended by straps inside the conning tower. His view was scary. As the *NR-1* rose sideways up the face of the oncoming wave, it rolled to the left and the OOD looked thirty or forty feet down into a gully that seemed deep enough to swallow a large building. Then as the ship slid over the crest and down the back side of the wave into the trough, he was looking up from a dark valley into a slice of the night sky, his sight limited all around by mountainous, moving walls of water.

During those long and stormy hours, we watch officers tended to sing to ourselves, loudly and not for entertainment, but shouting to stay vigilant and to assure ourselves that human sound still existed. It was easy to succumb to towline fever, a sort of involuntary hypnosis that left one just staring at the line stretching ahead, and withdrawing into quiet reverie, no longer really paying attention nor comprehending what was going on. To fight against such hypnosis, I sang every song I knew when I was up there, and wished I had learned more. The old World War I sing-along "It's a Long Long Way to Tipperary" was my favorite—an easy tune to bellow at the waves, and it carried a sense of starting out on a great adventure.

Eventually, things settled down as the direction of the seas changed. Then, in the middle of the ocean, we hit a tree.

A day or so after the storm, we were still getting fairly high waves and the boat would slide down into them and rise up again. While I was on watch, a big log, some thirty feet long, two feet in diameter, and stripped of all its bark and limbs, surged over the crest of an approaching wave and bore down on us like a battering ram. Before I could shout a warning, it banged into the boat, twisted, and wedged sideways between the bow and the towline.

I radioed the *Mizar* to stop, and Dwaine Griffith came up to the sail, as weary as the rest of us after the long Atlantic crossing. The captain simply had no patience for this latest nuisance. The skipper told me to stay put; then he strode out on the slippery fiberglass deck, as confident as a tightrope walker, while the boat rose and fell on towering waves. Balancing on the pointy bow, with nothing to hold on to, Griffith planted a boot on the huge log and gave it a mighty shove. The log broke free and the skipper, satisfied that his boat was no longer in jeopardy, went back below decks without comment.

The exhausting trip terminated at Ponta Delgada, where we found out we were not welcome. The Italian cable layer *Salerno*, the West German oceangoing tug *Helgoland*, the French drill ship *Terrabelle*, a scattering of other NATO vessels, and even the obligatory spy ship from the Soviet Union, this one an East German merchantman, were already there, but because we carried a nuclear reactor smaller than an office desk, we were not allowed to dock. For 94 days, from the time the *NR-1* left Connecticut until the day it returned, it would not tie up at any pier on land. Since the *Mizar* and the *NR-1* were the only United States ships in the task force, and we would work our tails off during that stretch, we considered the banishment insulting.

Nevertheless, there would be some extraordinary moments that we would never forget. When we surfaced, which we did only seven times from July 19 until August 29, crew members exchanged places, and after the rank conditions below, a full shower on the *Mizar* was pure heaven. Then it was off to sip wine with the French sailors, drink Azorian beer with the West Germans on ships that still had the awful swastika stamped on some of their gear, dine with the talkative Italians, and hit the port town with the only other Americans around, a team of navy Seabees doing AFAR construction work ashore. Cadets aboard a Danish tall ship expertly spliced our frayed towline as easily as sewing on a button, and rapid-fire poker games either made you rich or broke your heart.

On-shore dinners featuring São Jorge cheese, the freshest possible fruit, beefsteak, barnacles, and spider crab, and a wine that was once a favorite of the imperial Russian court helped us forget the TV dinners.

During one liquid evening, Roger Sherman and Steve Perry were invited aboard the West German ship for a few more drinks with the crew. The two, both possessing innumerable technical secrets, left when they figured out their hosts included some "cousins" from an East German ship moored nearby.

On their way out, they crossed through the bridge, and the technically curious Roger flipped a switch just to see what would happen. Klaxon horns erupted, lights flashed, sailors burst out of hatchways, and speakers blared. Sherman had sounded the general alarm, and he and Perry rushed for the gangplank as the angry captain screamed curses in German behind them.

Some of their drinking buddies were not ready to call it a night, and told them the East German ship was a training vessel for female attendants going into the marine services. "Come on. We're going to see the stewardesses," one sailor said.

Although it was four A.M., Perry and Sherman suddenly became quite confident in their ability to withstand any challenge of tall, blond

German girls who might want to pry loose the secrets of the *NR-1*. A jovial watch stander welcomed the rowdy group aboard, but just behind him stood an ominous figure dressed all in black and wearing a black homburg hat, just like in the movies—the political officer! With no sense of humor at all, he wagged his finger at them and slowly said, "No, no, no."

Sherman and Perry went away dejected, but woke up the next morning with massive hangovers and a strange sense of gratitude for the political officer. By stopping them from entering the communist ship and fraternizing with the crew, the man probably saved the careers of one American technical wizard and one U.S. Navy officer.

But the good times grew fewer as the mammoth AFAR project bogged down in a labyrinth of international miscommunication, equipment failures, bad planning, occasional stupidity, and a lot of finger-pointing. We worked less than 40 percent of the time and sat on the bottom for days, waiting for the big leaguers on the surface to do their jobs. The idleness was dull and grimy duty, and we preferred to rest on the side of some underwater volcano, playing cribbage or reading, than to be up there where multilingual chaos periodically overtook the task force. "To me this project looks like a shambles," Steve Perry observed in his personal log.

Although AFAR was a unified NATO operation, each country involved obeyed its own rules first. The West Germans, for instance, had seventeen divers for underwater work, but their rules were incomprehensible. Only two of them could be in the water at one time, they took extraordinary rest periods, and if there was even a slight chop on the surface, they simply would not go in at all. They looked terrific—tall and chiseled and bronzed, marvelous physical specimens in black Speedo-like bathing suits—but we stopped counting on them to do anything. If divers were needed, then Kam, Don, or I suited up and did the job rather than wait for the men we derisively called the Super Race, who spent a lot of time resting and catching up on their tans.

Diving eighty miles out in the ocean was an extraordinary experience, for the temperate current that swept around the Azores kept the water almost mirror clear for hundreds of feet down and we could see coral, rock outcroppings, and strange fish in the twilight glow. When swimming near the surfaced *NR-1* as it lay suspended as if in air, I was almost overwhelmed by the feeling that I might at any moment fall through the sunlit safety zone and into the yawning abyss.

The main problem for divers was that the surface fleet discarded a lot of garbage, and that attracted sharks. They constantly trailed the small fleet, cruising just beneath the calm surface with their white-tipped dorsal fins clearly visible. The *Mizar*'s beret-wearing, cigar-smoking Panamanian cook named Ché added to the problem by catching fish and some of the sharks, cutting off portions for steaks, then flinging the bloody refuse back in the sea. When I had to enter the crystalline water in my dive gear, my vision was limited to a narrow cone by my mask, and I knew that a shark could arrive from any direction–from below, behind, or my blind sides. I felt like a worm dangling on a hook.

On August 10, while we were submerged, a simple message was relayed to me aboard the *NR-1* by underwater telephone from the *Mizar*: "Your wife has given birth to a six-pound-eight-ounce baby girl. Both mother and daughter are doing well." We were back on the surface a few days later, and after a dive assignment, I swam to our barely submerged stern plane just forward of the rudder and climbed upon it like a seal onto a rock. There I rested, with an incredible ocean-level view of the sea, the ships, the sun, and the sky. The scene was as beautiful as an impressionist painting, alive with color. My mind was not on the mission or the boat, which, a hundred years after Jules Verne wrote *Twenty Thousand Leagues Under the Sea*, was matching some of the exploits of the fictional Captain Nemo. My thoughts were solely about my wife and our new daughter, Jennifer, whose name came from a popular song of the day, "Jennifer Tompkins," by The Street People. The entire birth, which took place at a navy hospital, had cost only $4.50, but it troubled me that a friend had to drive my wife there and that Johanna was told the navy could not get in touch with me. I realized that I had to make some decisions soon.

Project AFAR had been planned using old German charts, rather primitive in accuracy because they had been drawn for U-boats during World War II, and some other raw navigational data. When the *NR-1* surveyed the proposed sites, we found the actual landscape to be quite different from what was on the maps, and had to eyeball the bottom contours to find flat areas all the way down to our test depth of 3,000 feet. It consumed a lot of hours, but we identified good sites on three likely mountaintops in a rough triangle some 30 miles apart. The towers would be planted at depths of 1,200 feet, 1,700 feet and 2,800 feet.

The plan was for the *Mizar* to drop four fifty-pound electronic transponders that we would anchor on the bottom in a square. Those pingers would guide one of the towers into place. We used our manipulator arm to exactly place those base points, then got the hell out of the way as the ships carrying the massive towers moved into position overhead.

After working with these guys for a while, we had no desire to be anywhere near the drill ship, which carried the steel tower slung below her and dropped it down vertically. Each of the three-hundred-foot-tall towers weighed many tons and the slightest bump from one of them would crush us.

Only after a tower was on the bottom did the *NR-1* return to check that it was vertical, with its base in an acceptable position and with its attached cable streaming downslope in the right direction. Then we rushed away again so explosive bolts could be detonated and clamp the tower to the rocks. We figured there were about a dozen different ways we could die if we were not careful crawling around the ridges and flying a few feet above the ancient underwater volcanic cliffs, in this new forest of steel towers where explosions shook the mountainsides.

Our other task was to find a smooth path off the mountains for the cables that connected the towers to a clifftop laboratory the Seabees built on shore. It was another seemingly simple job until one considered that the water could be up to eight thousand feet deep in places and the entire area was treacherous. The rough terrain caused repeated wire breaks inside the British-made cables when they had to turn at sharp angles, and those ruptures required tedious and time-consuming repair. Everything involving AFAR seemed agonizingly slow.

Without doubt, the *NR-1* had more than its own share of problems. The jarring, vibrating tow across the Atlantic had severely damaged the mountings and vital pipes for our starboard propulsion motor, and that seriously limited our maneuverability. The diving planes and the rudder conked out at various times, forcing us to dive using only our ballast tanks and adjusting our position with only the four balky thrusters. We probably spent fifty hours maintaining the thrusters for every hour we used them.

Our first mission was a stern, real-world test of what was expected of us, and the various admirals had high expectations. Since we were the only boat on the NATO team with underwater capability, we caught a lot of undeserved criticism from the guys on the surface when things went awry, but in the end, we got each of those damned towers planted. Despite the problems, we did our job.

The entire experience was symbolized pretty well near the end of the mission when a swordfish attacked the *NR-1* while we were submerged. Even the fish were trying to skewer us. This one got its hard bill caught between the starboard anchor and its housing and thrashed about until the bill broke off. When we surfaced, Dwaine Griffith sent me and Kam over the side to retrieve the long sword, while Bob Lunt watched for sharks with the ship's .45 in his hand—the only time I ever saw the pistol out of the safe. Griffith later mounted the sword as a trophy over his fireplace mantel.

It took another two years for NATO to finish the AFAR project and put into operation the massive transmitter tower and its two equally large receiver towers, with their tiaras of electronic gear that could be turned in almost any direction. The system would operate until about 1986, but even today, its history and purpose are not of public record.

The *NR-1* headed for home on August 28. The sub's crew members who had gone aboard the tow ship took turns dropping their empty beer bottles into the churning wake so the glass containers would drift back and knock against the bobbing submarine, irritating whoever was standing watch on the bridge. But having been kept in the Azores until it was too late to avoid the North Atlantic storm season, the *Mizar* was soon barely able to make headway in the strong seas with the *NR-1* in tow, so the ocean tug USS *Kiowa* was summoned to take over. The *Kiowa* was used to rescuing huge vessels like battleships and messaged her first question, "How much diesel fuel do you have?"

"None," came the answer from the *NR-1*.

"Well, how long can you keep your power on?"

"Twenty years."

It took the tug's veteran chiefs a while to figure out how to work with the small nuclear-powered sub, but they adjusted, got the ships aligned, then turned the tug's blunt nose into the rough waves and headed for Connecticut. The *NR-1* bucked along behind in seas even heavier than those it faced on the way to the Azores.

About halfway back, the towline snapped, and the *NR-1* was suddenly alone, lurching around in angry seas. It desperately radioed, "*Kiowa. Kiowa.* This is Bottom Buggy. We have a problem." Hours passed before the *Kiowa* circled and made another hookup. The towline would break three times during the voyage home, and each time the trip was halted until the nylon hawser was laboriously spliced together again by U.S. sailors who were nowhere near as adept as the young Danish midshipmen who fixed it the first time.

The *NR-1* arrived back at the sub base at two o'clock in the afternoon on September 10. "The seas seemed endless," an exhausted Steve Perry wrote in his log. "There is a lot of ocean when you try to cross it like we did at nine knots."

Our first hurrah was not our finest hour, although we had most certainly done our part by getting the AFAR towers planted and finding paths for the cables. While still in a developmental stage for actual operations, we had been thrown into the deep end of the pool, and not only survived, but were successful.

People confined to the surface of the ocean could not comprehend the *NR-1*, nor could they see what was going on a thousand or two thousand or three thousand feet down below, where we had sweated among the dangerous tangle of volcanic peaks. We delivered results never before accomplished by any other submarine or submersible in an unforgiving environment, and our achievements were mistaken for merely routine procedures. The observers seemed unable to recognize that we were figuring out how to accomplish virtually impossible tasks as we went along, because no one had ever done it before.

13
TRANSITION

I flew back to the United States when our Project AFAR work was done, and avoided the latest misfortunes of the *NR-1* crew. The guys on the boat had a rough return, but we had some troubles of our own when the C-141 cargo jet got lost somewhere over the Atlantic and the crew of air force reservists decided, like Columbus, to just keep heading west until they found land. The United States had to be out there somewhere. While the *NR-1* was able to navigate around the unmapped ocean floor with enough precision to locate a fifty-five-gallon drum from thirty miles away, these guys were having trouble finding an entire continent.

It didn't really bother me, for riding in the cavernous cargo deck with the roaring engines vibrating the entire plane gave me plenty of time for some serious personal reflection. The *NR-1* was approaching still another important plateau, for within a few months, the original crew would start rotating off the ship for new assignments. It was time for all of us, and our ship, to move on. The boat was no longer "Rickover's Rubber Duck." It was a fully operational element of the U.S. Navy and, like it or not, the role of the plank owners was done. We had been present at the creation, but our baby was not really our property. The true plank owners of this submarine were not just the members of the navy's small original crew, but also the civilian workers at Electric Boat and the Sperry field engineers—Fred DeGrooth, Brian Wruble, and Roger Sherman, men who would continue working on it and riding it for years to come and provide the institutional memory for the ship, advising new skippers and officers and crewmen of the long road that had already been traveled, and carrying the verbal legends of the boat, as well as their technical expertise, with them.

"How would you like to be the OIC of the *NR-1*?" the personnel officer at Pearl Harbor asked a husky young submariner named Toby Warson. It was late 1970, and Warson, who had an outstanding, if unorthodox, record, had been running highly classified special ops work aboard the submarine USS *Queenfish* for the past two years. He answered, "What's the *NR-1*?"

The interviewer could only give a thumbnail description, since he wasn't cleared to know much about it himself. The term "cutting edge technology" piqued Warson's interest, but naval officers were careful in making career decisions and he already had wandered off the path once, by choosing postgraduate school rather than taking the standard tour as an engineer. Nevertheless, he had what is known in the navy as a magic ticket. Not only was he a graduate of the U.S. Naval Academy, but also he had played tackle on the Navy football team for two years and was married to the daughter of a four-star admiral, A. G. Ward, the commander of the blockade during the Cuban Missile Crisis. Warson's performance record with the fleet had been outstanding and the next logical step up for him was to become an executive officer aboard a fleet submarine.

"What about my XO tour?" he asked.

"Would you rather be the number one man on a ship or the number two man?" the interviewer countered.

Warson made the decision in a nanosecond. Every naval officer's ultimate dream is to captain his own ship. The personnel officer closed the folder, said Warson was one of three men under consideration, and instructed him to fly to Washington for an interview with Admiral Rickover.

Toby Warson recoiled at that, remembering his first meeting with the admiral, when he was fresh out of Sub School. He had spent the night before with his wife's family, and Admiral Ward cautioned, "For God's sake do not tell Rickover that you are in any way related to me. We've had some really cross words in the past. And don't tell him you played football, because he doesn't like athletes . . . and he doesn't like academy graduates." The warning was prophetic.

"You went to the naval academy?" Rickover had barked, almost in disbelief that his time was being wasted. "What the hell did you do in your first two years there?"

"I played football." The admiral didn't ask about the second two years, when Warson quit the team and improved his grades to rank near the top of his class.

"Football! You played football! What the hell! Get out of here!" As Warson left the office, Rickover called, "Tell your father-in-law that I said hello."

This time, the interview did not go much better. Warson received the usual harangue—"Jesus Christ! Did you think postgraduate school was better than being an engineer? Get out of here!"—and then returned to Pearl Harbor. The *Queenfish* was about to sail for the North Pole, which Warson figured was warmer than Rickover's office. Just before departure, he was instructed to report to the admiral again three days after the end of the Arctic mission. He had the job. Lieutenant Commander Toby Warson would be trained to become the second skipper of the *NR-1*, where he also would learn that "ass chewings by Rickover came with the territory."

The numbing noise of the big aircraft engines drowned out any possible conversation with others and left me alone in my own world for hours as the crew poured over their maps, trying to find America, then Virginia, then Norfolk.

I had once watched with great interest as a chief petty officer, a veteran of many years in the navy, reported back aboard our support ship, the *Sunbird*, after an extended shore leave. He arrived at the pier during a chill dawn hour in a bright, new automobile driven by a gorgeous young woman dressed in chic clothes. Their public farewell was long and the woman clung tightly to him, reluctant to let go, her face puffy from crying. Eventually, he gently patted her bottom, eased away, and boarded the ship. He crossed the gangway and saluted the duty officer, who gave him a quizzical look, for the girlfriend was still by the car, waving and weeping. "Aw, she'll get over it, sir," said the chief, never breaking stride. "I've got work to do."

Some single sailors might have admired his cool attitude, but I was now a family man, had been married for two years, and had very different priorities. My eight years in the navy represented approximately one-third of my entire life, and except for some odds jobs as a boy, it was 100 percent of my working career. I had to recognize that I was no longer the kid who went to sea aboard the *Sargo*—far from it.

A large part of my life had been consumed by nuclear training, being a prototype instructor, being chosen for the *NR-1*, and working for years to get the submarine running. I knew that the long endurance trial and the distant, confusing AFAR mission were only grueling examples of what lay ahead for the *NR-1*. Crews would be away from home for long periods of time in extraordinarily primitive working conditions, usually on missions that they would not even be able to tell their wives about when they returned.

My future career in the navy was limited. I could stay and choose to become an officer, but that would lead only to tours of duty in some submarine's engineering space. Never again would I have a chance to actually drive a ship, or command the boat from a stormy bridge, and the prospect of such limited duty was totally unappealing. Nor did I want to work with a crew ten times the size of that on the *NR-1*.

A logical alternative was to enter the civilian nuclear power industry and spend a well-paid career in some mind-numbing, land-based, windowless power plant that would not have a sense of adventure nor even the soothing motion provided by the rolling sea. Every member of the original crew, officer and enlisted alike, was facing the same problem. What next? What could possibly compare with duty aboard the *NR-1*?

The civilian world was not really very enticing at the time, compared with the security provided by the navy. The Dow Jones Industrial Average had shrunk to the mid–six hundred range as the economy settled into recession, and investors were cautious. The minimum wage stood at $1.30 an hour. The growth in the deep submergence industry had collapsed, which eliminated the option of my becoming pilot of one of those craft. John Craven, the navy's chief scientist, reported a White House meeting at which a top aide of President Nixon announced, "The oceans are not of commercial importance to the United States."

The military world was not much better. The situation had grown sharper in the Mediterranean as most Arab nations broke diplomatic ties with the United States and expanded the Soviet sphere of influence. Meanwhile, Vietnam had drained the U.S. Navy of funding, and before long Admiral Zumwalt would testify before Congress that there was only a 35 percent chance that the United States could win a sea war against the Soviet Union. Admiral Rickover told the congressmen that in case of such a showdown, he would prefer to command the Soviet submarine fleet, because he liked to win.

For a young man looking to the future in late 1970, the choices seemed pretty limited. My best option was to go back to school on the GI Bill, get a degree, and see what might be available a few years down the road.

The reservists eventually located the right airstrip and landed the plane, and I took a commercial flight up to New York, a bus to New London, then a cab home. Johanna and our baby girl were waiting, and that helped make my decision easy. It was time to turn a page in my life.

A ship in port is never really at rest, and there was a staggering amount of work to do in the maintenance, repair, and replacement of systems and equipment on the *NR-1* when it returned from AFAR. Half the life of any ship is spent in upkeep.

For the crew, that meant resuming the usual eighty-hour work-weeks, with no exceptions for weekends or holidays. From the time the reactor core was placed in the ship in the summer of 1968 until late 1970, none of us took a vacation. "Why don't you ever get any time off?" became a familiar complaint from all of our wives.

This time, however, there was a difference. More people were being added to the crew muster rolls to gain hands-on training. One hallmark of the *NR-1* was that you fully trained the person who replaced you, usually for six months, before the changeover took place. In fact, several new sailors were already in training with us during the Azores trip, doing support work because they were not yet fully qualified. Our staff of nine enlisted men and three officers had proven the *NR-1* could be run by a skeleton staff, but also had proven that was not the best way to get the most out of the ship. More men would be assigned in the future, although the minimum number still would be used for underwater work because there wasn't room for more.

Another sign that things were changing came on Thanksgiving of 1970, when three of us on watch that day staged a minor rebellion. Knowing official permission would never have been given had we asked for it, we took it upon ourselves to bring our wives aboard the *NR-1* for a visit. We sealed off and covered things they were not supposed to see, and the women who had felt the little orange submarine was a demanding rival for their husbands' attention finally got to go below decks, and were amazed at the tiny spaces. We put the baby, Jennifer, into the middle bunk and enjoyed a holiday picnic dinner on the boat's single small table. It seemed to be the most intimate of family gatherings, for my wife and daughter were helping me disconnect from the submarine that had been so much a part of my life for so long.

By Christmas, Johanna and I packed and shipped our household goods to our new house in Coral Gables, Florida, where I would attend the spring semester at the University of Miami to study for a degree in industrial engineering and computer science. I drove her and the baby to her parents' home in Pittsburgh, returned to Stonington, and filled our VW Squareback to the gunnels with the remaining household items.

There were no fond farewells, although Dwaine Griffith wrote up a nice commendation and many of my shipmates showed up at Fred De-Grooth's house for a New Year's celebration. We all realized this would be our final get-together before I signed off, and it was the last time I saw many of those with whom I had worked for so long. I got quite drunk.

On January 11, 1971, I was discharged from the U.S. Navy and left the sub base that same afternoon, consigning New London to my rearview mirror. For a full day, I drove, so emotionally drained that I hardly noticed the hundreds of miles the VW was covering as I headed south. In my mind's eye, I was back on that roller coaster of a wet bridge in the middle of a whistling gale, or diving with scuba tanks far out in the ocean, snooping through uncharted canyons, playing cribbage on the side of an underwater volcano, spying on Soviet ships, or doing a hundred other such things, part of the club. One day I was a member of the elite crew of a one-and-only navy ship, and the next I had lost my ticket to the party. I rolled into Miami a changed person, a civilian, a student, a husband, and a father, and spent a sleepless night on the hard floor of an empty house, agonizing over my decision.

Everyone who departed the boat felt lessened by doing so, although we knew the experience couldn't last forever. "I had a strong desire to spend the rest of my naval career on the *NR-1*," lamented Steve Perry.

"I was certain that I would never find anything so interesting and exciting, and I never trail-blazed again."

We had climbed a little-known pinnacle of mankind's technical achievement, and our training and experience transcended a number of realms. On the surface, we operated as any naval vessel, in accordance with centuries-old admiralty law. Under the waves, we were a submarine, but changed that half-century-old technology as radically as the biplane changed into the jumbo jet. When we flew over, landed on, or drove upon the bottom of the sea, we shared an experience in vehicle control accomplished only by the astronauts and other deep submersible pilots. We moved easily through all three phases, without giving it much thought, from standing watch as a nuclear power plant operator to flying the boat over the bottom, then surfacing and commanding the ship's operation from the bridge.

Unfortunately, like Cinderella, our time ran out. We had to choose our futures, and all paths led down from the summit.

Toby Warson's family moved to the East Coast while he was under the North Pole aboard the *Queenfish*, a patrol on which his executive officer suffered a nervous breakdown and retreated to his stateroom for more than a month. Warson took over as XO for the front of the boat while the engineering officer took care of the back end and the reactor.

When Warson arrived in Washington to enter the Prospective Commanding Officers School, the thirty-one-year-old lieutenant commander was thrown in among men of much higher rank and experience, and discovered his roommate was a senior captain on his way to a carrier command. "I was a naive and wide-eyed kid compared to the rest of them," he said. For the next thirteen weeks, Warson was immersed in an intensive course that centered on the intriguing small nuclear reactor and the equally small vessel that he was to command.

When he eventually stepped aboard the *NR-1*, he felt that he knew exactly what he was looking at, and was comfortable with the job. Dwaine Griffith welcomed his successor warmly and Warson liked the man on sight. "He really had his act together and I was nervous about taking over from him," Warson said. "He built this thing, knew every nut and bolt, knew all the bits and pieces, and knew how to run it. I walked in at an ideal time, because when I got there, it was ready to operate."

The change of command ceremony, with everyone dressed in whites, had to be held dockside because there was not enough room on the boat. Dwaine Griffith had made us proud that he was our captain, and proved the navy had chosen the right man. He went on to an illustrious naval career, rising to rear admiral, commanding other ships, including the missile submarines *Casimir Pulaski* and *Sam Rayburn*, working with intelligence-gathering groups, and becoming director of the navy's Deep Submergence Systems Division. Before he retired in 1991, Griffith had collected two Distinguished Service Medals, the Legion of Merit, and four Meritorious Service Medals. Not bad for an ROTC kid out of the University of Idaho. Dwaine died in 1996, admired by everyone who knew him.

Toby Warson soon discovered the inherent dangers of the *NR-1*. Few ships in naval history would have as many close calls, repeatedly, over many years, than its smallest nuclear-powered submarine.

One of his earliest missions, almost a training exercise, was another one of those milk runs up to Narragansett Bay, where the boat encountered one of the worst things that could happen to any submersible or submarine, almost as if the *NR-1* were saying "Welcome aboard!" to its new skipper.

The navigational problem of locating your place underwater had not yet been solved, although improvements had been made on the *NR-1*. It went out to test transponder ranges and techniques for recovering items on the bottom, tasks that would have to be mastered if the submarine was to participate in the dark, secret world at the bottom of the sea.

Roger Sherman of Sperry was recording data from some of the new instruments as the boat tracked along the bottom, using an electronic transponder planted as a navigational guide. A nor'easter churned the surface of the Atlantic, but a thousand feet down, the ride was smooth for the men aboard the *NR-1*. They never saw the line before it snagged them.

At some time in the past, a huge wire cage from a fishing trawler had got stuck on the bottom and had been cut free. One of the lines leading to the trapped debris waved like a slender thread in the current, and when the *NR-1* went by, the line was sucked into the number one thruster, where it became as entangled as a monofilament line around a fishing reel. In a moment, the boat was firmly lashed to the bottom of the continental shelf and was pulled right down to the floor.

"All you could see was mud," Sherman said. "Everybody was up by this time, Toby and Jack were in their underwear, and we saw this black cable going out of view. At first, we thought it was steel, and I started reviewing my life. We had just spoken to the support ship an hour before and agreed we would not be back in touch for another eleven hours. We were tied to the bottom, out of communication, and I thought, 'Our ass is grass.'"

Sherman climbed out of the view port area, and a new member of the crew, the irrepressible Jeff Davis, asked what was happening.

"We're anchored, baby," the tech rep replied, his eyes huge as he recounted their dilemma.

"Aw, don't worry," Davis reassured him. "They've got a contingency plan for this."

"What's that?" Sherman had been with the *NR-1* from the start and although he was certain that no rescue plan existed, he wanted to hope that maybe he had missed something. He knew that if something wasn't done, they all would die.

Davis grinned. "The navy's going to get the battleship *New Jersey* out of mothballs and come drag for us."

Although the idea was ridiculous, Sherman took comfort in the fact that crew members could joke about the situation.

After deliberating what to do, the officers decided not to drop the tons of lead that the boat carried to try to force a trip to the surface, and decided that blowing the ballast tanks also was too chancy. In either case, if the line didn't break they would be tethered to the bottom—nose down, stern up—possibly at an angle that would trigger an automatic reactor shutdown that would leave them without power.

The answer this time was the articulated arm, and Jack Maurer worked the manipulator's blunt metal jaw to gnaw at the snagged cable. Although the line turned out to be one-inch-thick polypropylene and not steel, as originally feared, it was covered with thick barnacles that fought the attempt to sever it with the blunt-edged jaws. Maurer spent about three hours biting on the line with the mechanical arm before it finally gave way. Today, he has a length of that line mounted on a plaque in his home, and the *NR-1* has sharp cutting-edge jaws for the manipulator arm.

Sherman wanted off the boat, but when the *NR-1* surfaced to transfer him to the support ship, the sea had gone wild. The *Sunbird* was still there, but other ships in the group had fled for port. Even the ever-present Soviet fishing–intelligence gathering ships had circled up in the distance, their big boats protecting the smaller trawlers, and were steaming slowly into the huge, oncoming waves. It was impossible to transfer Sherman in such weather, so the *NR-1* submerged again and resumed the transponder work in exactly the same area in which they had been snared only a few hours before. "I was not a happy camper," Sherman recalled.

The next day, the captain agreed to try the transfer again. Although the situation was still dicey, Sherman was ready to swim to the support ship if necessary, and departed in a wave-tossed small boat. He arrived aboard the bigger ship soaking wet, wearing civilian clothes with no insignia, but having a military-equivalent rank ID. The *Sunbird* sailors, who were never allowed on the *NR-1* and were never told what it did while submerged, thought he was from some sort of initialed government agency. The stormy ride back to port was a nightmare of seasickness for everyone on board the support ship, including everyone on the bridge, but to Sherman the wild seas represented safety, for he was no longer trapped on the floor of the ocean.

He finally walked into the kitchen of his home on Fishtown Road in Mystic, Connecticut, and found his wife, Karen, and her mother cooking in the kitchen. He wore a vacant stare and a terrified face that neither of them had ever seen before on this normally placid man. "I've been praying for you all week," said his worried mother-in-law. "I thought something terrible was going to happen." Roger sat down at the table, thankful the ordeal was over, but unable to tell his family what had happened. Keeping secrets was hard, and it took weeks of puttering around the house and garden before Sherman emerged from his personal fog. Then he went back to work aboard the *NR-1*, and dove again.

In late 1970, the always balky Mark XV computer seemed to go on strike during bottom searches. It would lock up unexpectedly, the automatic guidance would freeze, and all data-gathering functions would cease. A computer "crash" while running deep would stop the *NR-1* in its tracks.

After unsuccessfully trying to diagnose the problem, Sperry

reached out for the old pro, Brian Wruble, who was now involved in a Wall Street "research boutique," and asked for his help. His new employers gave approval but said it would cost the navy $3,500 per day to rent the services of the once low-salaried engineer.

While Sperry and the navy pondered the price tag, Wruble dug into his old manuals and spent about five hours of his own time sniffing through the problem. He tracked it through twenty systems and determined the Time of Mission counter used on the bottom was at fault. When he and his team had been programming the original computer, they had saved some memory space by designating the years with only a single digit, and had not set aside a designation for 1970. The computer simply no longer knew what year it was. Wruble told the Sperry engineers how to perform that simple adjustment, and gave the old computer another eight years of life.

The Y70 problem was an exact precursor of the Y2K problem that would bedevil computers worldwide thirty years later. Wruble solved it so quickly on his own that the navy was never charged a cent.

14
BLACK SAIL

"**C**aptain, we've got a problem." A second crew pilot was driving along the floor of the Mediterranean Sea and reached around to shake the shoulder of Toby Warson, who was sleeping behind the two pilot chairs, but not really resting at all. Warson blinked, looked at the screens, and shuddered. Every TV camera on the boat showed the *NR-1* was in the middle of a field of mines that had sunk to the bottom during World War II. The sonar, for reasons unknown, had not warned the pilot of the danger, and now the boat was surrounded by the ominous spines of the black mines.

"Jesus! Don't move! Don't do anything!" Warson was wide awake, knowing that high explosives become very sensitive when immersed over time in salt water. Every so often some unlucky fisherman hauls up an old German mine in his nets and is blown away. A mere touch by the submarine's hull on one of those ominous spines and the *NR-1* would share the fate of those fishermen.

The captain also knew his boat could not remain where it was on the bottom, because a sudden current could slide it into a mine. Gingerly, the downward thrusters were brought on line to press the ship firmly in position, while the pumps forced water from the ballast tanks. Everyone aboard was sweating bullets, for the submarine had to rise straight up, not very far, but exactly straight up. There were too many mines on the TV screens to count. As if recognizing the danger, the boat obeyed as if it also wanted to tiptoe out of danger, rose to a safe height, and flew away.

Life in the Mediterranean, or simply "the Med" in navy terms, has always been hazardous for mariners, and in 1971 it was perilous on the surface, along the shores, and, as the *NR-1* routinely discovered time and again, on the bottom. The boat came upon a grim reminder of the dangers when the cameras showed a line of strange shapes lying on the bottom sand. Warson had the boat move closer, and the objects turned out to be the canvas-shrouded bodies of a large number of dead people who had been buried at sea after some unknown disaster.

As he stared at the macabre scene through a view port, he asked one of his crewmen beside him, "Why don't we just go over there and shake one to see if someone is still alive in there?" The young sailor thought Warson was serious, and cried out, "No, Captain! Don't!" The skipper then had to talk the crewman, who was shaken by the thought that the *NR-1* might disturb the bodies of the long-dead sailors, out of resigning from the navy.

The *NR-1* would become very familiar with the Med, for shortly after Warson took command, the boat began to go "black" and entered the silent world of high-level intelligence work that deals more with shadow than with substance. As it began to sail in dark waters, the sub gradually disappeared from the navy's daily operational rosters. The escort ship, such as the *Kittiwake* or the *Sunbird*, would show up in lists of ships at sea, but not the *NR-1*, for the U.S. Navy had imposed a virtual cloak of invisibility on it. The ship was not even to be *seen* by outsiders on some missions. Riding so low in the water that it was hard to spot in a moving sea even when painted bright orange, on the missions when the sail of the *NR-1* was painted black, it simply disappeared in plain view.

The ship's very first Med mission for the navy was just such an assignment. The Mediterranean teemed with United States and Soviet warships, and Moscow had taken the strategic edge. In February of 1971, there were forty-eight Soviet warships in the eastern Mediterranean and forty-three American ships. A fleet intelligence officer observed, "This makes us definitely Number Two."

"The fact is that there is no longer a permissive environment where once the Sixth Fleet moved at will," wrote Admiral Ike Kidd, shortly after he commanded the U.S. naval forces in the Med.

The dramatic increase in Soviet heavy bombers flying in the area from land bases in Arab nations and an attempted coup in Jordan in late 1970 had brought the Cold War to a near-boiling point in the volatile region, which was known as the "Camel Crossroads." Many times, the two enemy fleets intermingled in a near-combat environment, as Soviet men-of-war shadowed U.S. aircraft carriers, and American vessels tailed major Soviet ships. At least on the surface of the water and in the air, the two sides could keep track of each other. Underneath the sea, things were different, and the Command History of the Sixth Fleet noted, "The number one threat in the Mediterranean is the Soviet submarine force."

The U.S. fleet updated the position of every Soviet surface ship every four hours because, as Ike Kidd observed, that was the best way to counter a sub-launched missile. "When a new one [radar contact] pops up, you know it's a sub," he said.

The Soviets felt the same nervousness about the American submarine force and geared a substantial part of their intelligence-gathering efforts to tracking our subs. Of particular interest were three narrow choke points—the Straits of Gibraltar at the mouth of the Med, and the two that separated the U.S.-dominated western Mediterranean from the large eastern portion where the Soviets were openly challenging our naval forces. The Sicilian Channel, between Tunisia and the island of Sicily, and the Strait of Messina, between Sicily and the very toe of the Italian boot, were of vital importance to the U.S. Navy.

Our subs had operated with impunity in the open oceans of the world and in the Med for many years, but things had changed. By 1970, when our boats entered the eastern Med, whether coming in completely hidden after weeks in the Atlantic or departing from the forward deployment tender at La Maddalena on the north coast of Sardinia, they often picked up a Soviet submarine tail just after passing through the narrows at either end of Sicily.

It was disconcerting, for it indicated that the Russians had vastly improved the passive sonar aboard their submarines, or had managed to lay some sort of listening device, perhaps a line of submarine-tracking hydrophones or sonobuoys, across the straits.

The U.S. operates sound surveillance systems (SOSUS) in similar bottlenecks, such as the GIUK Gap between Greenland, Iceland, and the United Kingdom, and both sides constantly tried to disrupt the SOSUS nets of the other. Since the Soviets did not seem to be tracking our subs well anywhere else in the world, analysts did not believe that Russian sonar capabilities had taken a huge technological leap. That put the odds heavily in favor of a bottom-mounted sound detection system, and one place that Soviet ears definitely were not wanted was across a narrows in the Med.

Navy intelligence began a quiet search for the suspected listening posts. Side-looking sonar systems were pressed into service to paint shadowy images of the seafloor and make any objects detected clearly stand out. For months, surface ships towing a number of detection devices prowled possible areas of interest, and transducers were mounted to the sides of submarines to further expand the reach of the system. Still, side-looking technology was in its infancy and the wet paper images produced were blurry and hard to interpret.

The hunt went on for months and was kept highly classified. Washington was not certain that there was such a listening device down there at all, since there could be other explanations for the Soviets' recent success in tracking our boats. We also did not want to let the other side, if they did have such a system, know that we were on to them. We definitely did not want them to figure out that we possessed the means to find objects on the seabed. In the arcane game of intelligence gathering and use, everything depends on not letting others know what we know, or don't know.

The searches eventually turned up something that could not be explained near the Strait of Messina—a narrow passage tortured by high winds and strong currents that has preyed upon unwary ships and sailors dating back to Odysseus and Jason and the Argonauts. In Greek mythology the monster Scylla lived on the rocks on the Italian side, ready to snatch up and devour seamen from passing vessels, while the deadly whirlpool Charybdis guarded the Sicilian edge.

The moist sonar readouts showed a long, straight, dark line stretched along the bottom. It appeared to be an underwater cable, but was in a location where no cables were supposed to be, and there was no indication where or how the cable terminated. Another, more ominous discovery nearby was a pattern of metallic objects, some close together and others scattered about. Intelligence analysts could only conjecture what they might be, and their conclusions raised flags of alarm.

The United States recently had developed an extraordinary weapon known as the "captor mine." It was deployed like a traditional mine, but that was where the similarity ended, for it contained sophisticated computer technology that essentially turned it into a smart, homing torpedo. Captor mines are programmed to lie on the bottom of the sea and they remain dormant for months or years until activated automatically at a specific time or by a given signal. They can even be programmed to attack one specific ship that has a certain acoustic signature and ignore all others.

The analysts had to consider that the Russians might have developed a weapons system similar to our captors and possibly have sown them in this choke point used by ships of many nations. A battery of well-located captor mines could deny U.S. warships access to the eastern Med at some future critical moment when the Soviets and their client states stirred up trouble among Middle Eastern flash points.

The entire delicate balance of the Cold War could be thrown off by such an action, and the political ramifications were frightening. Everything hinged on knowing what was down there, and naval intelligence could not verify what it was seeing on the faint readouts. U.S. submarines lacked the depth and bottom-operating capability needed to investigate the objects, and should a deep submersible be launched from a surface ship right over the suspect area, the Russian navy would know exactly what we were doing. The job was handed to the new kid on the block, the *NR-1*.

The first problem for the Submarine *NR-1* Advisory Group was to somehow sneak the boat into the Med with the Red Fleet prowling about. The sensitive nature of the mission ruled out another surface tow across the Atlantic, and underwater tows by other submarines, which eventually would become routine, had not yet even been tried. The navy chose to piggyback the sub over aboard a giant Landing Ship Dock (LSD), and that became the second problem.

For six months, starting even before we returned from Project AFAR, the LSD *Portland* sailed around Long Island Sound while engineers and naval personnel tried to figure out how to load the *NR-1* into the cavernous well in the aft portion of the ship. While the sub was being built, there once had been a plan to construct a special sled that would simply pick up the *NR-1* and carry it aboard an LSD, but that had been discarded in the financial crunch that surrounded the construction process. The latest version of that idea was for Electric Boat to build a wooden cradle aboard the LSD, which would then flood down as low as she could in the water and then have the *NR-1* move slowly and carefully over the cradle. The LSD would then rise back up by pushing out the excess water and be ready to go.

It took months of trial and error as the LSD kept having to go lower and lower and lower in the water, and risked her own stability as she did so. Tons of concrete blocks were brought aboard, and at one point, a small landing craft was even placed on the helicopter deck to push the big boat deeper, but she still was not low enough in the water. Eventually the LSD was sent to the shipyard at Portsmouth, New Hampshire, where the new aircraft carrier USS *Nimitz*'s giant anchor chain, weighing thousands of pounds, was brought aboard. The *Portland* had never carried anything as heavy as the diminutive *NR-1*.

The submarine's crew showed up for work wearing astronaut-like jumpsuits that were bright orange and emblazoned with shoulder patches. The new uniforms were a great morale boost for the *NR-1* crew, marking them as being somewhat special in their otherwise drab, confined, and overworked existence. "We pranced around the LSD and managed to piss everybody off. We thought it was cool, but the squadron commander didn't," Jeff Davis said. The unamused captain of the *Portland* barked at Toby Warson, "Get your guys out of those damned things! This is my ship and you are not going to make my men look second-rate!" Unlike the astronauts, the *NR-1* crew lacked the clout needed to stand out from the rest of the navy. Since the captain of the *Portland* wore four stripes on his sleeve and Warson was only a lieutenant commander, the jumpsuits were discarded and rarely ever worn again.

The LSD dipped her stern down to the maximum depth it could go and the *NR-1* inched aboard, stern first, and was secured on the wooden cradle. The LSD expelled the water from the aft well, leaving the submarine sitting high in a sort of floating dry dock. It was then covered by a tent that shielded it from prying eyes and set off on a mission that would cost $100,000 a day.

It was hoped that the LSD would provide a better method of transport than the debacle of surface towing on the AFAR mission, but the entire trip across the Atlantic was a nightmare. "The vibration was unbelievable," said Jeff Davis. Links of the carrier's anchor chain clanged like big cowbells, and timbers of the shoring cradle creaked beneath the strain while the submarine wiggled around so much that loose screws came out, inside cabinets collapsed, equipment failed, and some exterior gear actually fell off. Maintenance on the little sub, which was fresh out of the shipyard, became a major challenge.

On the way over, the sail of the *NR-1* was painted black.

The Red Fleet gave the *Portland* an extraordinarily hostile welcome, for the big tent on the back of the LSD meant that something was about to happen and they wanted to find out what. The U.S. Navy was just as intent that they would discover nothing, and tucked the *Portland* into the heart of a Sixth Fleet carrier battle group.

As the unarmed *NR-1* huddled out of sight beneath the tarp, sleek and nosy Russian gunboats rushed up to the *Portland* to try and see the mysterious cargo, and U.S. escorts would cut them off. "They came right up on both sides of the LSD and one closed in directly astern while their planes buzzed overhead," said Fred DeGrooth, the Sperry tech rep who wore a khaki uniform to disguise his civilian status. "If *Portland* had slowed down, we would have been rammed. We just gave them the finger and sailed on." Officers knew that an intentional collision might be attempted to force the *Portland* to stop and perhaps reveal her hidden cargo.

When the LSD reached a position that put the *NR-1* within range of the target area, the U.S. task force closed in tight around her while the Soviet hounds circled close by. Late that night, the *Portland* turned off her running lights, plunging the area around her into stygian blackness. The LSD flooded her dry well and dipped her aft section below the surface, and with handheld flashlights providing the only illumination beneath the tent, the *NR-1* slid into the warm, salty waters of the Med and immediately dove to the sanctuary of the bottom, where it came to a dead halt. The entire operation took only twenty minutes. As long as the *NR-1* remained deep, silent, and motionless, it would not be picked up by Soviet sonar, because the floor of the Med is a centuries-old junkyard. Ships of a dozen vanished civilizations litter the seabed and it is impossible to tell one from another.

The surface task force got under way and departed the area in a gigantic decoy operation that pulled the curious Soviet bird dogs along with it, while leaving the *NR-1* on its own. The battle group took a sweeping tour of important Med hot spots during the next two weeks, sailing from Sardinia almost to the entrance to the Black Sea, which alarmed the Russians who were following along. Getting your opponent to look the other way is the essence of an intelligence operation.

Once the surface boats were out of the way, the *NR-1* got to work. Because of its range, it did not have to be dropped right on the target. Not having to surface meant that it could fly almost anywhere on the compass. It had the ability to carry experts from naval intelligence to the true targets, in person or through detailed reports and photos of close-up examinations. It did not take long for the *NR-1* to find the suspect cable and follow it to a set of hydrophones, which were photographed thoroughly with the boat's 120mm handheld cameras and 35mm bow-mounted cameras. While looking at mysterious objects through the view ports, we could poke and prod them with the manipulator to reveal additional features. With the ability to rest on the bottom, we could gaze at them from any angle we wanted, for as long as we wished, and the ship took its time.

Fifteen days passed before the task force returned to a predetermined spot, not the drop-off point and far from the Straits of Messina, and the *NR-1* climbed back aboard the *Portland* in the dead of night and was under the tent before the sun rose. Toby Warson flew to the United States where he showed the photographs to a select group of analysts, then flew directly back to the ship. "They want more pictures," he told the crew. The entire sleight-of-hand mission was repeated and left the Soviets more mystified than ever.

Not even the crew of the *NR-1* was told much of what they were doing, even while they were doing it. With such clandestine operations, their job was to go to a certain place, find a certain depth or spot, and accomplish a specific task. The crew was made up of submarine and nuclear experts and most could not tell a hydrophone from a xylophone, or a mine from a melon. It was not necessary to be experts at all things, and in cases such as this the crew did not need to know the overall purpose of the mission in order to execute it. What they did not know, they could not reveal, even by accident. The work was done with no publicity, wives and families and friends were told nothing, and even when some job appeared rather obvious, it probably was not what it seemed.

Naval intelligence secured all of the photographs and records at the end of the first Med mission, and the cover story was that the hydrophone setup and the mines were only some relics from a distant war. It may be true. It may not. The mission was so compartmentalized that few ever knew the whole story, and the U.S. certainly was not going to reveal to the Soviet Union what had been found, where it had found it, how it was discovered, or even if anything at all was found.

That was the way the intelligence game was played. A good result would be for us to know where the hydrophones and mines were and what their capabilities were. An even better outcome would be if we gathered that information, but the enemy did not know that we knew. Somewhere in between is the foggy place where we would want them to think that we knew something, whether we did or did not, or vice versa. The truth is always elusive in the intelligence game and the cards are played according to what the other fellow is doing. You could go crazy trying to envision all of the possibilities. Deception and disinformation are powerful weapons.

In a scenario that would be repeated many times in the long life of the *NR-1*, the mission remained under such tight secrecy that the crewmen who were aboard that voyage thirty years ago still are not allowed to speak of it. Their job was to get there and back, and get the needed information covertly, and they did it well. What was found was left there, and fell beneath the firm cover of classified information.

While on the mission, the *NR-1* caught a glimpse of its future by seeing the distant past. On the floor of the Med, the submarine, with its view ports and TV cameras, was able to see things that had lain buried in the silt for untold eons. Steering through one passage, it rolled up on the skeletal remains of what was believed to be a galleon that had sunk during the years when the Italian peninsula was a mere province of Greece, perhaps even prior to the rise of that great civilization. The wood had disintegrated over the centuries, but the iron fittings were still there, as were remnants of the scattered cargo.

The discovery had nothing to do with the official mission, so the find was more of a curiosity than something to be studied. Jack Maurer reached the manipulator arm out, gently plucked up a vase, and put it in the collection basket as a unique souvenir. He thought little of the peculiar artifact as years passed, and left it on a shelf in his home until the day it was broken when the Maurers moved to Monterey, California.

An art expert spent three months carefully piecing it back together, and encouraged them to have it identified. A curious archaeologist from the de Young Museum in San Francisco determined that the beautiful vase, some ten inches in diameter and nineteen inches tall, was either a Greek or Phoenician amphora dating from the third or fourth century B.C. When experts wanted to know how such a rare piece of pottery had come into his possession, Maurer could only reply with a mystifying, "Sorry, I can't tell you."

He also did not want to reveal that after picking up that one small vase, the *NR-1* rolled right over a lot more of them as it continued on its true mission. Science still wasn't a part of the job, but the little vase was a harbinger of great discoveries yet to come.

15
THE SCIENTISTS

*T*he *NR-1* was expensive to run. The submarine had to be ready to sail on a twenty-four-hour notice when operational, and even when in dry dock, it usually was undergoing costly changes to prepare for new missions. At a time when the tactical and strategic concepts of submarine warfare were being revised, it was difficult to find the funding to keep the *NR-1* ahead of the technological curve.

Time had overtaken the most basic theme of attack submarines, which emphasized the single task of finding an enemy ship and hitting it with a torpedo. As years and wars passed, subs had grown and diversified, acquired new capabilities from nuclear power and weaponry, and vastly improved their electronics, sonar, and computers. The attack boats provided an important nucleus, but the undersea fleet had become more ominous as the subs became platforms that could deliver long-range missiles. Strategy was being conceived for global conflict, not a stealthy one-on-one battle between a submarine and another ship. Design work was under way not only for ICBMs, but also tactical Tomahawk cruise missiles and Harpoon antiship missiles.

Although the submarine force had an immense amount of influence in the navy, everyone frantically searched for worthwhile missions. What could the underwater boats do to earn their keep? The answer lay with the dark arts of stealth and cunning, the submarine's ability to gather and provide intelligence about current and potential enemies. American submarines were still tailing Soviet subs, and special warfare operations such as inserting SEAL commandos into strange places were coming of age, but the breakthrough came when U.S. subs began to tap the communications cables of the Soviet Navy, and to locate Moscow's submarine detection networks as the *NR-1* had done in the Med. We were able to read the other fellow's mail, listen to his telephone conversations, and find out what he knew about us, all extraordinary advantages for military planners.

Like every other ship in the fleet, the *NR-1* had to meet the changing times. Although it was virtually brand-new, its concept was almost a decade old, and the competition for dollars was made even more difficult for a ship that intentionally remained far in the background. Publicity might shower down on the surface fleet, but the *NR-1* stayed out of view in order to operate with maximum efficiency. Every crew member was indoctrinated that the less said about the boat, the better. That cocoon of silence had also been perpetuated within the navy itself, and some people were wondering about the hybrid submarine-submersible, the only one of its kind in the world—"Why do we need it at all?" The boat would have to adapt to the new budget realities and overcome the status quo if it was to survive.

Enter the scientists.

From the very start, the *NR-1* had been designed, built, and operated beneath the guise of being little more than a vehicle that could help advance the knowledge of oceanography. The time had come to make that a reality, to a very controlled degree, and bring science aboard. No one doubted that the *NR-1* could indeed benefit oceanographers, and it was a guaranteed method of adding value. Mission money would flow with the expanded role.

The hidden benefit was that such research trips would not hinder the true military work of the *NR-1*, while providing perfect cover for classified missions. That pattern, once begun, would expand over the years, and the boat would make historic scientific finds while still carrying out "black" work of purely military value. The camouflage was perfect. While in a canyon for a scientific survey, navy observers could poke around for such things as hiding places for enemy subs, Soviet listening posts, and enemy missiles and mines. On occasion, the scientists would be aboard just to deflect attention from the actual purpose. Rickover was adamant that the professors from the publish-or-perish world of academia not write a word that could give away any

NR-1 operational capabilities, such as its depth and endurance. They were passengers only, and the admiral's harsh rules kept many of them away. Why go out on such a mission if you weren't allowed to write about it?

Dr. Bruce Heezen of the Lamont-Doherty Geophysical Observatory at Columbia University and Dr. Charles Hollister from the Woods Hole Oceanographic Institution were the first scientists to come aboard, partly because they were already famous and did not need to write a book. They had already done that. The internationally known oceanographers had authored *The Face of the Deep*, a thick treatise hailed as a landmark study of the geological and sedimentary makeup of the ocean floor.

Most of their research had essentially been through interpretation of accumulated sonar data, mathematical probabilities, and the careful examination of bottom photographs. There were many things they still did not understand and time aboard the *NR-1* offered them the opportunity to explore firsthand the world they only knew on paper.

Heezen, whose three-bedroom house was chock-full of rolled-up charts of the world's oceans and seas, was a big man who boasted that he had not done anything physical since the seventh grade. It was a tight squeeze just to get him down the hatch of the *NR-1*, and once below, he was dismayed at the lack of personal space and the abysmal food situation. But he was willing to put up with almost anything to enter a new realm of discovery. "Heezen was gaga over the deep, and what it looked like down there," said Toby Warson, the sub's skipper during Heezen's first journey.

Hollister was an adventurer as well as a respected educator. While still a graduate student at Columbia University, he had organized and led a mountain-climbing expedition to Antarctica that was written up in *National Geographic*. A tall and handsome man, Hollister had a zest for life and was always ready for a prank or a party. He would charm admirals and sailors alike with his excitement about the things that the *NR-1* could do for science. But when he was at work, Hollister was totally focused. A serious academic and a master of many disciplines, he eventually became the dean of the Woods Hole Oceanographic Institution. The Heezen-Hollister sounding charts of the world's oceans would one day be on the walls of universities, ships, and naval offices around the globe.

Charlie Hollister had been a student of Bruce Heezen at Columbia. Similarly, one of Hollister's own graduate students was a personable and adventurous young scientist named Robert Ballard, who eventually would follow their footsteps aboard the *NR-1* and carve a swashbuckling reputation as an undersea explorer.

The *NR-1* took the oceanographers out to the largely unexplored continental shelf, where they lay immobile on their stomachs, staring with awe through the view ports as the boat dropped through several thousand feet, threaded into the canyons, and crawled along the sedimentary floor.

In and out of deep valleys, across cobbled ridges, flying over seamounts, turning this way and that, it hauled Hollister and Heezen wherever they wished to go. Warson was delighted by their first reactions, watching the men of science acting "like two kids with a new toy." About two days into the cruise, the ebullience of discovery was replaced by an ominous quiet as the tides and sudden bursts of currents from nowhere changed and chewed the contour of the ocean floor in minutes, right before their eyes. Eventually, there was no chatter at all as Heezen and Hollister studied the jutting rocks, strange craters, and shadowy, turbulent water.

"We were taking core samples off the canyon walls, picking up rocks, and they were just growing more glum," said Warson. The skipper was acutely aware that this voyage, which was no strain at all for the *NR-1*, was as important as any the boat had ever conducted, for the scientists were needed if there was to be any hope for future "dual use" missions. He stopped the dive, found a quiet place to park the boat, and had a talk with them around the single little table on board.

"What's wrong?" he asked. "What is it that we're not doing? What is it that you guys want? Just tell us and we'll do it."

Bruce Heezen and Charlie Hollister were both grumpy. "We got problems, man, but it's not you." Hollister rolled his eyes in futility.

"We've just spent eight years on this book and now we get down here where we can see what is really going on and we find out that we're wrong," explained Heezen. "We've got this book three inches thick that has been declared The Book on this kind of stuff and *we're wrong*! We've got to go back and rethink this."

With that kind of backward endorsement, the *NR-1* would never lack requests for use by serious scientists. A new mission had been crafted.

Heezen would become a particularly frequent and favorite rider, and the boat would change character when he brought aboard a cache of his own tasty cuisine and the boat went to sea with meats and exotic cheeses hanging from the pipes. It was fitting that a few years later, Heezen, with his loud shirts, fancy food, and friendly personality, died doing what he loved most, riding aboard the *NR-1*, studying the wonders of the ocean.

The turnover of the first crew was completed when Danny Gunter departed in late 1971 as the last enlisted man, and Jack Maurer, the final officer, followed a few months later in 1972. That cut the tie between the operational boat and those of us who had brought it on line, and the new crews would have no memory of those long, hard years and battles to get the *NR-1* into the water. All of us, including the boat, had new jobs.

My family and I had settled into a small, old house in Coral Gables, Florida, about a half mile from the tropic swamps, a place overrun with vegetation and large, peculiar bugs. One of the first words ever uttered by our daughter, Jennifer, was "Ooch," a baby-talk contraction for the large, flying, hissing roaches that were as much a part of Florida as the sunshine. I bought Johanna a copy of the book *Florida Insects* to help her identify whatever might be crawling across the floor.

Originally, I had considered becoming an oceanographer, but engineering paid a lot better, so I plunged into math and science, determined to get my degree from the University of Miami as fast as possible.

Although I was out of the navy and away from the *NR-1*, the sea still called to me, and by staying in touch with my old friends, I learned of things going on back at Electric Boat.

The yards were awash with projects. EB was building a dozen 688-class attack submarines, a new generation of missile subs was under construction, and a $400 million contract was in the works for a massive Trident missile boat (known as a boomer), three times as big as the 688. There was so much work going on, and more on the horizon, that parts of the new boats were strewn about like giant toys until the workers could get to them. My friends told me that David Lewis, the new head of EB's parent corporation, General Dynamics, had developed a special relationship with Admiral Rickover, and that the Old Man was steering contracts to Groton almost as fast as the ink could dry. It was boom time on the Thames.

Tucked within all of those grand plans for the new flights of big boats and even bigger boats was one much smaller project. Preliminary plans were being made to create an *NR-2*! I knew that I had to be part of it. I did the four-year engineering course in Miami in two and a half years, picked up my degree in the spring of 1973, and went to work for Electric Boat. Home again.

The SOSUS networks were a particularly odd battleground in the early 1970s, as the opposing American and Soviet fleets went to great trouble to plant lines of their own hydrophones while trying to wreck those of the opposition with tactics as simple as dragging anchors through them.

In years to come, the U.S. Navy would build sophisticated ships for the sole purpose of finding, repairing, and burying those valuable detection lines, but at the time, such missions perfectly suited the *NR-1*. "We could pick up a cable, roll along with it until we found a break, then bring it up where a waiting repair ship would patch it," said one crewman. After the trip to the Med, the navy recognized that the *NR-1* could graze at will among the cables, moving along the seafloor like some giant, curious lobster.

But the *NR-1* had not been built to handle the specialized, demanding work on the underwater network, and many of the problems that Toby Warson would weather during his three-year tour as skipper would involve refitting the ship for its new role. "Toby's second crew had a lot of problems," said Chuck Chorlton, the nuclear engineering manager at EB. "There was hell to pay at some of those meetings with Admiral Rickover and he was throwing people out of the office right and left."

The boat spent a lot of time in dry dock as it was modified to do jobs that its creators had never envisioned. Such refits would become frequent in the future as the little sub was constantly adapted to new technologies and needs during its long life span.

One point in the original operational instructions specifically stated,

"The *NR-1* is capable of recovering/implanting objects, within size and weight limitations, and assisting surface ships to recover/implant heavier objects to test depth." That anticipated that the manipulator arm could do the lifting, but it was soon discovered that the arm was unable to pick up more than a hundred pounds. A guy in a gym could lift much more. To improve on that, a set of forklike, interlocking tines was installed in the belly of the boat to give it a heavy-lift capability. This grasping device, supported by the entire lifting ability of the ship, would be able to pick up enormous loads.

Another major change was the addition of a "Jetter," a cumbersome device that shot water through special nozzles at immense pressure to dig through bottom soils, the same way a garden hose can plow up a garden. The device expanded the boat's cable-tending abilities and let it quickly dig up or bury items on the bottom. Today the navy has a special cable repair ship, the USNS *Zeus*, that carries an undersea tractor and a sea plow equipped with a modern, multinozzled version of the Jetter, but at the time, the addition of the device to the *NR-1* was a closely held secret.

Admiral Rickover, who had his plate full with his battles to get the 688-class subs built, was drawn back into the orbit of the *NR-1* as his boat was changed and modified, and it was as though he had never left. As the alterations unfolded, he made life hell for EB in general and Toby Warson in particular. The young captain would be abruptly summoned at any time, day or night, to explain why something had happened, or might or might not happen. "I would pick up the phone and the cord would start to uncurl from all the liquid fire coming down the line. He would scream at me for thirty seconds or more and slam the telephone down," Warson recalled. A personal confrontation usually would earn him "a napalm burst" as soon as he walked through Rickover's door. The admiral, although saddled with enough other projects and controversies to break the back of an ordinary mortal, was single-minded in overseeing every design change of the *NR-1*, right down to personally trying to reconfigure the electronic circuits. The little boat was more than a passion with him—it was an obsession. One morning Rickover's secretary telephoned Warson with some sad news. "Mrs. Rickover passed away last night," she said. "So unless you have something really important, please don't call the admiral until after lunch."

* * *

Despite modifications over the years, one thing never changed for the *NR-1*. It always sailed close to the razor's edge. Time and again the sea almost took the small and vulnerable ship, and time and again the crew found some way to extract themselves from danger. It could happen in some distant undersea canyon, or right on the front doorstep, and almost every cruise encountered a heart-pounder.

A strong side current kept the *NR-1* pinned helplessly to the wall of a canyon for hours on one trip. On another, the lead weights stored aft fell off while the boat was being towed, forcing the stern up, the bow down, and the *NR-1* into a steep and dangerous dive. Fortunately, that happened while the bridge was unmanned, so no one was trapped there when it suddenly went down. In another incident, an inexperienced pilot drilled the ship into a mud barrier two thousand feet down, and then, because he was not making headway, increased his speed and pushed the nose deeper into the mud. A cable wrapped around a bottom rock the size of a garage became entangled in the thrusters, and in a similar incident, the boat snagged a SOSUS cable when it tried to dodge beneath it.

Returning home from one job, the *NR-1* made it safely to within sight of the Thames, but was prevented from getting through the Race by the monstrous seas of a hurricane. Instead of trying to dive in the shallow water, the boat sought refuge behind the coastal islands at the tip of Long Island.

The lookout who was strapped into the bridge was having the usual problems of being trapped topside as the heavy seas broke over the rolling boat when he spied something large moving toward them through the rain. He called Warson on the ship's phone: "Captain, there's an aircraft carrier up here!" The big ship seemed to be bouncing around as badly as the *NR-1*, and was drifting nearer.

Toby Warson could not dive the boat because of the man stuck on the bridge, there would be no way to dodge out of the carrier's path if it closed on them, and there was no way to outrun it. As the huge ship and the little boat shared that small area of storm-tossed sea, a bit of calm moved across the area. The *NR-1* recovered its man on bridge watch, hurried out to deeper water, and dove to safety.

The mystery ship above was later found to be the British carrier HMS *Ark Royal*, which had been visiting New York when it tore loose from its anchorage in the hurricane and drifted up the Connecticut shore without power. Had it even bumped the *NR-1*, the carrier would never have felt the impact, but the submarine would have died within a few miles of its home.

Danger was always a companion, and it is extraordinary that the only fatality on the boat thus far in its long career happened when scientist Bruce Heezen suffered his heart attack. Every crew came back with stories, after every voyage, and anyone who ever served aboard the *NR-1* well understood the meaning of a plaque that rested on the desk of President Kennedy, a former PT boat skipper: "O, God, Thy sea is so great and my boat is so small."

In January 1973, one of the stars of the Prospective Commanding Officers course was Chuck Larson, who eventually would wear the four stars of a full admiral and twice serve as superintendent of the U.S. Naval Academy. At the time, he was already an experienced captain, and was therefore somewhat surprised to find that his PCO roommate was the most junior guy in the course, an ebullient young lieutenant commander named Allison J. Holifield. But they had something in common, for both held orders to become the new skippers of two of the most unusual submarines in the navy. Larson was headed out to command the USS *Halibut*, the boat that in 1971 first placed a tap around a Soviet naval communications cable lying on the floor of the Sea of Okhotsk. It was one of the biggest intelligence coups of the Cold War and gave American analysts the ability to actually eavesdrop on conversations between top Soviet naval officials. The *Halibut* was a legend in the murky world of intelligence gathering, and not just anyone could be her captain. Holifield also was headed for a rather clandestine assignment, having been chosen as the new officer in charge of the *NR-1*.

Born in Mississippi and raised in Florida, Holifield originally was drawn toward aviation because his father had been an officer in the U.S. Army Air Corps. Submarines became attractive when his cousin, who was in the navy, arranged for him to crawl all over an old diesel boat. When the time came for college, he chose the Naval Academy, because upon graduation he would be able to choose between planes and subs. A training flight that let him experience landing on an aircraft carrier, often likened to a controlled crash, convinced the midshipman to pursue a career in nuclear power and submarines. Admiral Rickover chewed out Holifield during his selection interview for not studying hard enough, but he actually stood number sixteen in his class of more than seven hundred when he graduated in 1961. President Kennedy handed him the diploma.

His career had followed normal patterns right up until he finished a tour as operations officer–navigator aboard the USS *Narwhal* and it was time to take a turn as executive officer aboard a large attack sub. Instead, he was selected for the *NR-1*, which he knew only as "the supersecret minisub that was painted orange and tied up north of Pier 15." Like Dwaine Griffith and Toby Warson before him, Holifield jumped at the opportunity to have his own command rather than serve as number two on a bigger boat. The only real drawback was that Warson, an enthusiastic diver, insisted that Holifield also qualify as a navy scuba diver, which forced him into that exhausting course at the age of thirty-four, when the next oldest man in it was only twenty-two.

The normal transition for a new man aboard the *NR-1* was to work for six months beside the person who was being replaced, so for the rest of 1973, Holifield was slowly introduced to his new ship and learned every trick in the book. He was totally intrigued by what the boat could do.

The change of command ceremony in which the broad-shouldered, athletic, boisterous Warson was replaced by the small, slim, quiet Holifield was held in December 1973, in a little briefing theater at the New London headquarters of the submarine fleet. No invitations were issued.

Toby Warson, despite an outstanding record, would see his navy career end a few years later. "You screwed up one time too often," Rickover told him before exiling him from the boats to a desk job in Washington, never explaining why. Although he had worked only in submarines before, Warson was intrigued by what he found in the corridors of power, dealing with influential people and thinking up out-of-the-box solutions to intricate and important problems. He was eventually selected to become a captain, but he chose to retire with the rank of commander after nineteen years of naval service. He accepted the lowest-paying civilian job offer he received, a midmanagement post with Honeywell, and then skyrocketed in the private sector. Before he was done, Toby Warson held civilian titles such as chief executive officer, general manager, and managing director of Fortune 500 companies, and had private offices that were larger than the entire working space aboard the *NR-1*. One of Rickover's major failings was that he helped drive away a large number of such very talented officers, costing the navy several generations of leaders. That was all in the future, for long after he left the boat, Toby Warson would have one important and final mission with the *NR-1*.

Al Holifield felt on top of the world when he took command. He loved his new boat and how the men called him "Captain." He could only imagine where they would go, and what they might do, and there was a definite bounce to his step as he and his wife, known to all as Mugsy, went home that night to their house in nearby Gales Ferry. The new skipper did not know he would soon be facing "Black Saturday."

*L*ate on the Friday night before Easter in 1974, Al Holifield was asleep at home, untroubled that the *NR-1* had been delayed from casting off for its next mission to Europe because the tow ship was not ready. He could use the extra rest before having to spend several weeks sleeping on the deck behind the pilots' chairs.

The bleating of a warning horn on the sub base a few miles away roused him only slightly, and he thought, "Wow, they've got a fire somewhere," then went back to sleep. The telephone rang at about eleven o'clock. His wife answered, listened for a moment, then thrust the receiver at him with a look of horror on her face. Holifield could barely make out the muffled voice of his engineer, Rick Furest, gasping through a mask, "We have a problem . . ." Holifield was out of bed, dressed, and racing out the front door in minutes. His ship was burning.

The *NR-1* was nuclear powered, but as a backup, it also carried 150 silver-zinc battery cells in an aluminum well beneath the decking in the forward area of the ship, just at the bottom of the ladder to the sail. Crew members had long believed the makeup and maintenance of the high-power-density cells was more art than science, and were unaware that the negative battery plates had been impregnated with mercury to get more use from them. Mercury in any form is specifically prohibited on submarines and in all confined spaces because, if released into the atmosphere, it can be a deadly poison.

On virtually every voyage, a cell or two would short out and over-heat, requiring someone to pull up a square of the deck plating and rewire the cables around the hot cell. The crew had learned to live with the problem by yanking out the faulty unit and dunking it into a bucket of water to cool it down.

On the night of April 12, when an enlisted man on watch heard the buzzing of the alarm for the test circuit that ran through the entire battery section, he reset it to be sure the trouble was not just a blown fuse. When the alarm immediately resumed, the duty crew started looking for the problem. A whole section of the deck plating above the batteries became red hot even as they stood on it, and when they unscrewed the four big screws and removed one of the plates from its rubber gasket, they saw a churning hell of boiling smoke. The potassium hydroxide electrolyte fluid in the batteries had overflowed, and one cell after another shorted out and buckled, spreading incredible heat. They wrestled the deck plate back in place and sounded the alarm as acrid smoke spewed through the ventilation system.

Holifield saw the plume of pale smoke rising from the hatch in the orange conning tower, and men were rushing fire extinguishers to the boat, which was under a shield of bright lights. When he climbed aboard, he found Rear Admiral Paul Early, the commander of Submarine Group Two, already standing on one of the fairwater planes, which extended from the sides of the sail. The admiral was looking into the hatch with a worried scowl on his face. There were no open flames, but the interior of the submarine was a dense cloud of white smoke. Holifield knew that men—his men—were down there fighting for the life of the ship. Although the docked boat was operating on shore power, they were below in that thick, poisonous cloud, sucking air through protective masks and monitoring the nuclear reactor. Because of the extremely close quarters aboard the *NR-1*, only a few people could be inside at a time to fight the fire.

Rick Furest popped up the ladder, his head emerging from the smoke, and reported to his skipper that the battle below was still raging, and they were pumping carbon dioxide from fire extinguishers through the ventilation system into the battery well. The rapidly expanding carbon dioxide cooled the reaction, and the quicker they could dump it in the better.

Holifield suggested trying to get the top of the battery well open so the CO_2 could be pumped directly into the compartment. When Furest and his men tried to raise a deck plate, it bulged ominously from the internal pressure, and they quickly screwed it back down. When he reported back, Holifield had the sickening feeling that unless this tremendous heat could be contained, he might lose his ship, while knowing there was little more that could be done. His crew was already down there, performing heroically.

As Friday night turned into Saturday morning, sailors brought every fire extinguisher they could find on the sub base to the *NR-1*, including the 101 CO_2 canisters from the *Polaris* missile boat tied up behind it.

There was evidence below that some silver had melted, and Holifield knew that a temperature of 1,700 degrees was needed to do that. As the intense heat melted cell plates, mercury was released, creating a major health hazard. And still his men fought on, taking turns as waves of toxic fumes spiraled out of the ship. The caustic vapor skinned the paint from the aluminum van in which the Sperry engineers stored their electrical gear, leaving portions of it shining in the morning sunlight.

There was nothing more to do. Either the ship survived, or it didn't. Had this emergency happened at sea, where the boat should have been on this date, the men would have been forced to surface and abandon ship, and the submarine probably would have been lost.

The skipper and the admiral stood on the wing of the bridge, watching helplessly, as men handed full fire extinguishers down the hatch and pulled up empty ones. It took hours for the fire to finally peter out and for Holifield to see his crew emerge, filthy and exhausted, but still alive and wearing grins of satisfaction for having barely averted disaster.

The cleanup phase began the same day, but was painstakingly slow because the atmosphere had been so contaminated in the boat that each crew member could only work four hours out of every twenty-four. Everyone involved was tested for possible mercury poisoning during the weeks to come, and the *NR-1* spent the next six months being repaired. Every inch of the boat was thoroughly scrubbed clean. Almost all of the electronics had been destroyed and they had to be replaced. The Sperry engineers found that when they removed a circuit board and blew on it, the gold leads on the transistors would flutter away like particles of shiny dust.

* * *

While the *NR-1* was laid up in the shipyard, work was continuing on creating the *NR-2*. The new boat would be changed little in basic design from its predecessor, and the nuclear power plant would be the same. The hull would be built this time from HY-100 steel, an upgrade from the original HY-80, to give the new boat a greater depth capability. The major changes would be in the front end of the ship where the instrument and control system was to be upgraded to house the latest electronics technology, which had advanced so much in the past six years. The plans showed that the *NR-2* would be able to go deeper and do much more, opening a whole new layer of the ocean to manned exploration, work, and military applications.

I had been hired by Electric Boat as both an engineer and an expert on the *NR-1*, and was one of eight people on the design team for the *NR-2*. Henry Furuno, who spoke with a thick Japanese accent, was again the structural engineer and Jack Leonard still the top man, so we had veterans of those awful *NR-1* construction and design wars in charge. There was every reason to believe that this time, things would go much easier.

The high confidence level was enhanced because business was booming at EB. Things could not have been better for the largest employer in both Connecticut and Rhode Island, and the 688-class attack boats and the monster Trident submarines were pulling in a seemingly endless supply of money. The yard was filled with twenty thousand people and the thunder of their machines. Large facilities to first fabricate, then assemble and launch the boats had come on-line and a new sub was being completed every few months.

So it was a great surprise when I discovered that the shiny apple was rotting fast on the inside. I was among some three thousand engineers on the EB staff who worked jammed together in a pair of five-story brick buildings. Management offices occupied the outside edges near the windows, while in the center area the desks were arranged end to end in long rows. Each engineer was given thirty square feet of space and the desk took up twenty-five of it. There was only eighteen inches of space behind each desk–just enough to pull open the drawers. If a person in the middle of a row wanted out, everyone between him and the aisle had to stand and push his chair in. We on the *NR-2* design team counted ourselves fortunate to have a small glass-enclosed space. It really set us apart, and we guarded it zealously.

However, the tight quarters was not the main problem. Ironclad union rules clashed with an unrealistic workload in the design departments and in the shipyard. This brewed a recipe for disaster. Engineers, for instance, were only allowed to make freehand sketches of their projects. Any straight line had to be drawn by a union draftsman. All typing, no matter how few lines or characters, had to be done by a union secretary. As a result, schedules slipped. The backlog of subs to build grew, design changes accumulated, costs mounted, and the navy grew impatient. EB had too much work, but also idle, inefficiently applied resources.

After years of unrelenting, fast-paced effort, first in the navy and then at school, the enforced slowdown left me shocked and bewildered. Union representatives would creep by our offices and peer through the glass partitions to insure no contract rules were being violated, while midlevel managers would also frequently check to see if any engineers were slacking off. Therefore, we kept the appropriate props in plain view, usually a stack of blue line drawings with pencil marks scrawled all over them. If you wanted to stretch your legs, you picked up a sheaf of papers and walked somewhere quickly, as if on an urgent mission, because strolling casually was frowned upon.

A friend warned me to take care when sitting at my desk with a pencil in my hand, because if I fell asleep and my head dropped forward, I might poke out my eye. At first I thought it was a joke, but within two weeks I was so overwhelmed by the lack of productive work that tears of boredom streamed down my cheeks as I sat at the desk, busily doing nothing. It seemed inevitable when I learned that if the design and construction of the *NR-2* somehow managed to proceed on schedule, which rarely happened in the shipbuilding business, it would be twelve years before the boat could be launched.

Twelve years? On the personal front, our second daughter, Catherine, was on the way and it occurred to me that she would be entering junior high school before the new boat ever touched the water. To take care of my family, I decided to stick it out at EB for a while longer. Perhaps things would settle down. I naively could not imagine how they could get worse. Just in case, I enrolled in an after-hours course leading to a master's degree.

As bad as things were for the engineers, the incredible amount of wasted time in the shipyard was killing the company, for down by the Thames where the work was being done, restrictive union rules affected everyone. A welder needing to move a heating element just one inch to complete a job was required to inform his boss, who had to schedule a union electrician to show up and do something the welder could have taken care of in a moment. Almost two dozen trade unions protected their contracts with a vengeance, and the slightest violation resulted in a grievance. The average worker who welded or installed equipment in the hull sections spent only two hours a day actually on the ship performing his job because of the continual coming and going involved, and that little bit of time was often ineffective because the workplace was so crowded. The yard was working three shifts, but much was not communicated from one shift to the next, and even more time was lost to rework. In order to speed up the delivery of subs, more people were hired, but that only made the situation worse.

The result was an extreme lack of productivity and mounting costs that far exceeded the specified lucrative sub-building contracts. At one point, Rickover became so frustrated with the situation that he ordered padlocks placed through the coin slots of every vending machine in the entire shipyard in the hope that workers would spend more time on the job and thus get the ships out sooner. Even though the locks remained in place for years, that and similar quick fixes didn't seem to improve matters, and tensions mounted among the titans at the top levels of EB, the navy, and General Dynamics–EB's parent organization.

The unions walked out on an extended strike in the fall of 1973, and for three months, I went into the yard to work as an electrician, pulling cables through the partially completed hull sections of the several ships then under construction. It wasn't that difficult, without the unions around. When the strike ended, EB management was saddled with expensive new contracts while simultaneously engrossed in a war to recoup some of their escalating costs.

The *NR-2* project eventually was presented to Admiral Rickover, but he was not about to climb out on a limb that was even longer and weaker than the last time he built this kind of boat. Furious at the gigantic claims being made by EB, Rickover was in no mood to give them an extra nickel. He erupted when he saw the *NR-2* proposal, the twelve-year construction schedule, and the estimate of how much money would be needed to build a ship that would be almost structurally identical to the *NR-1*. It made the $100 million spent on the first boat appear to be a bargain. The project was also under simultaneous attack by skeptics who claimed the *NR-1* had not lived up to the admiral's promises, and blamed him for the massive cost overruns on the first boat, just as he blamed almost everyone else for overruns on other projects. His allowing the mystery sub to be used as a science vehicle did him little good, for as one official charged, "I don't know what that submarine has done for science, because whatever it does is kept classified."

Rickover, still keeping most operations of the *NR-1* from reaching the light of day, knew he could not win the battle for a new and improved version of the expensive boat. He looked at the proposed price tag and fulminated, "You guys think that Congress is going to give me a *billion* dollars for another toy? A *billion*?" And that was the end of that.

The shipyard would have been more than happy to take a contract for the *NR-2*, but with no navy money on the horizon for the project, our funding was slashed to a fraction of the original budget. To keep a foot in the door, the project was downgraded to something called a Nuclear Hull Test Vehicle, an HY-100 hull structure that would be crammed full of instruments and towed around at great depths to see how well it survived. The *NR-2* never had to face the perils of the ocean, because it sank before it ever got off the drawing board.

A period of confusion and conflict killed both the *NR-2* project and, temporarily, the government's confidence in Electric Boat as its premier submarine builder. Company management struggled to control a massive, well-funded organization that seemed to have a mind of its own. In the grinding upheaval and battles between EB and Admiral Rickover, Jack Leonard lost his job. I felt that if such a man, so long a key player in the tight world of submarine construction, had been sacrificed, there was little chance that EB could pull out of its nosedive. I arranged a transfer off the hull test project.

Following its lengthy overhaul after the battery fire the *NR-1* returned to active service late in 1974, as good as new, and set out on a new schedule of missions that once again blended science with secrecy.

Al Holifield was proud that his crew had not lost a step in the six months of work. They were as sharp as ever. It had become common-place for some enlisted men on the boat to qualify as officers of the deck, and many of them eventually moved into higher ranks. During a tow into the Atlantic, the *Sunbird* sent word that a couple of the *NR-1* guys were on the new promotion list, but Holifield was startled to learn that 25 percent of his people had been simultaneously selected as war-rant officers and limited duty officers. "I used to have to stop every once in a while to remember that any of my guys could go aboard the next ship down the pier, where they would think he walked on water. These people were all handpicked," he said.

The *NR-1* came back on duty at a time when it was needed more than ever on the military front. The Vietnam War was grinding to a close, and that country, once unified, would allow the Soviet Union's navy some much needed warm-water ports in the Pacific, from which it could significantly expand its reach. That would balance out the sub-stantial blow they sustained in the Med when the Russians were or-dered to leave Egypt. No matter what the formula, there was no reduction in the formidable presence of the Red Fleet, as Admiral Gor-shkov proved by launching Okean II, a naval exercise bigger than Okean I, and causing even more alarm.

To improve the U.S. ability to track enemy submarines in this tense time, the *NR-1* was sent on a sixty-day mission to Scotland in 1975 to examine the SOSUS networks in the area, and while doing so, discov-ered that a basic assumption of the submerged listening posts had been wrong. "Everyone thought the SOSUS lines lay flat on the ocean floor, but we found them all over the place. One was dangling across a valley, just suspended between the peaks of two underwater mountains," one crewman recalled. That degraded the information that was transmit-ted. It also made the lines vulnerable to the dragging anchors of Soviet ships purposely trying to snag and break them.

Rectifying that situation became a primary and urgent *NR-1* mis-sion. The wife of an officer heard her husband refer to "cable work" so often that she thought the navy was somehow working for the tele-phone company. That was not far from the truth, since when the navy considered buying an underwater plow similar to the one AT&T had used to bury the TAT-6 transatlantic telephone and telegraph cable, the *NR-1* was sent out to examine the plow's work. The cable, which ran between Connecticut and Spain, was supposed to be safely and securely buried, but actually snaked far away from the intended trench in many places, and at times was entangled with and dangling over abandoned lobster pots and other junk on the bottom. The navy decided to build a plow of its own.

In 1976, shortly after the United States celebrated its bicentennial in July, the *NR-1* headed for Scotland on classified missions called Spacious Sky and Jib Sheet. This time, it was towed across the Atlantic underwater, and porpoises happily kept pace by riding the unseen wave created as the bow of the *NR-1* pushed through the sea.

The *NR-1* worked quietly out of the picturesque bay of Holy Loch, Scotland, where the U.S. submarines rotated in to change crews and be serviced by a single sub tender and a floating dry dock with beefy cranes. In those days, working so far from everyone, the *NR-1* was very low on the list of priorities for the limited facilities. When a missile boat came in, the *NR-1* was bumped aside and lost its place in line. The brass felt that it was more important to keep the boomers at sea, so patching up the smallest submarine in the fleet could take a long time. It wasn't such a bad deal for the crew, however, for it gave them plenty of time to enjoy Scottish hospitality. They rotated on and off the *Sunbird*, "played in the mud" as they called the classified SOSUS work, and counted the days until they could return home.

The last item before going home would be another change of command ceremony, this time to be conducted in Holy Loch. Al Holifield was finishing his three-year tour and would be replaced by Mike McQuown, a thirty-five-year-old Naval Academy workaholic from Nebraska. His striking resemblance to the comedian Johnny Carson contrasted with the formal and humorless way he did his job—an approach that did not sit well with many of the more experienced crew members. But McQuown was said to be on the navy's fast track and had served as flag lieutenant to the commander of submarines in the Atlantic. He considered getting command of the elite *NR-1* akin to winning the lottery, and his wife remembered that after his first trip on the boat, he came home as enthused as "someone who had found religion."

Holifield was running out of time to finish the SOSUS work, turn the boat over to McQuown, and head for home. Already, poor visibility and strong currents were kicking up choppy seas. He knew that this was only a preview of the wicked weather that plagues the North Atlantic in winter. Then a broken shear bolt on the Jetter forced the *NR-1* to suspend its work and put into Plymouth, England, for repairs. The navy was anxious to finish upgrading the vital SOSUS array system that was operated out of a town in Wales, and ordered the boat back to the network again, officially extending its tour.

Racing the weather, the *NR-1* scurried out of Plymouth, and on September 14, as it was busy digging in the muck at the bottom of a channel, the world changed.

17

TOMCAT DOWN

Seventy-five miles northwest of Scotland's port of Scapa Flow, a massive naval exercise called Teamwork 76 was under way. Some two hundred ships from ten NATO countries were staging joint maneuvers in the North Atlantic, the English Channel, the Norwegian and Baltic Seas, and along the Jutland Peninsula. The exercise was Cold War posturing at its extreme, and mixed among the allied warships were Russian spy ships, including a pair of Kresta II–class cruisers and seven Soviet-bloc electronic intelligence ships. Only a week before, a U.S. Navy frigate collided with a Soviet submarine in the Mediterranean, and now America's big boys and the Soviet spooks were at work again, this time on the dangerously surging seas of the North Atlantic. The *NR-1* was not far away, but much too small, hidden, and valuable to be involved.

The centerpiece of the exercise was the battle group of the aircraft carrier USS *John F. Kennedy*, whose planes were running realistic strike operations. Everything had gone according to schedule for the first week of the exercise, but by September 14, bad weather was on the way, and a strong wind ripped apart the gray clouds and rushed across the flight deck as the carrier turned into it to launch planes. Among those watching the exercise from the carrier were dozens of news reporters and photographers, for it was Press Day, and NATO was counting on some good publicity. Pictures of sleek warplanes catapulting off a carrier deck would not only build public support, but also send a message about readiness to the Soviet bloc.

A twin-tailed Grumman F-14 Tomcat was being readied, its Pratt & Whitney afterburning turbofan engines humming in idle. From its needle nose to its tail fins, the sophisticated F-14 was the hottest thing in the sky and was unsurpassed as a fighter jet. It also looked good on camera.

What could not be photographed, however, was the heart of the Tomcat, its powerful AWG-9 radar, a machine of near magic proportions. The AWG-9 could pick out and track six individual targets simultaneously from more than a hundred miles away, no matter what the weather or the enemy's electronic jamming ability, and at any altitude from fifty feet above the wave tops to eighty thousand feet, at the rim of outer space. While doing so, the radar simultaneously painted an accurate electronic picture of the developing battle zone that was transmitted back to the carrier commanders. The reporters did not even know the AWG-9 was aboard the plane.

The F-14 normally would be armed with Sidewinder missiles for its primary mission of destroying threats far away from its home aircraft carrier, but for today's war games, a new missile called the Phoenix had replaced the Sidewinders. It was a solid-propellant rocket designed to be especially deadly at long distances and was undergoing tests to become the navy's primary air defense weapon.

A Phoenix streaking through the air, answering the commands of the Tomcat's AWG-9 radar, would give the navy pilot a particularly long arm in aerial combat. It could reach out a hundred miles and close on its target at a top speed of close to three thousand miles per hour. The F-14 was the only combat aircraft capable of carrying the Phoenix, which also could be fitted with a nuclear warhead.

Together, the Tomcat and its Phoenix payload formed perhaps the most technologically advanced air combat system in the world. Each aircraft cost $14 million, the missiles were half a million apiece, and the combined technology was priceless.

Lieutenant John Kosich was at the controls of a Tomcat from the VF-32 Squadron, and had taxied close to *Kennedy*'s number three catapult, stopped, and put on the brakes. Sailors wearing colored shirts that designated their jobs gave his aircraft some last-second adjustments, and armed the Phoenix missile on the belly rails. The wings of the F-14 were extended straight out as it sat on the black deck, but after the launch, the pilot would tuck the wings sharply back and the fighter would tear through the sky at fifteen hundred miles per hour.

As he ran through the final checks, his engines suddenly roared and Kosich felt the plane begin to move on its own. He had not given it any commands, and it was moving! He stomped the brakes and checked the throttles, which were still in idle, but the engines had somehow gone berserk, producing full power and pushing the F-14 forward on the angled deck. As he fought to control it, the plane ran over a crewman, breaking his ankle, and its right wing clipped two more parked planes. The pilot tried to shut down the throttles, but they did not respond, and he used the nose wheel to steer his out-of-control aircraft away from an entire line of other planes. The fighter jet moved inexorably toward the edge of the 252-foot-wide angled deck, leaving thick rubber skid marks and injuring two more men.

The pilot and his backseater pulled their ejection levers and rocketed out of the plane, both coming back down onto the flight deck without injury. But the F-14 Tomcat, watched by members of the world's press, went over the side with its big engines still screaming. It immediately sank out of sight. "There goes fourteen million dollars," the British Broadcasting System reporter told his audience.

The astonished officers on the bridge of the *Kennedy* took a navigational fix to mark the spot, as did the equally amazed Soviet intelligence ships that were shadowing the exercise. The plane and missile had splashed into international waters that the charts said were about 1,850 feet deep. Instead of being the exclusive property of the United States Navy, both top secret weapons, under laws of the sea, were now available for salvage by anyone. One of the biggest prizes of the Cold War lay on the ocean floor, and could be taken by anyone who could find it and pick it up.

Almost lost in the excitement was Lieutenant Kosich's claim that his Tomcat had jumped to full power all on its own. That suggested a serious design flaw that could jeopardize the entire frontline defense system, and correcting the problem in every F-14 in the fleet might cost millions of dollars. The only way to determine whether the machine was at fault or the slide overboard resulted from pilot error was to actually view the positions of the cockpit switches and levers.

News of the F-14 and Phoenix going into the water was included in a routine report passed along that evening from the *Sunbird* to the

NR-1, which was down deep, working on the SOSUS submarine-detection network. Commander Al Holifield thought the situation was interesting, but since it did not concern his ship, he went back to work.

The *Kennedy* seemed to be jinxed that day. A few hours after losing the F-14, the carrier collided with the destroyer *Bordelon* during refueling operations, injuring seven men and damaging the smaller ship enough to force her into port for emergency repairs.

The U.S. Navy had no choice but to go after the F-14 wreckage with everything it had. If they did not, the plane and its missile, both crammed with classified electronics, would certainly become the targets of a Soviet salvage operation. Moscow recently had lost one of their MiG-25 Foxbat fighter jets when a pilot defected to Japan, and would leap at a chance to even the score. For the U.S. to lose such a package of cutting edge military technology would be a catastrophic setback.

The Teamwork 76 task force, which was not equipped to recover the missile and plane, sailed away, and for once, they were happy that the Soviet spy ships followed. As long as the Red Fleet tagged along, they could be accounted for, but the big worry was that a Soviet fishing trawler might gather the downed aircraft in its nets and pull it up. While figuring out its next step, the U.S. Navy decided to keep the area of the crash under the surveillance of long-range P-3C patrol planes from Keflavik, Iceland.

The task of finding and recovering the plane and missile was given to the Navy Supervisor of Salvage, who assembled an experienced team of civilian experts and appointed a civilian to be in charge of the at-sea recovery units. The navy's search contractor was Seaward, Inc., of Falls Church, Virginia, and that company added a subcontractor, Hydro Surveys of Fort Lauderdale, Florida, to run the side-scan sonar needed for the search. The navy loaded the latest model of its unmanned, remote-controlled CURV submersible on a plane for a flight from San Diego to London, where it would be taken aboard the *Constructor*, a Norwegian salvage vessel.

The *Constructor* had side thrusters that could maintain a specific position at sea, even in heavy weather. Also signed up was the *Oil Harrier*, a British vessel with powerful winches that could haul up the heavy weight of the plane. The navy's oceangoing tug USS *Shakori* joined the recovery task force to tow an array of robotic "fish," acoustic detection devices that could scan wide paths of the ocean floor with sonar.

The combination of Press Day on the carrier and the presence of so many civilian vessels and workers erased any hope of keeping the operation from the public. In a most unusual move, the navy decided to be totally open about the search and recovery operations. They would represent it as a mere salvage job, and downplay the vital nature of the objects they were desperate to get back.

The weather was a more immediate problem than keeping the Soviets away from the site and dampening the curiosity of the media. The North Atlantic would become one of the most inhospitable places on earth when winter came, and although it was still the middle of September, strong winds already were singing through the rigging of the ships and vicious seas were piling up. Planners believed that unless the foul weather abated, the tumultuous waves, wicked currents, and frigid temperatures would make it almost impossible to bring up the plane. They said the recovery effort had to be completed by November 1 or it would be abandoned.

That left less than seven weeks, and the first of those passed before the *Shakori* could load the necessary equipment and emerge from the Firth of Clyde on September 21, headed northwest from the Orkneys. The huge tugboat spent three days fighting through the blustery seas and found the search site shrouded in rain and fog, with winds of forty knots churning up waves twenty feet high.

Nevertheless, the *Shakori* managed to lower her "fish," which started gathering sonar data and messaging it back through a long cable to the bridge of the ship. The results emerged on a paper printout. While the fish was hauled through the area in which *Kennedy* reports indicated the plane went down, the *Shakori* was pummeled by a furious storm. Seas slammed the tug so hard that she popped rivets and required continual pumping, and the sonar operator had to be strapped to his chair as the ship lurched in thirty-five-degree rolls. For ten days, the sonar search found nothing while *Shakori*'s crew hung on for their lives and studied the unrolling printouts. They finally got a sonar picture of something that looked like it might be a plane on October 3, but by then the battered tug, pitching and rolling violently, was low on supplies and limped back to Scotland. The weather grew worse by the day.

Another week went by before the *Shakori* could go out again. She strung along the robot at the end of eight thousand feet of line, but again the plane was nowhere to be found. It was not where they had left it, and navy officials worried the Russians might have somehow snagged the F-14 while the tugboat was gone. The chief of naval operations in Washington received a string of depressing reports.

"12 October–Heavy weather over the weekend hampered *Shakori*'s search..."

"14 October–Heavy weather and navigational problems continue to hamper search operations..."

A message was sent throughout the navy for personnel "knowledgeable in search operations." They were grasping at straws.

To Sperry engineer Roger Sherman, this was all nonsense. "For God's sake," he thought, "the *NR-1* is parked at Holy Loch, just down the street from the crash site!" He had closely followed reports as the operation bumbled along for several weeks and finally made a decision.

On the same day that the *Kennedy* was providing air cover for a mock amphibious assault by marines across a windswept beach near Esbjerg, Denmark, Sherman stormed the ramparts of the U.S. Navy. He left his office in Building 16, walked down two flights of stairs, and entered the headquarters of Submarine Squadron Two. Hey, he said, you guys are letting a golden opportunity slip away here. The *NR-1* is part of your own squadron, it's over in Holy Loch, only a hundred miles from the scene, it has just what is needed for this job, so why don't you use it? The same answer came back from each of the various officers with whom he spoke: "What's the *NR-1*?"

Sherman realized at that moment that he, a civilian, knew more about the boat than the senior big-boat officers with whom he was talking. They were barely aware of the small sub, and none had ever been allowed aboard. They had no idea of what it really was, or what its capabilities were. The *NR-1* had been kept *too* secret.

Since having been launched seven years earlier, its missions had been run under such deep cover that many officers now in positions of responsibility were unaware of its presence. And it was orange. Everyone knew it was orange. Eventually, Sherman was asked to brief the squadron commander and went into a conference room filled with somber men festooned with enough gold braid and polished brass buttons to blind the naked eye. For more than an hour, he used his substantial storytelling prowess to describe the boat, what it had done, where it had gone, and the things he had seen while rolling along the ocean floor.

It is nuclear powered, so it doesn't have to pop up for fuel and air! It can make a continuous sonar bottom search and stand rock-steady a half mile down, much deeper than any other sub, no matter what is happening on the surface! Then it can actually eyeball anything it finds! It can photograph it or grab it, your choice! Eyes widened as he described its exploits, and how it was just finishing up a SOSUS duty tour in Scotland. The officers decided to send the issue up the chain of command. Sherman was optimistic when he returned to his office, but after waiting for several hours, his optimism faded to anger when a rather diffident duty officer called from downstairs.

"We raised the issue to COMSUBLANT [Commander of Submarines, Atlantic] and when he passed it on, he was told in no uncertain terms that the surface community would take care of the problem and make the recovery on their own," he advised Sherman. "They don't want any help from the submarine force."

"This is crazy," Roger protested. The navy had kept the power of the *NR-1* secret from the very people who most needed to know about it, and now a turf battle had erupted during an emergency that had national security implications. Instead of using the navy's own unique asset, the admirals of the surface fleet were allowing civilian and foreign companies handle what could be one of the most sensitive projects in recent naval history. Even the project manager on the scene was a civilian.

Sherman was furious. It was almost as if they *wanted* someone else to recover the plane and the missile. Frustrated, he dialed a local number at Electric Boat and talked to Captain Art Francis, who was in charge of the Naval Reactors field office at EB, and therefore a direct conduit to Admiral Rickover. Francis listened attentively to Sherman's explanation of what was taking place both in the cold waters north of Scotland and in the hot waters of naval political intrigue. After a few questions, he had heard enough, and said, "Thank you, Roger. I understand the situation. I'll get back to you."

Francis immediately telephoned Rickover in Washington, and played the shrewd card of jealousy. "I believe whoever the admiral in charge of the F-14 recovery is may be an anti-Rickover guy, Admiral," he said, stoking the fiery temper of his boss. "You know how they never want you, or anything you are involved with, to succeed. They're wasting a good bet on this thing."

Art Francis hung up with a smile, imagining the next few conversations Rickover would have with the boys in the Pentagon. He could not actually tell the admiral to get on the phone to the CNO, but there was no doubt that Rickover was already burning up the phone lines.

Within two hours, Roger Sherman got a breathless call from the flustered squadron duty officer. "Quick. Come on back down here," he was told. "The *NR-1* is on."

Only twelve days were left until the drop-dead date of November 1.

Toby Warson was in Groton. He had been promoted into the big black boats and was the commanding officer of the Blue Crew on the USS *George Washington Carver.* As such, he was one of the most powerful men alive, for his ship packed enough nuclear missiles to level any enemy in the world. He picked up the ringing telephone and was surprised at the urgency in the voice of Admiral Joe Williams, the salty, hard-driving commander of submarines in the Atlantic. Like all good submariners, Williams held aircraft carriers in quiet disdain. Any ship that is not a submarine is simply a target.

"The Airdales have lost an F-14 and a Phoenix missile," COMSUBLANT told him. "Can the *NR-1* find them?"

Warson's thoughts flashed back to the years he had spent as skipper of the little boat, and his answer came quickly. "If they have good navigation data, they should be able to."

"Good," snapped Williams. "You're on a plane tonight for Scotland. I want you in charge of the recovery effort."

More than three years had passed since Warson had last set foot on the *NR-1* and now he was being ordered to leave one of the biggest and most vital subs in the fleet to work again with the tiniest nuclear-powered ship in the navy. For the moment, the *NR-1* was more important than his boomer.

The USS *Batfish*, only three years old, was a shadowy warrior involved in the hush-hush Ivy Bells espionage program that specialized in tapping Soviet communications cables. It owned a Naval Unit Citation for outstanding clandestine work.

In the middle of October, the nuclear-powered attack sub received an urgent, peculiar message, broke away from its mission, and headed for a spot north of the Orkney Islands. The new orders stated that the *Batfish*, which was loaded with war-shot torpedoes, was to "sanitize" the F-14 crash site area prior to the arrival of the *NR-1*. The orders did not specify what "sanitize" meant.

While the *Batfish* lurked below, the HMS *Blue Rover*, from the Royal Navy, went in to run interference on the surface. The Soviets were not welcome in the area.

The open information policy and the visible salvage operation that had been treated as some sort of public relations sideshow were back firmly beneath the umbrella of military control. The navy might be late in closing the door, but they were now slamming it shut hard.

Warson, a military officer, was taking command of the operation. The *Batfish* and the *Blue Rover* were on guard duty. After a Pentagon memo glumly pointed out "the loss and search generated considerable public affairs interest," a heavy hitter, a full captain, was dispatched to London to shore up media relations.

The *NR-1* crew had paid little attention to what was going on with the search. They had completed the SOSUS work and were back at Holy Loch, getting ready for the change of command ceremonies. Al Holifield called his squadron commander to advise that they were ready to make the swap—Mike McQuown would become OIC and Holifield would fly back to the States and prepare to become the commanding officer of the USS *Pogy*, an attack boat out of Pearl Harbor.

Holifield was informed that Admiral Williams had vetoed the changeover. A new task was on for the *NR-1* and COMSUBLANT had said, "I don't want a new guy to do this." Instead of going home, Holifield was to head out to sea again, right away, to try to find the missing F-14 and its Phoenix missile. McQuown would remain on the ship to assist Holifield.

The civilian ships would still be involved, and high navy officials would have sketchy overall command, but the past, current, and future skippers of the *NR-1* were taking over the mission.

18
NETS

*T*he wardroom on the USS *Shakori* was crowded, but the talk among the gathered military personnel and civilians stopped as Al Holifield and his executive officer, Joe Nolter, stepped inside. They had been rushed over from Holy Loch to Aberdeen to meet with a panel of technical experts about the F-14 and the Phoenix. The main thing the *NR-1* officers wanted to know was if the missile, which was armed when the plane dove off the carrier, might blow up when it was touched. "I was a little worried about parking alongside a live missile with an explosive warhead," Holifield recalled. They were assured that the Phoenix would be safe, particularly since it would still be solidly attached to the aircraft. Raise the plane and the missile comes up with it, the experts advised. There would be no safety problem. They were so certain the missile would still be attached that they did not even tell the men who were going after it what the Phoenix looked like.

A representative from the plane's builder, Grumman Aircraft, said the sub would find the plane sitting right side up, almost on its wheels, as if ready for takeoff. The swing wings were extended when it went overboard, so it would have glided down, much like a coin dropped into a glass of water, rather than tumbled.

The discussion turned to the structure of the aircraft to determine where a line would best be attached to hoist it. The tail hook was the strongest point, but did not provide a good place for a linkup. Instead, it was decided the *NR-1* could use its manipulator arm to poke a line through the strut of the nose wheel, which was sturdy enough to catapult the heavy fighter from the ship. Then the submarine would move away and the salvage operation would haul up the plane. It would be, they thought, a relatively simple job.

Holifield and Nolter went back to their boat with a bit of skepticism. Both knew that the best-laid plans made around a table during a large meeting probably would mean little when the *NR-1* actually arrived at its target. What was found on the floor of the sea seldom matched what was imagined above.

The *Shakori* returned to the crash site and joined the *Constructor* and the *Oil Harrier* for an attempt to locate the plane by using the CURV III, which had been flown out from California. It was a very quick outing, for when it was deployed from the *Constructor* the remote control vessel only got down to 1,500 feet before its main power cable shorted out. It was pulled back in and all three ships, unable to stay on station because of the high seas, returned to port.

The *Batfish* arrived in the area and reported "no contacts of interest" after an initial sweep of the perimeter. That did not mean that the Soviets were not around, for a covey of their salvage vessels and oceangoing tugboats was about to arrive, and the *Blue Rover* would stay busy shouldering them out of the way while the *Batfish* kept close watch from below the surface.

Toby Warson stood on the bridge of the *Sunbird* as she headed out through the Firth of Clyde, towing the *NR-1* behind like a baby elephant in a circus parade. It was a wicked time to be going to sea, and he dug his hands into the pockets of his foul-weather jacket for warmth. The skies over Scotland were gloomy, a brisk wind and hard rain pelted him, and the seas were building. "Nothing ever happens when the weather is good," complained Warson, whose code name for the operation was Big Daddy.

Ed Craig, the *Sunbird* skipper and a Naval Academy classmate of Al Holifield, agreed with Warson as the ship bucked through heavy seas, heading for the deep waters 100 miles from shore. The *NR-1* would soon be able to dive and be towed submerged, in calm waters 150 feet below, but the *Sunbird* would still be on top, bouncing around on the tempestuous sea.

* * *

Just knowing where to look was a problem. The coordinates given by the *Kennedy* were not reliable because the carrier used her internal navigation system more to coordinate the instruments of the planes with the level deck than to pinpoint an invisible spot on the moving ocean. The system had not been reset for some time, which meant the given position was suspect. The rough guess could be off by miles.

The age-old problem of finding something that falls into the water is not only that it disappears from sight, but also that it does not drop straight down. As the Grumman representatives had explained, even something as big as an airplane will wobble and sail as it falls through water. The problem does not end there, because strong currents can play havoc with anything lying on the bottom. Therefore, the location of the sunken F-14 was truly unknown.

Nineteen days after the plane went overboard, robotic sonar fish pulled around by the *Shakori* made a "high probability contact" on October 3. But after the ship was forced back to port by the storm, she had to spend more days trying to reacquire the plane. The target was not found again until October 15, a month and a day after the incident. Somehow during the two-week interval between contacts, it had moved. Weather again drove the fleet tug back to shelter, and six more days passed until she was able to find the contact for a third time, and she dropped an electronic transponder overboard to mark the spot.

No one really knew where it was nor why it was moving about. The best hope was that the turbulent seas, and not the nets of some Soviet ship, had pushed it to the new location.

On October 21, the same day the transponder was dropped, the *NR-1* loosed its tow from the *Sunbird* and settled to the bottom, coasting lazily through a cloud of millions of tiny, iridescent jellyfish that stretched as far as the eye could see. Once on the floor, some 1,800 feet down, it took range and bearing checks with the support ship, then rose up and began to fly a careful, expanding box search pattern.

A hundred feet off the floor, the *NR-1*'s side-scan sonar could cover a wide area, which resulted in more contacts than expected. The bottom was littered with large boulders, each of which bounced back a solid sonar signal that confused the readings aboard the *NR-1*. There were no recorded sonar patterns of what an F-14 would look like underwater, because the supersonic Tomcats were supposed to be up in the sky, not stuck in the mud, and there was nothing with which to compare the returning signals. Whenever an interesting reading came up on the sonar, the boat had to slow, turn, drop down, and hover to look and verify that it was not the plane.

After a detailed exploration of an entire square mile around the transponder, nothing worthwhile had been discovered, and Holifield felt they were wasting time. If they had to eyeball every rock in the area, they might as well just be down near the floor and do it the hard way, by inspecting the bottom through the view ports in fifty-foot swaths.

Visibility was excellent and the thallium iodide lights painted the water around the boat as a pale, wavy blue green that showed up well for the television cameras. Holifield was in the right-hand pilot seat and his engineering officer, Mike Riegel, was driving the boat when they circled to investigate still another strong signal.

The captain saw something peculiar on the screen, a shadowy, moving presence about fifty feet out, just at maximum range of the forward-looking bow camera. It did not look like marine life, nor did it look anything like a plane, and as the boat drew nearer, the camera image stretched far upward and expanded in width until he could see neither the top nor the bottom of it. The image undulated in the water.

When Holifield suddenly realized what he was looking at, he made an instant decision and, for the only time in his career on submarines, shouted: "ALL BACK EMERGENCY!"

Eighteen hundred feet beneath the surface of the ocean, the *NR-1* was driving straight into a tangled wall of fishing nets.

The engines jerked into reverse, but forward momentum kept the *NR-1* moving toward the nets, which loomed closer by the second, so close that Holifield could make out the individual squares of rope and the big cork floats that pulled the ends of the nets up vertically in the water, making them tower above the submarine. The boat finally coasted to a stop about twenty feet from the menacing mesh, came to a hover, and backed slowly away.

The submarine cautiously made its way to the bottom to find what anchored the nets, and the F-14 swam into hazy view, swaddled in the thick cordage, one wing mangled, and upside down, exactly the opposite of what had been expected. Deep troughs of drag marks showed the plane had been hauled some distance along the floor, and the mud caked in the wheel wells indicated that it had flipped. Some deep-sea trawler had snagged the aircraft and, unable to lift the heavy burden, cut free its nets. Which trawler, and of what nationality, was unknown.

The other startling discovery was that all of the weapons stations on the bottom of the plane were empty. The Phoenix missile was gone. Al Holifield picked up the microphone and called the *Sunbird.*

"Big Daddy, this is Bottom Buggy. I got good news and I got bad news, which do you want first?" he asked.

"Give me the good news," replied Warson.

"The good news is that we found the F-14. The bad news is there ain't no Phoenix missile!"

"Say again?" Warson was stunned. Every civilian and military expert consulted had sworn that once the missile was loaded on the plane, there was no way that it could shake free. Holifield repeated his report, and Warson relayed the news up the line.

The *NR-1* was parked 1,850 feet down, sitting on the floor, with its camera trained on the upside-down Tomcat when Warson came back on the underwater telephone with the word from headquarters. "Bottom Buggy, this is Big Daddy. They say that's impossible, that the missile could not have come off the plane, so it must be there. They want you to go look again."

Holifield stared at his TV screen. The bottom of the plane was in clear view, as clean and white as the belly of a fish. "Goddammit! If they don't believe me, tell them to come down and take a look themselves. It's not there!"

Big Daddy laughed. He was on the side of the *NR-1* all the way, and if Holifield said the missile was gone, then it was truly gone. Warson decided the boat had enough problems down there without having to listen to absurd conclusions from distant nitpickers. From now on, he would take any heat from the landlocked experts and let the *NR-1* get on with the job.

With its wheels down, the *NR-1* crawled near to study the partially buried plane from several angles. The nets almost blanketed the plane, floating high above it like some bizarre flag. Holifield would be working the manipulator arm, which required that the submarine get closer to the plane, but he had to allow a safety margin. To be caught in the nets would be a catastrophe.

"I've got to be very careful, because if I get it tangled up in the screw, I can't reach back there with the manipulator," he thought. "If we get caught in front, I can cut it, but not behind. If it gets caught up back there, I'm in trouble." Although the bow would have to be almost directly above the plane to secure the lift line, Holifield was determined to keep the stern as far away from those menacing nets as possible, and there was no room for error.

Even as the captain was having that conversation with himself, the newest man aboard the *NR-1*, Frank Smith, was at a view port and didn't believe what he was seeing. Something was coming at them, disturbing the sea life and combing through the rocks and mud as it pushed forward like some invisible force out of a Hollywood movie. It shimmered before his eyes like heat waves rising off an asphalt highway on a hot day and hurried inevitably closer by the moment. He shouted a warning just as Joe Nolter, the executive officer who was driving the boat, heard a strange, low sound coming from the side-scan sonar, a sort of moan, and saw the thermometer that measured the outside temperature drop five degrees in as many seconds.

A huge underwater wave of a type that no one even knew existed hit the stationary little boat broadside, plucked the *NR-1* off its wheels, and bounced it sideways several times like a ball, every bounce pushing it closer to the fluttering nets.

Nolter fought the force of onrushing wave with the thrusters, but with only a thousand pounds of pushing power, they were no match for this surging tidal force. Out of options, he skewed the nose of the *NR-1* directly into the heavy current, which meant shifting the stern propellers closer to the nets. That stopped the bouncing, and the boat was able to hang there, vibrating, as the churning, mad water swept past, tearing up the ocean floor as it went.

The phenomenon was unknown to science, was not noted on any chart, and had never before been experienced. Like so many *NR-1* encounters, it arrived as an unexpected surprise and the crew had to deal with it the best they could. The peak force passed quickly, but a strong following current made further work on the F-14 impossible until the water settled. To get the plane hooked up for lifting, the *NR-1* would have to contend not only with the possibility of being trapped in the nets, but also with a sea-bottom storm. The crew christened it Nolter's Maelstrom, and it would torment them for the rest of the mission.

"It hit us twice a day, every frigging day," said Mike Riegel. "About every ten hours, here it would come like gangbusters." They learned to anticipate the powerful flood, and just before it was due the submarine would point into the oncoming wave, flood its ballast tanks to get as heavy as possible, raise the wheels, and rest on the bottom, trying to become rock solid as the surge swept by. The recurring problem forced a timetable change in working on the recovery, since the submarine could be nowhere near the barricade of nets when Nolter's Maelstrom was due. The *NR-1* might have more lives than a cat, but this combination could use them all up in a hurry.

On the surface, there was more bad news. Cold gray waves were surging high and the bleak weather report indicated things were going to get worse. The cluster of Soviet vessels was nosing closer, "playing cat and mouse games," according to one officer, and there could be no question of abandoning the recovery effort. If the allied ships headed for port, the Soviets now had a good idea where they could fish for the missing plane.

There was great concern about the origin of the nets that had snagged the airplane, and although the *NR-1* got close enough to read marking numbers on some of the floats, the ownership question became as tangled as the fishing gear itself. Some said they were French, although no French ships were near the scene. Some said they were the property of a British fishing fleet. Others claimed the nets belonged to a company that was a front for the Soviet Union, while still others said the markings on the floats contained Russian Cyrillic characters. The truth became lost in that world of military intelligence in which nothing is necessarily what it seems. The only thing known for certain, even thirty years after the event, was that Soviet trawlers were the only ones actually seen near the accident site. As one member of the search team remarked, "The water was about 1,800 feet, and that's kind of deep for fishing, particularly in an area where there aren't many fish."

It was a moot point anyway, for now that the *NR-1* had located the wreckage, it wasn't about to let it go.

On the surface, the clock and the calendar might mean something, but below where there was no sun nor moon, time was measured only in the six-hour shifts on duty. With its nuclear heart, the *NR-1* stayed down for the entire mission, never once coming to the surface, relying on its strength of staying power to do what no other ship in the world could. Passing hours meant nothing, and when the skipper and crew needed sleep, they parked the boat on the bottom and shut down for a while.

The job of lassoing the F-14 belonged to Holifield, while the crew maneuvered the boat and held it steady, hovering near the bottom but careful not to disturb the sand. Visibility would be critical during the coming hours of detailed work. In the past few years, Holifield had become a virtuoso at working the now ancient Westinghouse manipulator, a single arm controlled by push buttons and switches. The claw on the end could open and close and turn, but had nowhere near the dexterity of the grasping mechanisms that had been made for other submersibles in the years since the *NR-1* went to sea. This was not much more than a big pair of pliers on a stick, and using it to snare the F-14 was, in the words of one crewman, like "wrapping a Christmas present in a cupboard with one hand while wearing a boxing glove."

Since the nose landing gear of the plane was clogged with mud from being dragged, Holifield instead looped a rope pendant over one of the main wheels, then the *NR-1* backed off and cinched it tight around the strut. On the end was a shackle that could be attached to a lifting line, but several days passed before that could be done because the *Constructor* could not hold steady enough in the heavy seas to lower the line that would connect to the pendant.

The *NR-1* spent the empty hours searching for the missile around the fallen plane, but did not find it. The alarming possibility had to be considered that the same sort of trawling nets that had wrapped the plane might have been able to retrieve the secret Phoenix.

The chief of naval operations received a dismal report on October 25. "Weather conditions continue to hamper salvage operations. If weather continues to deteriorate, *NR-1* and *Sunbird* will proceed to Scapa Flow Bay, Orkney Islands, for safe haven and remaining surface units will proceed to Kirkwall."

But Warson kept the task force at work, unwilling to abandon the site to the watching Soviet trawlers, and the weather gods finally gave them a break. After several unsuccessful tries, the *Constructor* lowered the lift line accurately enough on October 26 for Holifield to snap it to the pendant around the main landing gear. Ship and plane were now connected.

As the line tightened, the Soviet trawlers realized something important had happened, and the fishing vessel *Rion* charged across the storm-tossed seas, heading for the recovery site to get a better look. The allied ships closed frantically into position to block the *Rion* from reaching the *Constructor*, and the Soviet vessel backed off, but it was clear that if the task force now gave up and went back to port, the enemy fleet would surely pounce. The Russian intelligence-gathering ship *Krenometr* edged uncomfortably close, but did not interfere.

The *Constructor* passed the lift line to the *Oil Harrier*, which would use her strong winch to pull the plane from the mud, but the North Atlantic would not stop pounding the operation. As the *Oil Harrier* came about, she was rolling violently on seas that were twenty feet high, and the stern rose and fell that much with each wave. At the end of the towline, more than a thousand feet down, the F-14 was nothing more than a big piece of metal, a gigantic sea anchor. The constant pull and tension created incredible stress, and before the ship had gone three miles, the line parted with an audible crack and the F-14 plunged back to the bottom.

This time it flipped over again on the way down and landed right side up, with its wheels digging into the bottom muck, not only trapped in the nets, but also wrapped with a section of the parted line. It remained deep, at 1,410 feet, and the *NR-1* was called back to do the dangerous job all over again.

This time, the boat flew carefully over the open cockpit, and Mike McQuown burned several rolls of film photographing the switches and the instrument panel. Data from those pictures would define the condition of the aircraft as it went off the deck, and determine if the accident was caused by a mechanical problem or pilot error. It was fortunate that they spent so much time taking those pictures, because the jinxed plane was about to encounter even more problems. On October 28, the *NR-1* hooked up the line for a second try, and again left the area. The *Oil Harrier* pulled, the surging seas again fought against the lift, the line snapped once more, and the F-14 returned to the mud for the third time.

"*NR-1* is presently searching the bottom to relocate the aircraft and assess the situation," the CNO was told. They were out of time. The November 1 drop-dead date was only a few days away, the weather was growing more evil, and the Russians were watching for a sign of weakness. Nothing as heavy as the F-14 had ever been raised from such a depth before, particularly in vicious seas, the cost of trying to pull it up was nearing $2 million, and everything they had tried had failed.

The plane was still on the bottom, and the missile was gone.

19
PHOENIX RISING

At least the *NR-1* had a good starting point this time, and could begin work at the place where it had found the F-14. From the furrows made by the plane when it was dragged by the nets, they could tell exactly the direction in which it had been moved. The boat had already spent many hours scouting back along that track, and had found nothing.

No longer involved in trying to haul up the plane, the *NR-1* could refine its search, and the starting point remained where the aircraft had been discovered. A geographic area of high probability was determined, then divided into *x-y* grids on the plotting chart, and the search began.

It was a fact that the missile was still on the plane when it went overboard, but the same experts who guaranteed the Phoenix would still be attached had made another major error. Because the Phoenix was such a top secret piece of weaponry, very little information about it was shared with the *NR-1* officers during the briefing. That need-to-know doctrine now stymied the recovery effort because the submarine crew had not even been given a description of the missile, nor shown a photograph. They had no idea of what it looked like.

So they had wasted many hours poking into the mud immediately around the fallen plane, hunting what they believed to be a small, sleek missile similar to the Sidewinder, which weighs only 190 pounds and is less than ten feet long. The disturbed sea bottom easily could have swallowed something of that size.

Only when it became obvious that the Phoenix search would be a separate operation were the details passed along. In sharp contrast to the Sidewinder, the explosive warhead of the Phoenix weighed 135 pounds by itself, and the missile's overall weight was in excess of a thousand pounds. It was thirteen feet in length and fifteen inches in diameter, and had tail fins that measured three feet across. The chances were pretty small that something that size had slid out of sight into the muck.

Those broad, flat tail fins added to the location puzzle. When the missile broke free of the plane, the fins would have guided it off on its own spinning course. Once on the bottom, the big fins would have helped the currents, including Nolter's powerful and repetitive Maelstrom, roll it about. It could be anywhere.

No matter how big or small it might be, no matter what its weight or shape, the crew of the *NR-1* figured there was only *one* missile down there, if somebody else had not already snagged it. Whatever they found would be the Phoenix.

The boat came to a hover about 25 feet off the bottom and began flying in methodical patterns. There was no surface light 1,800 feet beneath the storm-tossed ocean waves, so all of the sub's lights were on to pierce the obsidian blackness. Two men lay prone in the view port area to personally examine the vast flats of mud, while the sonar scanned for objects in the distance. Big rocks once again registered false alarms.

As the sour weather battered the topside support ships with gale force winds, the submarine "mowed the lawn," as the crew called the tedious exercise of following the forward-and-back track. At the end of each leg of the search, they extended the reach, pressing to cover a little bit more territory on every pass, for time had become critical.

Toby Warson, aware of the approaching deadline, had already called down instructions to bring the search to a close, but Holifield coaxed him to allow a little more time, at least to complete the current pattern. Holifield, however, knew they had used up the clock. November 1 was less than forty-eight hours away.

The current and former skippers of the *NR-1* also realized that the crew had done arduous and continual duty since it submerged on October 21 to find the F-14, and were exhausted. They had patrolled every possible patch of sea bottom without success, and it was time to report to Big Daddy, "We can't find the Phoenix missile." The *NR-1* swung into the final turn of an extended sweep that had lasted seventeen hours straight.

Once again, Frank Smith, at one of the view ports, caught an unexpected glimmer off to one side. *Something there!* He took a harder look. From the distance, at the edge of the bubble of hazy light, lay an object that looked like a model rocket from his high school science class.

"I see it!" he shouted. "I see the son of a bitch. I see it!"

"What?" called back Mike Riegel, who was driving the boat.

"The missile! I see the missile!" Smith moved so quickly in his excitement that he bashed his head on the low overhead. The newest enlisted man aboard, who had not been qualified to do anything yet on his maiden voyage except look out the window, had found the Phoenix missile. As Riegel brought the boat close, Smith got a better look at his find, and whispered, "Jeez, it's big!"

Holifield ordered the boat to stop and hover, then lower cautiously to the bottom so as not to kick up a curtain of mud. The forward TV camera was trained on the missile, and he could make out the words stenciled on the side of the Phoenix: DO NOT ROLL, TUMBLE OR DROP.

The discovery set alarm bells ringing in the recovery ships, Washington, and London, and Toby Warson on the *Sunbird* was suddenly inundated by unwanted advice from surface fleet officers about how to raise the missile. They did not understand the *NR-1*, but wanted to be back in the game when credit was handed out. "A bunch of Airdales are trying to tell me how to do this and that," he complained in a call to Admiral Joe Williams, the COMSUBLANT. Williams, who was determined not to let the turf war erupt again and jeopardize the mission, started making Rickover-style telephone calls. Within twenty minutes, the irritating suggestions ceased, and Warson began receiving only the technical data that he requested.

The *NR-1* babysat the Phoenix for hours while a plan was formulated. Retrieving the missile by itself had not been part of the original recovery plan, but now that it had been located, the navy wanted it brought back. The missile seemed to be relatively undamaged, except for a hermetically sealed collar located just behind the warhead. That section contained the electronic brains of the missile and had been crushed like a tin can by the deepwater pressure, lending still more unknowns to the situation.

Fail-safe mechanisms encased in that area prevented the Phoenix from being automatically armed until it reached a certain speed or had traveled a safe distance from the plane that fired it. If those important controls had been damaged in the accident, the risk factor was substantially increased.

Holifield would not go after the missile if he thought it would endanger his men and his ship, but no one knew what would happen until he actually grabbed it. No matter what decisions were being made elsewhere about this recovery, after carefully examining the missile, he was confident that the safeties were still intact. They would go for it.

Toby Warson made an emergency call to the United States, and a team of Explosive Ordnance Disposal experts was hustled aboard a plane for an emergency flight to Scotland. Specialists would be needed to finally secure the powerful weapon.

Although the decision had been made, the sub could not simply grab the Phoenix and go, for other factors were involved. Below, Nolter's Maelstrom continued to pelt the sub periodically and added more risk to recovering the missile. They would have to work around it. Further, the navy wanted the missile to reach the surface under the cover of darkness to limit spying from the Soviet intelligence ships.

The vessels of the surface recovery task force closed in on a spot above the *NR-1*, and when the next maelstrom passed, Joe Nolter and Mike Riegel cautiously maneuvered the boat, guided by television cameras and men at the view ports, until it was centered exactly over the missile. Both the missile and the submarine's bow were pointing in the same direction. Then the massive tines in the belly of the boat were opened, and the boat settled deeper, inch by inch.

The open fingers were designed to lift much heavier loads, but it plucked up the missile as gingerly as if it were an egg. The crew took their time locking it in place, for no one wanted to take a chance on crushing or losing the weapon.

Once secure, the *NR-1* made a slow-motion climb to the distant surface, carrying in its belly a missile that contained enough explosive power to destroy the entire ship. The submarine broke onto the open sea just before midnight on October 30, in the midst of the salvage task force that had circled about to block the Soviet trawlers.

Warson was on the bridge of the *Sunbird*, which was rolling so heavily on the waves that he once again felt the strange onset of seasickness that sometimes affects submariners when they pull surface duty. There was little light, because storm clouds tearing through the skies obscured the moon. He saw the *NR-1* rise in a sudden flash of foam, but when that wash died, the sail of the tiny ship was only a small, dark spot on the ocean surface, almost invisible on the heaving sea.

Warson had to assign someone to actually dive into the chill and roiling midnight water, swim beneath the *NR-1*, and check out the missile, and of all the people aboard, he deemed himself to be best equipped to do that job. He was a qualified navy diver, and he knew the ship and the situation as well as anyone could. The heavy lift device had been installed during his command, and he knew how to avoid the unshielded "hot" radiation area around the reactor compartment, which was close to the tines. Together with Al Holifield, he could determine the next step. Rather than risk the life of another diver, the commander of the entire operation strapped on scuba gear and plunged into the North Atlantic waves.

Once below, swimming alone in the sea, he examined the long white missile from tip to tail by the narrow beam of a handheld light. Its white shell gleamed from where it was nestled snugly within the grasp of the lift device. The Phoenix was secure, and although it still looked menacing, Warson was satisfied that it was safe. It was time for him to move aside.

He went back aboard the *Sunbird* and sent their divers over the side. They attached special clamps around the missile and tied them to sturdy lines that were ferried back to the support ship. When everyone was clear, the *NR-1* opened the tines, and the big missile swung away on its cradle of ropes and clamps and was hoisted aboard the fantail of the *Sunbird*.

The only remaining problem was to make it completely safe. The demolitions experts had not arrived from the States, and a long series of complicated radio messages about connecting alligator clips to certain circuits provided only rough guidance.

There is a strong belief in the navy that a veteran chief petty officer can do almost anything, and now one stepped forward and took over the job of romancing the explosives package, although he had never before seen a Phoenix missile. He studied the engineering drawings, talked things over with experts on shore, and declared, "Okay, I can do this."

With Warson looking over his shoulder and everyone else cleared away from the fantail, the chief picked up some wire cutters and, without hesitation, snipped some circuits deep in the guts of the Phoenix missile. He then turned to Warson and reported, "Well, sir, it didn't go off."

His name may have been lost to history, but his actions polished the halo of the chiefs a little brighter that night. Chiefs can indeed do anything.

NR-1 RECOVERS PHOENIX MISSILE

The black headline over an Associated Press story from London jumped out at readers of *The Day* newspaper in New London, Connecticut, on Monday morning, November 1, 1976. Pictures would follow in coming days showing some of the officers and men of the *NR-1* and the *Sunbird* posed around the missile, with an American flag waving in the background. "Once in a while a submarine makes headlines and warrants extra attention, if not awe. Such an exceptional mission has just been completed by the *NR-1*, a small nuclear research submarine crewed by only five men," an editorial in *The Day* declared. "All in all, it was a great piece of work. Even the Russians must be applauding, however grudgingly."

The unexpected, joyous telling of the great adventure was notable for several reasons. As one news report noted, the failure of the F-14 recovery had been "a bit of an embarrassment to the navy." So plucking the missile from 1,800 feet beneath the surface was trumpeted as a huge success, and quieted the fact that the fighter plane was still down there. Moreover, it was a substantial intelligence coup to show the missile lying dry and in one piece aboard the *Sunbird*, for that let the Soviet Union know the United States Navy possessed a boat that could operate at depths unreachable by any submarine in their own inventory. It was something else for them to worry about.

Importantly, the stories and photographs brought the *NR-1* out from the dark world in which it normally sailed. Details, including calling it a "research submarine" and saying it had a crew of only five, kept much of the disguise in place, but the boat was now a visible entity that demanded watching by other fleets. How long had it been around? How deep could it *really* go? And if it could get that missile up intact, what else could it do?

By the time the newspapers appeared, the *Sunbird* already was towing the *NR-1* back to Holy Loch. The navy had abandoned all hope of getting the F-14 up in one piece, because trying to haul up a twenty-ton plane by a single strand of cable in those heavy seas was never going to work. The job was redesigned for pure muscle, not finesse, so the *NR-1* was no longer needed.

A British trawler was hired to simply haul it in, much as if it were a school of fish. The *Boston Halifax* snagged the plane in her steel trawl net twice, and both times the net broke and the plane again toppled back to the ocean floor.

Two West German salvage boats were brought in for a try. The "heavy grab ship" *Taurus* and the work ship *Twyford* spun out steel cable between them, let it sink to the bottom, and pulled the slack cable through the area until it snagged on the plane. With the *Taurus* maintaining a steady position, the *Twyford* sailed in circles to wrap the plane tightly in a shroud of steel. A fifty-ton shackle was lowered to tighten the knot, and the *Taurus* lifted the whole package to within five hundred feet of the surface. It was towed eighty miles, into waters that were shallow and calm enough for hard hat divers to get at it.

On November 11, nearly two months after it plunged from the *Kennedy* deck and eleven days after the deadline, the remains of F-14 number 159588 broke the surface, almost an unrecognizable chunk of junk from being bounced, dropped, and dragged along the bottom for so long. The wreckage was sent to Norfolk, virtually useless to the investigators trying to determine why the throttle stuck and caused the accident in the first place. The future of all F-14s remained in jeopardy until the problem could be fixed. Since the plane was utterly destroyed, the *NR-1* photographs of the switches, gauges, and open cockpit became the primary source for the information needed to identify and correct the problem and get the F-14s safely back into the skies.

The long and complicated operation had cost $2.4 million, which an article in *Reader's Digest* several months later judged to be "a small price to pay to keep invaluable secrets in American hands."

About the time of the recovery, former nuclear submarine officer Jimmy Carter was elected president of the United States—a development that guaranteed continued enthusiastic White House support for his mentor, Hyman Rickover, by now a full admiral. In Scotland, on the windswept deck of the *Sunbird,* another leader was also being put in place. The delayed change of command ceremonies finally were held for the *NR-1,* and Al Holifield handed the job over to Mike McQuown.

Holifield was the third consecutive skipper of the smallest nuclear submarine in the navy whose future career would be a series of successes, a trait that marked most of the men who served aboard the *NR-1.* He flew back to the United States immediately after the brief ceremony and began three months of study at Naval Reactors to learn the propulsion plant of his new ship, the USS *Pogy,* a full-size submarine that dwarfed the *NR-1* and had a completely different reactor. He would lead the *Pogy* for two years, proceed to command the Gold Crew of the USS *Ethan Allen,* and then rotate into the slot of intelligence officer on the COMSUBPAC staff. Holifield rounded out his career as commander of the Naval Intelligence Support Center in the Pentagon. His final boss, prior to retirement in 1991, was Admiral Dwaine Griffith.

McQuown took over a ship that was in dry dock. After the long tour working on the SOSUS network, the grueling search and salvage effort for the missing plane and missile, the underwater cyclones of Nolter's Maelstrom, and the punishment of the North Atlantic, the *NR-1* had a number of problems that needed repair and replacement before it could return home. The work was done at Holy Loch against a background of success, for the little boat had proven its capabilities even to its most severe critics and by doing so ensured its own future. The events of the past few months guaranteed funding, not the scrap heap.

The new captain, however, represented a major change, for he was not the usual low-key individual who led this unique crew.

McQuown was an intense, chain-smoking workaholic who delighted in tearing apart and putting together his MG sports car, survived mostly on coffee, and was entranced by the early computers. "You don't understand," he would tell people who were baffled by his passion for computers, which were steadily becoming smaller and more powerful. "One day everybody will have one of these on their desk!" No one questioned his integrity, his ability, or his brains, for no man was chosen to serve aboard the *NR-1* as a reward for being stupid. The Nebraskan had the same birthday, January 27, as Admiral Rickover, whom he considered to be not only God, but the entire Holy Trinity. They also shared an abrasive style of management that worked for Rickover, but proved to be McQuown's Achilles' heel.

Although he thought highly of his crew, his abrupt command style grated on some of the men from the beginning, particularly the Sperry field engineers. He believed his crew was experienced enough to handle the boat on their own and felt the civilians were more of a hindrance than a help. In the space of only a few months, both Fred DeGrooth and Roger Sherman would ask to be transferred from the boat that they had helped design, build, and run. Sherman stayed with Sperry at Electric Boat, but moved to the Trident program. Fred DeGrooth left Sperry and went to work for Electric Boat, where he remained assigned to the *NR-1* project, but in a different capacity.

McQuown had been stung and embarrassed when ordered to stand aside and let Al Holifield run the F-14 mission, one of the most important jobs ever given to the *NR-1*. And although he played an important role, he had been a supernumerary, just another member of the crew, and now as captain, he felt the need to prove something, at least to himself. When the boat cast off from Holy Loch and headed home, the new skipper was determined that his ship would be run with the precision of a Swiss clock, even on a milk run like being towed from Scotland to Connecticut.

The *Sunbird* turned her blunt nose into the Atlantic in the first week of December beneath a canopy of dark, angry skies. From her stern, an incredibly strong double-braided Samson nylon line, seven inches in diameter, was hooked to a heavy ball that was held intractably snug in the cowcatcher on the bow of the *NR-1*.

Ahead lay some 2,500 long miles of groaning, towering waves, whistling wind, and the bitter cold of a gale that was growing to hurricane strength, and as always when caught in big seas, the boat rolled and pitched, even before reaching open water. The tow ship might have to ride it out on the surface, but the *NR-1* did not have to. As soon as possible, McQuown took the submarine beneath the horrid weather, until it reached sanctuary at a comfortable depth of about 150 feet. Down there, he felt, there would be nothing but smooth sailing.

* * *

About a week after the *NR-1* left Scotland, a young sailor hurried through the corridors of Admiral Rickover's charm school in Crystal City, outside of Alexandria, Virginia, until he found the right door, knocked, and stuck his head inside. "Commander Holifield, there's a telephone call for you from Captain Darby," he said.

Al Holifield, studying in the prospective commanding officers' course, picked up the phone. "Hi, Jack," he told his old shipmate, with whom he was staying. Darby was stationed at the Pentagon. "What's up?" Darby curtly told him to hold the line, and a new voice came on, that of Admiral R.L.J. Long, the deputy chief of naval operations for submarine warfare.

"The reactor has failed on the *NR-1*," Long tersely told him. "What do we do? What do we do?"

20
LONG RIDE HOME

*L*arge waves exploded over the *Sunbird*'s bow and frothy green water sluiced along her sides as she lurched through the outer fringe of the hurricane that had taken position directly in her path across the North Atlantic. As the hours passed, the *Sunbird* pitched and rolled with increasing violence in the massive waves south of Iceland, and the ride became so rough that some smart off-duty sailors climbed into the decompression chamber, which was low and on the centerline of the ship, and the most stable place aboard. In the opinion of one officer, "The ship was getting the shit beat out of it."

From the stern of the *Sunbird* stretched the long braided nylon cable that reached far beneath the surface and was tugging the *NR-1* along the endless miles. Even 150 feet below the storm, the *NR-1* could feel the surge of the large waves, but it glided smoothly ahead, no matter what hell was descending on the tow ship. Being sheltered from foul weather was one of the best things about submarines.

The *NR-1* crew preferred being right where they were, coasting comfortably along, rather than being up where the *Sunbird* was being slammed. The *Sunbird*'s sailors were a bit envious, but that feeling came to an immediate halt when the ship got an emergency call on the underwater telephone from Mike McQuown.

A circuit breaker had blown on one of the control rods in the submarine's nuclear power plant, safety mechanisms had simultaneously dropped the rest of rods, and the reactor automatically "scrammed," or shut down. In the middle of the ocean, hovering in waters some eighteen thousand feet deep, the *NR-1* went virtually dead. As the ships came to a sliding halt, the *Sunbird* sailors reevaluated their situation—they would rather be seasick any day than trapped below the surface aboard a malfunctioning nuke.

The *NR-1* switched to battery power and when the dim emergency lights flickered on, Engineering Officer Mike Riegel and two reactor control technicians searched for the problem, tracking it to the blown circuit breaker. Riegel, a neat and deliberate professional, always chose his words carefully, and based his opinions only on facts. His quiet report to the new captain was pessimistic. "I don't know the extent of the damage for certain, and I don't know how long it will take to fix it, so we need to get the electrical load down as far as we can."

The loss of reactor power was not in itself cause for alarm, for the batteries could provide temporary emergency power. All nuclear submarine crews trained rigorously for such a situation, and under established procedures, the decision to restart the reactor had to be made within an hour of the shutdown. If it could not be brought back on line during that time, then the ship must be taken to the closest available port.

The *NR-1* had run numerous tests, both at dockside and at sea, to determine how long it could operate just on the batteries. With careful conservation and minimal power use, the ship could, in theory, last a couple of days.

Al Holifield briefed the admiral in Washington on the procedures for handling a scrammed reactor, and when he learned that an hour had already passed before he got the news, he believed that the emergency was probably already over. "You don't do anything. If you haven't heard from them by now, they've either fixed it or have already committed to be towed to the nearest port. Everything is probably okay."

But Holifield had not been given the entire scenario. There was no nearby port, for the *NR-1* was trapped beneath angry waves, a thousand miles from anywhere. Even if the tow was resumed, the process of reaching safe shelter would take much longer than the few days the *NR-1* could last submerged, operating only on batteries, and coming to the surface in such a storm-whipped sea was out of the question. The established procedures were unworkable.

Riegel and the reactor control technicians worked in near darkness on the breaker panel while a worried Mike McQuown hovered nearby, writing detailed notes about what they were doing, what they found, what they thought. The captain knew he would face an official inquiry when they finally arrived at the sub base, and he would need precise answers. Rickover would have questions!

After removing the failed circuit breaker unit from the panel, Riegel searched through the ship's spare parts inventory and found that they had no replacement aboard. It was a common item with a low failure rate, and designed to be replaced as an entire unit by one carried in the equipment van, not disassembled on ship and repaired piece by piece.

The engineer told the skipper they now had only two choices—figure out how to repair it with the tools and materials on hand, or abandon ship.

There was a growing sense of urgency. Every moment that passed, the precious, irreplaceable electric power supplied by the ship's batteries was draining away.

McQuown ordered all unnecessary electrical loads secured. There would be no warm drinks, nor heated food. Even small panel lights that were not essential were unscrewed. Without the heaters, the frigid temperature of the surrounding sea penetrated the submarine's hull with ease, and warmth vanished. Everything inside grew cold to the touch, and in the dim light, the crew saw their exhaled breath in the thick, moist air, and each breath sucked up a bit more of the life-supporting oxygen.

"This is lovely," Frank Smith muttered to himself as he crawled through the boat, unscrewing little light bulbs, disconnecting fans, and hunting any small electrical load that could be disconnected. His first trip on the NR-1 had turned into something he would remember forever.

"We're lost down here and have no electrical power," he thought as he climbed into a bunk and pulled up a blanket. The narrow interior of the NR-1 seemed smaller than ever when lit only by dim battle lanterns, the utter silence was disconcerting, and the air was getting funky.

Lithium hydroxide, a white powdery substance carried aboard all submarines for emergency atmosphere control, was spread on the forward compartment decks to absorb the rising level of carbon dioxide, and everyone not on watch or necessary to fixing the problem was sent to the bunks or view port pads. No one could close their eyes, but at least they stayed warm under blankets, were out of the way, and produced less of the suffocating CO_2.

They tried not to envision the danger of abandoning ship, climbing out of that single hatch while the boat was being thrown about in a hurricane.

The time passed slowly as Riegel and an electrician continued to dissect the breaker and finally discovered that one of the solid silver contacts that allowed electricity to flow had partially burned away. Using a file, the engineer carefully began shaping the burned contact so that it would once again exactly fit its mating counterpart so as to reestablish the circuit.

As McQuown watched the slow process, he was alerted by a crewman when more than half of the electrical power stored in the fully charged *NR-1* battery had been consumed. It was still another critical moment, for the life support system was not the only important need. The sub was nearing the point at which there would not be enough battery power left to get the reactor started. That would create a virtually impossible situation in which the reactor could not restart without sufficient battery power, and the weakened battery could not provide the electrical current needed until the reactor was back on line to recharge it.

Riegel and McQuown discussed the deteriorating problem. When the breaker was repaired, there probably would be enough battery power left to take the reactor critical, but the officers knew that a lot of additional electricity would be needed to run the reactor pumps, motors, and instrumentation when they pulled the control rods to get the nuclear power plant back to a self-sustaining condition.

Once the nuclear reaction began, it would heat the cooling water within the reactor vessel, and it could quickly reach a boil unless it was kept under sufficient pressure. The readings in the pressurizer unit had dropped well below the limits for safe operation while they worked, and the disappearing electrical charge meant there was not going to be enough power available to raise pressure to those limits again.

"We got as much out of the battery as we could to get the pressure back, but that was it," Frank Smith said. "We weren't there."

Without adequate pressure, the water inside the reactor would boil and create bubbles that could cause massive surges in the power level, which could trigger a catastrophic steam explosion.

Such a detonation could fracture the reactor vessel itself or rupture the coolant piping. Then the highly radioactive cooling water would run out into the ship, and a core meltdown would begin within the reactor.

The fate of everyone on board would be sealed. They would be forced to surface and abandon ship immediately, no matter what the weather conditions. The *NR-1* would sink and become a radioactive hulk at the bottom of the sea.

There was no way to know how the plant would react during the dangerous period before it was able to produce enough electricity to fully heat the pressurizer. Never in the history of the nuclear navy had such a risky restart been tried.

Riegel eventually finished his delicate task and placed the reassembled breaker back into the panel and wired it up. Now the decision was up to the captain. Using the underwater telephone lash-up to the *Sunbird* and Washington, McQuown had earlier obtained permission to deviate from the established procedures in order to fix the breaker, and to abandon his ship if he could not. But things had grown much more serious—they had passed the point of no return. There was no time to ask permission again. They would only lose more precious battery power if they had to wait, perhaps for hours, for people who were far away to make a decision.

What confronted Mike McQuown was far beyond the sacred parameters of the manual. He could follow the rigid reactor plant rules, in which case he must surface his powerless submarine immediately and try to abandon ship in the fierce storm waiting above them. That would almost certainly result in the loss of life among the crew, as well as the loss of the first ship under his command.

Or he could tempt fate by starting a nuclear power plant that was not sufficiently pressurized. It might work, but even if it did, he would have violated ironclad safety procedures and placed his ship and his men in jeopardy. Either way, he almost certainly would lose his job. He knew of no instance in which the careers of the captain or the engineer of a nuclear power vessel had survived a violation of the written reactor plant procedures. There were many well-documented cases where they had not.

He was faced with a situation for which there was no right answer. But at least trying to save the ship was preferable to abandoning it as a powerless hulk in the midst of a hurricane. Things would be easier to explain if they managed to bring the boat back under its own power. He did not want to contemplate what would happen if his choice was wrong.

"Well," Riegel asked, "How ballsy do you feel?"

McQuown had mulled over all the possibilities many times and made up his mind. He barked, "Maneuvering, commence a reactor start-up!"

The engineer moved to the reactor panel, normally the station for an enlisted man. Riegel would do this himself. "No sense spreading the blame," he thought, and started pulling the rods.

The reactor went critical and started heating the coolant while all eyes locked on the gauges and dial indicators. No one spoke as Riegel nursed the temperature up. Carefully, they started the turbine generator, began to make electricity again and heated the pressurizer. There were no surges, no sudden spikes, and no explosion.

They made it!

The *Sunbird* passed the word to Washington that the *NR-1* reactor was back on line, but neither they nor the Pentagon knew the details of what had happened. They tugged the slack out of the towline, felt the *NR-1* pull at the far end, and the tow got under way again. The seas were still raging, but they figured to be home in a week.

At the other end of the towline, McQuown started composing the most important message of his life—the one explaining to Admiral Rickover just how far over the line he had gone to bring the small reactor back to life. It felt as if he were writing his own epitaph. When he completed the draft message, he slept fitfully for a while, and went to the table and edited it again before picking up the telephone and reading it to Ed Craig, the CO of the *Sunbird*, for relay to Washington.

After transmitting the message, acknowledging his violations of The Book, McQuown could not sleep at all. He simply withdrew inward as he waited in agony for a response. The silence from Washington was ominous.

When the distant emergency was over, Al Holifield again buckled into his studies at the PCO course in Crystal City. Then came another knock on his door, and once again, a yeoman entered with a message. "Commander Holifield, you have a telephone call." This time, Admiral

Long was already on the other end, and wasted no time with pleasantries. The news was even worse than before.

"We've lost the *NR-1*!" the admiral said. "What do we do?"

Holifield wanted to know what was meant by "lost." There had been some sort of accident at sea—the towline snapped, both propellers and the rudder on the submarine had become fouled in the line, and nothing had been heard from it since it submerged. The *Sunbird* had lost all contact.

Again, Holifield counseled prudence and patience. Remember that this is not only a submarine, but a submersible too, he said. It can trim up at a precise depth and just sit there, if the reactor is still providing power, for as long as necessary. "They're probably down there playing cribbage," he advised. "All you have to do is keep track of them."

That's the problem, the admiral responded. There was no sign of her—none at all. The heavy seas had separated the *NR-1* from the *Sunbird* and it was not responding to calls. All along the eastern seaboard, submarines and surface ships began putting to sea. Their mission—find the *NR-1*.

A day after the reactor incident, and even deeper in the Atlantic, the towline had parted where it chafed at the stern of the *Sunbird*. The severed rope had snapped back so hard that it knocked out a sailor on the support ship. Two shipmates had to grab him before he was washed overboard.

The titanium ball to which the other end of the line was attached was still hooked in the cowcatcher on the bow of the submerged *NR-1*, and the loose Samson line drifted aft alongside the submarine. While under tow, the *NR-1* left its engines idle, but the water passing through the screws kept the two propellers spinning freely. As the drifting line came down the starboard side, it was sucked into, then through, the turning propeller, which wound it up like a fishing reel. The submarine was forced to surface and try to free the screw and to establish a new tow.

They came up in the middle of the hurricane. Winds sliced off the tops of huge waves, and the little boat was barely able to keep forward momentum with its single operable propeller. It was being hurled about by the mountainous seas, but managed to keep contact with the *Sunbird*, which frantically tried to stay close. If they could free the tangled line, another would be shot across and reattached.

McQuown pulled on foul-weather gear, snapped into a safety harness on the bridge, and edged over the side of the conning tower to the dancing hull. Water sluiced over, around, and above the boat as the captain worked his way forward step by agonizing step to the cowcatcher, moving slowly and using every handhold he could find along the smooth, slick fiberglass deck.

As the boat rose and fell, nosing into the waves, water pounded him and the wind tried to blow him away. McQuown unfolded his navy pocketknife and with one hand keeping the safety line in a death grip, he used the other to hack and slice at the long white nylon hawser that was stretched tight as a banjo string. Progress was measured strand by braided strand, but the cut got deeper, until, with a final chop, the line popped apart and disappeared over the side.

Instead of relief, McQuown felt a growing sense of horror as the big rope was caught by the rushing seas and ripped toward the stern, not on the starboard side, where it was already entangled, but on the port side. In seconds, it was swallowed by the one remaining spinning propeller, which grabbed it hungrily and tied it into knots. As it caught, the line was stretched tighter and tighter across the rudder, and the *NR-1* went dead in the water.

With its skipper still clinging to the foredeck, the ship lost all forward momentum and slewed sideways, at the mercy of the oncoming seas. One crewman swore the waves were fifty feet high, and by the time McQuown reached the safety of the bridge, the boat was wallowing in dangerous, violent rolls.

There was only one thing to do—get off the surface—and the submarine dove for safety, without any propulsion or steering power. As soon as the hatch was closed, the boat flooded its ballast tanks and sank beneath the storm. At least they were off the raging surface. Although the seas above were tormented, there was very little motion within the ship.

Again and again, McQuown called the *Sunbird* on the underwater telephone. There was no response. Ed Craig on the support ship had also been trying to establish contact with the *NR-1*, with the identical result. While they had been separated, the ships had been pushed farther apart by the unyielding winds and heavy, rolling seas. Once the boat submerged, radio communication was impossible.

Within minutes, the *NR-1* was caught by the powerful Gulf Stream, which was as potent below as the hurricane was above. The submarine, with its propellers and rudder inoperable, was pushed one way by the underwater current, while surface winds shoved the *Sunbird* farther away by the minute.

"Okay, so we're completely helpless. We've lost communication and we can't steer," Frank Smith told himself, as once again, he was ordered back into a bunk. All they could do now was wait it out.

Holifield's prediction was accurate, that there was no danger of sinking. Barring some other disaster, they could just bob there indefinitely. Sooner or later, the storm would calm and they could go up again and fix things and go home. "The people above us are going to be more nervous than the people here in the boat. Somebody will find us."

After the first day below, rocking and helpless, he wasn't so sure.

"There has been an incident," Admiral Joe Williams picked his words carefully as he spoke to JoAnn McQuown. To the wife of the captain of the *NR-1*, the gruff voice of COMSUBLANT seemed to carry mixed feelings of sympathy, optimism, and worry, and it was all she could do to keep from dropping the telephone.

"We've tried everything, but we have lost communication with the *NR-1*," he said. "We have deployed people from Connecticut to Florida to search for it. Thirty boats are out there."

The admiral had a request. As the captain's wife, it would be better if she, not some unknown man, even some admiral, called the wives of the other crew members to tell them what was going on. Bad news was easier to take when delivered with the sensitivity of a woman.

Mike McQuown had proposed to JoAnn five days after they met, when she was teaching at Fitch High School in Groton. She had said "yes" five days later and they were married a week after his boat, the USS *Flasher*, was commissioned at New London. When he flew to California for his next assignment, she traveled across the country aboard a Greyhound bus, and for ten years, she had been a submariner's wife, following him to Hawaii to Newport News and back to Connecticut. She was well versed in the rules and lingo of the trade, knew not to ask where he had been for months while off on some spook mission, and didn't make improper inquiries when he brought some mysterious stranger into their home.

JoAnn McQuown had been part of the *NR-1* family from the very start because her father was the materials supervisor at Electric Boat when it was being built and had regaled his family with tales of a small, secret submarine. She had been pleased when Mike got command of the boat, which she felt would be worthy of his extraordinary skills, but she also watched it change him. When he returned from his first training mission, he was not able to get comfortable in his bed, but slept instead on the floor, wedged tightly between a couple of chairs with a loud alarm clock right next to his ear. As much as anyone, and more than most, she knew this small boat was dangerous.

She realized that her husband's duty also carried a terrible responsibility for her, too. "Yes," she said, "I'll call them all. That's my job." The final words of Admiral Williams were like an icy stake through her heart. "Be proud of him," he said.

It sounded so . . . final.

Mike McQuown was feeling totally jinxed. This was the cruise from hell. First the reactor scram would have to be explained, and now he also would have to describe for the admirals how he personally managed to hog-tie his own boat in the middle of a hurricane. By the end of the second day, the captain thought that if by some miracle he got back to the United States, he probably would not have to worry about his job because the navy might just march him in front of a firing squad.

Even the normally affable engineering officer, Mike Riegel, began to worry as the long hours passed. He kept a close eye on the reactor because he knew that if they lost power again, they would have to surface and abandon ship. Without the *Sunbird* around to help, there would be no hope of immediate rescue, and no one could last long in that terrible freezing sea. He noticed that they had run out of coffee and so to take his mind off a problem he could not solve, he spent hours rummaging through the dry Vietnam-style long range patrol rations to remove the packets of instant, and divided them equally among the coffee drinkers aboard. They could only wait for conditions above to change.

It took another three days before the weather eased enough for the *NR-1* to once again surface. The boat came up, still crippled by the lines, but able to radio for help. The *Sunbird* heard the call and Ed Craig pushed his ship hard to get back to where the *NR-1* was wallowing in winds and weather. What the surface boat regarded as relatively calm was a pitching nightmare for the little sub.

The first job was to reestablish a towline, and the *Sunbird* prepared to shoot a ball over. In the churning seas, there was no chance at all of looping the new line over the sub where it could be grabbed and locked into the cowcatcher. Somebody needed to go into the water, and Frank Smith, a qualified navy diver, volunteered. Wearing a life vest, he hooked a safety line to the deck and leaped into the angry ocean.

As soon as he hit the water, a big wave collapsed onto the *NR-1* and the submarine disappeared beneath it. Smith, a tough sailor who was confident in his diving ability, suddenly found himself alone in the sea, far from the *Sunbird*, and felt the safety line attached to the submarine tighten. He took a big gulp of air just before the boat pulled him beneath the surface. Down he went, praying that he could hold his breath until the *NR-1* could come back up.

The men aboard the *Sunbird* wrapped the ball in ten life jackets and floated it toward the sub. Smith scrambled to reach it, and it took all his strength to get enough slack in the line to force the ball into the cowcatcher—a feat he later would consider to be physically impossible. He worked his way back to the bridge and went down the hatch, wondering if every voyage he took on the *NR-1* was going to be like this.

Smith later would marry the dark-haired niece of Mike McQuown's wife.

A lurching tow was restored and the *Sunbird* hauled the *NR-1* to a rendezvous with other search vessels, and in the protected waters provided by the lee sides of those ships, divers could unsnarl the lines that hobbled the submarine. Mike Riegel made certain that the first diver who swam over carried a waterproof package of coffee. McQuown anxiously asked the *Sunbird* captain if there were any messages from Rickover or his NR people regarding the reactor incident. There were none.

Working with saws and knives, five divers clustered around the screws and chopped away the entangling lines as waves swirled about and over them. The line was cut free, but severe damage had been done. When the *NR-1* got under way again, its rudder was stuck in a position that forced the submarine to veer to the right, while the whole ship listed sharply to the left.

As the slow tow progressed, a peculiar convoy formed around the two ships. The attack submarine *Narwhal* was stationed to one side, and another sub, the *Billfish*, went to the far flank. A fleet oiler positioned herself in front, the submarine rescue vessel ship *Kittiwake* joined up, the ammunition ship *Mount Baker* took station, and as the *Sunbird* completed the final leg of her journey, more and more ships clustered about in a tight escort. They were determined not to lose the *NR-1* again.

For Mike McQuown, the remaining days spent in transit were torture. Home meant nothing but trouble, and the captain was morose as he stood on the freezing cold bridge while the *NR-1* made its final turn out of the Race and was pushed up the Thames by a tugboat toward its home pier. He knew that he had much to answer for, and had heard nothing from Rickover. Frankly, he wished that this final part of the trip had lasted longer, storm or no storm, so as to delay the inevitable. He was certain that the end of the ride would also be the end of his career. At least he could take some comfort in the fact that his ship and his men had made it back. It was Wednesday, December 15. They would all be home for Christmas.

He could not make out the bustle going on around Pier Eight of the sub base as the boat came into the Sub Squadron Two area. There were a lot of people there. Waving. Color. Flags. A change of the wind brought the sound of music. Trumpets and drums. He picked up his binoculars.

A line of women and kids were at the waterfront, standing and waving before a row of white-capped naval officers. The families were all there, and each held a cardboard square with a letter on it, spelling out WELL DONE NR1. Admiral Williams stood forward, a white scarf tucked into the neck of his blue winter coat. In the hands of his aides were medals and awards for every member of the crews of both the *NR-1* and the *Sunbird*, and he personally planned to pin a Presidential Meritorious Service Medal to the chest of Mike McQuown.

The *NR-1* had arrived home, and with the full approval of Admiral Rickover, it received the first brass band welcome given any American submarine since the end of the Second World War.

21
ENDGAME

*T*he *NR-1* had accomplished its most difficult and successful military missions to date during the 101 days it spent working out of Scotland in 1976, proving its versatility at the very time the U.S. Navy was evolving into a new role.

Vietnam was over, but many years would pass before the navy fully escaped that war's impact. To save money, Presidents Lyndon Johnson, Richard Nixon, and Jimmy Carter all wielded sharp knives on the Pentagon budget, particularly on the costly building of new ships.

That gave new importance to maintaining the ships that were already in existence, and each ship was examined to see what role it might play in the future to justify its cost.

Eleven years had passed since Electric Boat delivered the *NR-1* to the navy, and although it was never an official part of the war fleet, the boat had carved its own niche, a role so vital and unusual that the navy was willing to spend precious dollars on it, sometimes at the expense of bigger ships.

The *NR-1* not only could point to its special and covert operations, but also to its growing popularity among scientists, whose home institutions such as universities and research labs helped pay for its missions. The sub had proven that it could still perform military jobs while simultaneously advancing the frontiers of science, and anything the scientists learned on the bottom of the ocean might have potential military applications. New minerals, underwater pathways, currents, and photography techniques, and the use of robots and advanced sonar and computers all promised substantial military benefits. The smallest nuclear submarine in the U.S. Navy would help blaze a trail into a new generation of naval operations.

When the time came in the 1980s to decide the future of each of the navy's 119 submarines, the *Nautilus*, the historic pioneer of nuclear power, was decommissioned at Mare Island, while the *NR-1* was updated and assigned new missions. The *Sunbird* became its primary support ship.

During 1977, oceanographer Bruce Heezen died on board, and his passing seemed to mark the end of the strict military usage of the boat. He and Charles Hollister of Woods Hole had been the first scientists allowed to use the *NR-1*, and their ability to keep secret any military matters they encountered bridged a gap of Pentagon skepticism. Their book, revised to include what they had learned while riding aboard the *NR-1*, became an ocean industry standard. Although the official navy still did not encourage "dual use"—both scientific and military—of its warships of the line, the *NR-1* was proving that such a role was possible. Its roster of embarked personnel had for some time regularly included oceanographers, marine biologists, geologists, geophysicists, engineers, technicians of various sorts, and even graduate students, and none had surrendered any secrets that jeopardized security.

The navy's gradual acceptance of new ideas mirrored exciting discoveries that were being made in the deep oceans. The latest version of the *Alvin*, from Woods Hole, found warm springs on the crust of the Pacific seafloor that teemed with unexpected life forms such as tube worms, then encountered mineral chimneys that spewed black smoke and water that was hot enough to melt lead. Once again the unknown beckoned from the deep, and the *NR-1* was one of the few vessels that could answer the call.

By the dawn of the 1980s, the boat once again had faded into that comfortable dark background where it operated best, becoming a dim presence even while taking selected scientists on voyages of exploration. It ran two special ops of a completely classified military nature in the Atlantic during 1981, and while it was gone, a monumental change occurred.

Ronald Reagan became president of the United States that year and brought in John Lehman, a young and brash fighter pilot, as his secretary of the navy. It was Lehman's task to reverse the decline of the fleet, and backed by the deep pockets of the Reagan administration, he laid plans for a six-hundred-ship navy that would feature fifteen carrier battle groups and one hundred nuclear-powered attack submarines. That fleet would be able to project U.S. presence and power anywhere on the globe.

The emphasis would not only be on carriers and their escorts, for Reagan's arms buildup would also expand espionage and intelligence activities for undersea craft. An accompanying decision to extend the nation's offshore rights in a U.S. Exclusive Economic Zone in effect doubled the size of the country and reversed the Nixon doctrine that there was nothing down there worth exploring. The announcement immediately fueled new military, commercial, and scientific interest in undersea exploration, creating even more work for the *NR-1*.

Lehman, who personified the "New Navy," recognized that there was only one man who could derail his dreams—a singular officer who had bedeviled shipbuilders, contractors, governmental officials, and big-ship admirals for decades, a man who viewed Lehman to be nothing more than an upstart, a passing nuisance. The man had accomplished great things, had committed grievous sins, and, in the view of many, had outlived his welcome and his usefulness.

Admiral Hyman Rickover would have no place in Lehman's navy. He had to go.

On a wintry day, the old man wandered aimlessly around the grounds outside the West Wing of the White House, having been summoned by Lehman to a meeting with the secretary and the president. Rickover's hatred of showing his credentials, having to prove who he was to underlings, was sharply tested that day at the big gates, where uniformed Secret Service guards demanded his identification. They knew who he was, and he was on the expected list, but nevertheless they required him to show his ID.

He walked slowly down the curving black driveway toward the small West Wing portico where two marine guards in dress blues stood at attention, flanking the entrance. He had visited many presidents and knew that inside that portal were more Secret Service guards, a small desk where he would be required to sign in, and phalanxes of aides, escorts, functionaries, and political folderol. For a man who could pick up a telephone and shake giant corporations with one of his famous tirades, the admiral considered having to jump through such hoops to be a gratuitous insult. He circled about the cold lawn as a chill breeze picked at his sparse gray hair, and huddled deep into his long black overcoat. Rickover was not scared. He was angry.

A passing reporter recognized and greeted him. "What are you doing out here all alone, Admiral?"

"Can you get in there?" Rickover nodded toward the guards.

"Sure, but I don't go through that door."

"Take me in," Rickover said.

The reporter escorted the admiral through the nearby unguarded entrance to the pressroom and every newsman and newswoman present snapped to alert as the thin old man walked through the back corridors and was handed off to an astonished White House staff member. Within minutes, he was in the Oval Office, having bypassed several layers of bureaucracy, and the news was out. Rickover was meeting with Reagan. *What's that about?* Notes were made, telephones were dialed, questions were asked, and word spread to Capitol Hill and the Pentagon. Any hope of keeping the meeting secret evaporated.

What followed was perhaps the most antagonizing and explosive session Reagan ever encountered in his private office. Shortly after the handshakes and cordial welcome by the friendly president, who could charm anyone, things went to hell. Lehman tried to couch the official firing in glowing accolades and promises of perks, but Rickover would have none of it. He snarled, "Mr. President, that pissant knows nothing about the navy!"

That sort of language was never used in Reagan's Oval Office, where decorum covered even the harshest political disagreements. Rickover flew into full rage. "He's a goddamn liar," Rickover bellowed. "He knows he is just doing the work of the contractors! The contractors want me fired because I am the only one in the government who keeps them from robbing the program!"

Lehman would write in his autobiography that he couldn't believe his ears. He and Rickover had met several times to discuss the retirement and the navy secretary thought the admiral had already come to grips with his fate. This White House meeting was supposed to be little more than a photo op during which Reagan shook hands with and profusely thanked Rickover for his long service to his country.

That part of the event had been carried out with only a bit of polite chatter.

When the photographers were gone, Rickover bored into Reagan with a vengeance and Lehman silently prayed for a hole to open into which he could just disappear. Senior presidential aides were looking at the secretary of the navy so sternly that Lehman needed a double shot of whiskey that night to calm his nerves. Rickover's tirade went on for five minutes, the insults getting ever more strident. "Are you a man?" he demanded of the president of the United States. "Can't you make decisions yourself?" He compared the similarity of their ages. "They say you are too old and that you're not up to the job either."

When Reagan tried to diplomatically say that Rickover wasn't exactly being fired, that the administration could use his services in other ways, the admiral snapped, "Aw, cut the crap!" He demanded and got a private fifteen-minute meeting, but Reagan refused to retreat in the face of the onslaught. When it was done, Rickover returned to his Spartan office and had aides hunt up the official photograph of John Lehman and a portrait of the traitor Benedict Arnold. He hung them side by side.

Rickover could have retired in 1952 at three-quarters pay, but instead, thirty years later, he had to be forcibly kicked out of his powerful position, and chose to go out with guns blazing. Without his work, the admiral withered. Hyman Rickover died in 1986 and was buried with full military honors, eulogized as a paradoxical visionary.

A by-product of the admiral's infamous confrontation with the president was that the *NR-1* lost its grumpy godfather, but by then, things were changing so rapidly that Rickover's stormy departure was hardly noticed. The USS *Ohio*, first of the new generation of massive Trident submarines, was launched, and within two years the Tomahawk cruise missile became operational from submarines. Subs were no longer mere shoot-and-scoot vessels, but formidable strategic weapons with global reach.

An unknown author named Tom Clancy published his first book in 1984, and with the success of *The Hunt for Red October*, the public became hooked on the drama of underwater military operations. Buried deep in that popular book was a passing mention of the *NR-1*.

About the same time, an enigmatic scientist named Robert Ballard was allowed to use a U.S. Navy submersible robot, the *Argo*, to find and photograph the sunken submarine *Thresher*. In the years to come, Ballard would strengthen his work with naval ships and publish almost as many books as Clancy.

The intelligence community felt that the work of both men sent messages to Moscow that the Soviet Navy could not compete with the undersea capabilities of the Americans.

While Clancy branched off into other fields of fiction, Ballard stayed with the underwater world, a talented modern explorer with the deft public relations touch of Jacques Cousteau and the media savvy of Carl Sagan. When he used the *Argo* to discover the broken wreckage of the *Titanic*, two miles below the surface, Ballard's professional legend was secure, but the fantastic discovery only whetted his appetite for more. He was a young man at the time, and his career was far from complete. Within a few years, he would direct the *Argo* to descend three miles, where it found the World War II German battleship *Bismarck*.

One of the most horrendous scenes ever televised live occurred in 1986, when the much-publicized space shuttle *Challenger* blew up shortly after it was launched from Cape Kennedy. Pieces of the doomed spacecraft splashed into the Atlantic, and a navy task force was assigned to the recovery mission, for somewhere on the ocean floor was the reason behind the tragedy. In a familiar scenario, the surface ships were scattered by foul weather, but on the bottom, the *NR-1* crawled and flew around and recovered significant pieces of the wreckage, including part of the solid rocket booster engine containing an intact portion of the failed O-ring that caused the disaster.

President Reagan almost reached his goal of having a 600-ship navy, but at a fantastic cost. In 1987, the fleet had 594 active units, including 139 submarines...not counting the *NR-1*, which was still off the books. The defense budget had ballooned to $274 billion, more than 27 percent of all federal spending, and the government was operating with a soaring deficit. The finances of the country were being strained.

Reagan-era defense spending will be debated for many years to come, both for the impact it had on the federal budget and for the way it presaged a sharp reduction in the military threat of the Soviet Union. Moscow's wobbly economy could not match such a spending spree. Communism wavered, then collapsed, and by 1989 the Cold War was over.

The value of such work as Ballard's finally tilted the navy, which no longer faced the possibility of a pitched Midway-style battle at sea, to embrace the "dual use" concept and led to a growing partnership that allowed not only robots, but also ships of the line, to participate in missions that were not totally of military value. Even attack subs soon would be carrying scientists to regions and depths to which they never before had access.

It was inevitable that Bob Ballard would ride the *NR-1*, and when he decided to inspect ancient shipwrecks in the Mediterranean, he entered the home turf of the navy's littlest Cold Warrior.

The personable Ballard coaxed the navy into lending him the boat as a way of keeping it ready for military operations, then talked financial supporters into sponsoring his exceptional searches and adventures. He had been familiar with the boat for some time, for as a naval reserve officer, he had worked in the intelligence world under the command of Dwaine Griffith.

After his early serious undersea scientific work and his find of the *Titanic* and other vessels, Ballard saw the *NR-1* as a way to expand his brand of exploration. Able to carry more than one or two scientists at a time to extraordinary depths and linger indefinitely over a shipwreck, the boat was a natural match for the man. He would come to call the *NR-1* the Rolls Royce of undersea vehicles. They first partnered up on the "Jason Project," and in the final decade of the twentieth century, the explorer and the revolutionary submarine would dive many times to study the remains of vessels that plied the ageless trade routes of the Med.

Their success was overwhelming. With the nuclear staying power, the view ports, the recovery apparatus, and the modern sonar and communications, Ballard personally was able to study ships that were more than two thousand years old and had sunk long before Christ was born. Many civilizations had sailed these very routes, and Ballard and the *NR-1* made so many discoveries they could not log them all. Archaeology and oceanographic research had never had a tool that extended its reach into such places, and Ballard noted in wonder after one mapping project, "We were finding a Roman ship every other day with this submarine, until we finally said, 'Stop.'"

At one point, he was allowed to bring reporter and author William J.

Broad of the *New York Times* aboard, and Broad made the first full public report of the boat and its characteristics in 1995. With navy approval, the sub emerged from the secrecy in which it had spent so many years, and publications ranging from college alumni magazines to *Popular Science* to *National Geographic* would pull that curtain further aside. Some diehard admirals in the Polaris Marching and Chowder Society perceived such stories to be a breach of security, with a touch of treason.

But the navy knew it could still impose secrecy when it was needed. All the *NR-1* had to do for a covert mission was paint the sail black, hook up to a support ship, and go away for a while. Without the Soviet intelligence trawlers around to track and molest its operations, it was easier than ever to carry out special jobs.

Over time, some of its secret missions would come to light, such as the search for the sunken Israeli submarine *Dakar* and the recovery of equipment from a downed F-15, but many more of the submarine's assignments continue to be classified. Ballard and other scientists would uncover history, but never give up the boat's secrets. The mystery has been maintained for decades.

Crew members usually fared well after their tours aboard the *NR-1*. They had the aptitude and attitude needed to become successful anywhere when they were selected for that special ship's duty, and the responsibilities thrust upon them while on board tested their mettle and honed their skills. The path for most officers leaving the *NR-1* led to command of a full-size nuclear submarine and swift elevation in rank. A number of admirals have had *NR-1* experience in their background.

The men chosen for the original crew—the plank owners—continued to achieve. Admiral Dwaine Griffith ran the navy's deep submergence operation for many years, even after he retired, and played an important role in navy intelligence. Captain Jack Maurer was CO of the USS *Parche* and of Submarine Development Group I, and some of his daring exploits were detailed in the book *Blind Man's Bluff* by Sherry Sontag and Christopher Drew.

Captain Steve Perry became vice president for operations of a major utility with multiple nuclear power plants in the Midwest after commanding both a submarine and a submarine tender.

Many of the enlisted men became officers. Bob Lunt became a lieutenant commander and was appointed to the selection board for enlisted personnel seeking to become warrant officers and limited duty officers. He believed that "being on the operating crew of the *NR-1* was an automatic" when it came to making those appointments. Dan Gunter qualified as OOD on board the USS *Whale* and exchanged his silver dolphins for gold; he eventually rose to the rank of commander and was the officer in charge of the Submarine Support Group at the huge U.S. Navy base at Subic Bay, in the Philippines, after the Mount Pinatubo eruption. Other plank owners, including Larry Kammerzell, Dean Paine, Dave Seaton, Don Marks, and Jim Turner, went to work in the civilian nuclear power industry, where they moved into management and consulting positions. John Claytor became the manager of information technology for a large library system in central Florida.

It was the same for the three original Sperry field engineers. Roger Sherman remained with Sperry and became the manager of the Trident Submarine Navigation Subsystem field office at Electric Boat. Fred De-Grooth worked for Electric Boat on the *NR-1* project until 1994. Brian Wruble left Sperry in 1970 and went to Wall Street, where he founded an investment management firm that grew to $40 billion in assets.

I left Electric Boat in 1977 to become project manager of the Sperry Marine Systems Iranian Navy Gyrocompass Repair Facility being constructed at Bandar Abbas. In November of 1978, I landed in Tehran en route to inspect the site near the mouth of the Persian Gulf, and right away realized things had gone wrong in a big way. The next day, with fundamentalist Islamic leaders fueling a rebellion and riots in the streets, the Shah of Iran abruptly left the country.

My bosses back in the States, who were watching television news reports of hotels being sacked, furniture being burned, and the hostile treatment being given Westerners, called and ordered me to leave as soon as possible. I had come a long way and wanted to complete my assignment, so I delayed one fateful day, long enough to have an Iranian soldier arrive at the hotel and point a machine gun at my stomach as I was leaving for the airport. By then, all of the U.S. airlines had halted their flights, and only with luck did I manage to reserve the last available seat on the last British Airways plane out.

It was a first-class ticket, but I no longer cared about the expense account. The cabin was jammed with the most unlikely refugees, as wealthy Iranians fled the new regime carrying as much as they could in gold, cash, furs, and jewels.

In my remaining time with Sperry, I designed and tested navigation equipment for the Swimmer Delivery Vehicles that were used by our scuba diving Special Forces in Panama and Grenada, and in raids on Libya. I helped prepare the vehicles for those missions. By the end of my career with the company, I was the marketing manager for Sperry submarine periscopes and navigation equipment sales.

Later, I built a fifty-person software development firm that specialized in navy financial management applications, sold it, and decided to write a book about a little submarine few people knew even existed. From the start of my working life until today, through many places and jobs, I have always been, and will always be, a submariner.

The years of the late twentieth century seemed to pass with increasing swiftness. The once feared Red Fleet was reduced to something in the history books, and the U.S. Navy's emphasis changed from blunt-force confrontation on the high seas to stealth and the ability to assert power in regional conflicts.

At least one thing stayed virtually the same—the *NR-1*. Although it has undergone many modifications and improvements over the years to perform new tasks, it still looks about as it did on the cold launch day when it first slid into the Thames River. Its orange conning tower is no longer a curiosity, but a point of pride.

It has become one of the oldest operational boats in the navy. Not in a ceremonial sense like "Old Ironsides," the USS *Constitution*, which sits tied up at a wharf in Boston, or the *Nautilus*, which is on display at the Submarine Museum in Groton, Connecticut. The *NR-1* is actually working a busy schedule today that is unknown to most people.

Plans are once again being circulated to build an *NR-2*, a modern deep submergence submarine that will be needed to eventually replace the *NR-1*, which cannot last forever. But for now, the *NR-1* still sails. It has survived almost four decades in an unforgiving and hostile environment, with danger never far away, and continues to operate out there today, crawling through shadowy valleys and flying through dangerous canyons far beneath the surface of the sea—unseen, unknown, and virtually unstoppable.

NR-1 Roster from 1966 to 1977
(Includes rate and rank when reporting aboard)

Initial Crew: 1966–1970

Officer-in-Charge	LCDR Dwaine O. Griffith
Executive Officer/Engineer	LT J. Stephen Perry
Ops/Navigation Officer	LT John H. (Jack) Maurer Jr.
Sperry Field Engineer	Roger M. Sherman
Sperry Field Engineer	Fred DeGrooth
Sperry Field Engineer	Brian F. Wruble
Nav/Comms/Deck	ET1 Robert T. Lunt
Reactor Controls	ET1 Dean Paine
Reactor Operations	ET2 Danny O. Gunter
Ship's Electrician	EM2 James Turner
Interior Communications	IC2 John Claytor
Sonar/Food Service/Photo	IC2 Lee H. Vyborny
Mechanical Division	MM1 Larry L. Kammerzell
Reactor Laboratory	MM2 David Seaton
Auxiliary Division	MM2 Donald E. Marks
Supply	SKC Robert A. Steinseifer

1971–1973

Officer-in-Charge	LCDR Toby G. Warson
Executive Officer/Engineer	LCDR Bernard D. Greeson

Ops/Navigation Officer	LT John F. "Dugan" Shipway
Sperry Field Engineer	Roger M. Sherman
Sperry Field Engineer	Fred DeGrooth
Electronics Material	ET1 Merrill Holden
Reactor Controls	ET1 Jeffrey A. Davis
Reactor Operations	ET1 Michael Barrett
Reactor Operations	ETR2 Bruce G. Arbogast
Sonar/Nav Division	EM1 Jeffrey L. Consolatti
E Division	EM1 John D. Harritt
IC/Food Services	IC1 Thomas L. Hall
Electrician	EM1 Chris H. Finehout
Electrician	EM2 Harold F. Dicer
Mechanical Division	MM1 William R. Willis
Reactor Laboratory	MM1 William M. Glidden
Auxiliary Division	MM1 George O. Smith
Mechanical	MM1 David F. Britt
Mechanical	MM2 Alan Demerath
Supply	SKC Henry Linster
Supply	SK1 Peter K. Clanton

1974–1976

Officer-in-Charge	LCDR Allison J. Holifield
Executive Officer/Engineer	LT Richard G. Furest
Ops/Navigation Officer	LT Joe Nolter
Sperry Field Engineer	Roger M. Sherman
Sperry Field Engineer	Fred DeGrooth
Crew Members Added During Period	
	EM2 James M. Condon
	MM1 Gary W. Pehling
	ETR2 Joseph A. Hansen
	MM1 Harry N. Tenaro
	EM2 Michael J. Mann
	ET1 Gary L. Wade
	ET1 Gary L. Willis
	MM1 David R. Bates

1976–1977
Officer-in-Charge
Executive Officer/Engineer
Ops/Navigation Officer
Crew Members Added
    During Period

LCDR Michael McQuown
LT Michael Riegel
LT Wayne Hollings

MM2 Mark R. Brown
MM2 Lawrence Lawson
ETN2 Everette Coats
IC2 Robert S. Miller
EM1 Frederick Comstock
ET1 Gerald Brinkman
ET1 Michael Marlow
EM1 Gregory Stanosz
IC2 Clyde F. Smith
MM1 Patrick Habel
ET1 John Richmond
MM1 Daniel Hudnut
MM1 Robert Lillge

AUTHORS' NOTE

This book is the product of many interviews conducted from Washington, D.C., to Washington State with participants in the saga of the *NR-1*. In addition, a great number of government publications were consulted, as were a large selection of newspaper and magazine articles, official research sites on the Internet, and the journals, scrapbooks, photographs, and letters of men and women involved in the ship's creation and operation. Occasionally, conflicting points of view arose as various people described a single event, and the authors chose what they considered to be the most likely description. The authors recommend the following books that were valuable in our research.

Craven, John Piña. *The Silent War: The Cold War Battle Beneath the Sea.* New York: Simon & Schuster, 2001.

Davis, Vincent. *The Politics of Innovation: Patterns in Navy Cases.* Denver: University of Denver International Studies, 1967.

Duncan, Francis. *Rickover and the Nuclear Navy.* Annapolis: Naval Institute Press, 1990.

Lehman, John F. *Command of the Seas: Building the 600 Ship Navy.* New York: Charles Scribner's Sons, 1988.

Maydew, Randall C. *America's Lost H-Bomb.* Manhattan, KS: Sunflower University Press, 1997.

Polmar, Norman, and Thomas B. Allen. *Rickover.* New York: Simon & Schuster, 1982.

Rockwell, Theodore. *The Rickover Effect: How One Man Made a Difference.* Annapolis: Naval Institute Press, 1992.

Sontag, Sherry, and Christopher Drew, with Annette Lawrence Drew. *Blind Man's Bluff: The Untold Story of American Submarine Espionage.* New York: Public Affairs, 1998.

Tyler, Patrick. *Running Critical: The Silent War, Rickover, and General Dynamics.* New York: Harper & Row, 1986.

ABOUT THE AUTHORS

Lee Vyborny has been involved with the U.S. Navy submarine force for more than thirty years, serving aboard a fast attack submarine and being chosen as one of the initial twelve members of the *NR-1* crew. He was an instructor at the Nuclear Power Training Unit in Windsor, Connecticut, and a navy diver. He later became a design and production engineer at the Electric Boat Division of General Dynamics, and a program manager for the development and manufacture of navigational equipment at Sperry Aerospace and Marine Systems. Vyborny, who is retired, owned a software company specializing in the development of financial management programs for use at headquarters commands of the U.S. Navy. He lives in Virginia.

Don Davis has written eleven books, three of which have become *New York Times* best-sellers. His most recent work includes *The Last Man on the Moon* with *Apollo 17* commander Gene Cernan (St. Martin's Press, 1999), and *JonBenét: Inside the Ramsey Murder Investigation* with Detective Steve Thomas (St. Martin's Press, 2000). *Death Cruise* (St. Martin's Press, 1996) has been reissued as a "True Crime Classic." Other major titles include *The Milwaukee Murders* (St. Martin's Press, 1991), *Fallen Hero* (St. Martin's Press, 1993), and *Hush Little Babies* (St. Martin's Press, 1997). As a news correspondent for twenty years, Davis covered stories ranging from the Vietnam War to the White House.